Crafting Poems and Stories

CRAFTING POEMS and STORIES

A GUIDE TO CREATIVE WRITING

Ethel Rackin

broadview press

Broadview Press – www.broadviewpress.com
Peterborough, Ontario, Canada

Founded in 1985, Broadview Press remains a wholly independent publishing house. Broadview's focus is on academic publishing: our titles are accessible to university and college students as well as scholars and general readers. With over 800 titles in print, Broadview has become a leading international publisher in the humanities, with world-wide distribution. Broadview is committed to environmentally responsible publishing and fair business practices.

Library and Archives Canada Cataloguing in Publication

Title: Crafting poems and stories : a guide to creative writing / Ethel Rackin.
Names: Rackin, Ethel, author.
Description: Includes bibliographical references and index.
Identifiers: Canadiana (print) 20220221979 | Canadiana (ebook) 20220222258 | ISBN 9781554814947 (softcover) | ISBN 9781770488625 (PDF) | ISBN 9781460407981 (EPUB)
Subjects: LCSH: Creative writing.
Classification: LCC PN187 .R33 2022 | DDC 808—dc23

Broadview Press handles its own distribution in North America:
PO Box 1243, Peterborough, Ontario, K9J 7H5, Canada
555 Riverwalk Parkway, Tonawanda, NY 14150, USA
Tel: (705) 743-8990; Fax: (705) 743-8353
email: customerservice@broadviewpress.com

For all territories outside of North America, distribution is handled by Eurospan Group.

Broadview Press acknowledges the financial support of the Government of Canada for our publishing activities.

Canada

Edited by Tania Therien
Designed by George Kirkpatrick

PRINTED IN CANADA

contents

acknowledgments

THIS BOOK BEGAN AS an idea shortly after I started teaching multi-genre creative writing courses at Penn State University's Brandywine Campus (then Delaware County). I am grateful to Adam Sorkin, who was instrumental in hiring and mentoring me in that position and to Nancy Sorkin, who simultaneously hired and mentored me as a writing tutor at Jefferson University (then Philadelphia University). Stephen Minot's *Three Genres: The Writing of Poetry, Fiction, and Drama*, was the first creative writing text I used, and the one that has most inspired me to write this book.

Marc Sherman and Sarah Touborg were first to encourage me to pursue the project, and a sabbatical from Bucks County Community College afforded me the space and time needed to begin to develop it.

I am grateful to the many colleagues, friends, and family who have been instrumental in lending their ideas, feedback, proofreading skills, general support, and enthusiasm along the way, including Mary Biddinger, Christopher Bursk, Stephen doCarmo, Kasey Jueds, Joanne Leva, Elizabeth Luciano, Anne Marie Macari, Carole Maso, Dean Rader, Hassen Saker, Christopher Salerno, Elizabeth Savage, Luanne Smith, Adam Sorkin, Gerald Stern, John Strauss, Rebecca Hoenig, Phyllis and Donald Rackin, and especially Dan Spirer.

Anonymous readers helped me to hone my ideas, and I am particularly grateful to Broadview editors Brett McLenithan and Marjorie Mather for their astute attention to this project throughout the process of its development.

This book is dedicated to the many various and wonderful students I have had the privilege of working with over the years: first at Penn State, Brandywine; then at Haverford College and Princeton University; and, most recently at Bucks County Community College. Special thanks to Carly Ceo, Kaden Unger, and Emily Bazelak, who contributed their fine writing to this book.

introduction to creative writing

a great adventure

THERE ARE SO MANY reasons you may have picked up this book. Maybe you've decided to take a creative writing course. Maybe you're taking up creative writing on your own or have been writing for a while and want to sharpen your skills. Whatever the case, you've embarked on an adventure. So often we're too bogged down fulfilling requirements for school, work, home (the list goes on) to make the space and time we need to pursue this path of passion and discovery. By deciding to focus on your creative writing, you're deciding not only to focus on your story and your life, in its various mysteries and meanings, but also to connect with others' lives in a way that is intimate and emotionally rich.

Before we embark on this adventure together, let's start at the beginning by asking: what exactly *is* creative writing, and how does it differ from other kinds of written communication, such as news stories, argumentative essays, scholarly articles, scientific studies, and so on? For one thing, as the title of the discipline implies, the writing we'll be studying and practicing is creative in nature, meaning that it involves producing something, which previously did not exist, through an act of imagination or invention. As creative writers, we don't have to stick to existing facts, prove a point, teach a lesson, or test a hypothesis. We have the freedom to raise questions, explore, paint a picture, rap, chant, howl, sing. The possibilities are seemingly endless.

This may lead us to believe that all bets are off: that no rules exist. After all, if we're creating something out of nothing, something truly original that emanates from our own lives or imagination, *why* would we want to impose order or follow a tradition? Actually, although there are no hard and fast rules when it comes to creative work, there are many reasons we may want to *stretch*: to become aware of those writers who have come before us and those who are our contemporaries, to try out different ways of doing things even if we're happy with how we've begun. There may be a high level of subjectivity when it comes to judging creative writing, but this doesn't mean that just anything will communicate to readers in a way that they'll find moving.

As an analogy, think of baking. A truly wonderful baker has created their very own recipe for outstanding cupcakes. When we take the first bite of that divine delicacy, we may pronounce it genius, and it very well may be. But for our baker to have crafted this masterpiece, they most likely engaged in some combination of learning from others, trial-and-error, hard work, experience, and talent. The craft of creative writing, like baking, can be learned. We can get better at it. With thought, experimentation, playful work, and feedback from others, we can develop our skills over time.

All of this assumes that your purpose is to write enduring work that readers will want to revisit. There's nothing wrong with having a more immediate goal of venting your emotions or creating a piece of writing that can be given to someone to communicate a specific message. If we consider the popularity of journaling and greeting cards, for instance, we'll quickly recognize the importance that writing plays in our everyday lives. This text, however, will push you beyond writing done solely for yourself or for a particular individual.

Although the creative writing we do is *always* in some sense for ourselves as well as for others, *Crafting Poems and Stories* will give you the critical skills you need to become better writers, capable of touching more lives than you may have previously thought possible. Think of this guide to creative writing as your GPS, navigating some of the routes available on your journey, pointing out which roads might be scenic, fast, or enriching, and steering you away from road blocks, traffic jams, and dead-ends. Although some of the roads I'll suggest you take—the writing models for you to check out, the exercises for you to try along the way—may surprise you, by the end of our time together, you'll be closer to finding your own unique way of doing things. Ultimately, it's up to you and your instructor, if you're taking a class, to decide how to use this book: which parts to focus on, which parts you may want to return to later. In other words, there's more than one way to productively and happily make use of this text. Speaking of the text, you'll soon notice that key terms are set in **boldface**, so that they're easy to find throughout. The purpose of offering these terms and their definitions is not to suggest that you dryly memorize them. Instead, use them as you like: as reminders, clarification, or to help you build a vocabulary you can draw on for class discussions.

Though the adventure you're about to embark on may interest you, you may be wondering if your life is exciting enough to write about. The simple answer is *Yes*! In fact, sometimes the things we find most mundane, boring, or perplexing about our own lives make for the best creative writing. Although you'll be inventing, it's often the actual details of your particular world that will bring your writing to life. For instance, if English is your second language, you may choose to incorporate your native language into some of your writing. Or if you work long hours as a server in a restaurant, you may choose to describe some of the smells, tastes, and voices from your workplace. Rather than shy away from your lived experience, *lean in*. In some sense, all creative writing begins with careful observation. And, at times, you may learn something about yourself that you didn't know; your writing may surprise even you. Maybe this is because creative writing offers the freedom and space to say what otherwise might be difficult or impossible to say.

So, how will you get started? Since you may get ideas anywhere and anytime, you'll want to keep a notebook small enough to carry with you, or get in the habit of using your phone to jot down observations and ideas. And it's always a good idea to immerse yourself in works by others—by reading ahead in this text, picking up a favorite book, and finding something new. Almost all of the reading you do has the potential to jump-start your own creative work. And hopefully, you'll have a chance to read strategically too: to find writers with whom you feel an affinity. This is the writing that may have the most to teach you in terms of its subject matter, vision, or form. However, even the writing that you find off-putting has a lot to teach you about what not to emulate or what you would never want to try. This process of getting started is a lifelong process. Even very experienced authors constantly jot down new ideas and search for new work to read.

You're probably used to reading literature in English classes or on your own, and, if so, you've learned how to analyze those texts within their historical contexts, for their deeper meanings, and in connection to each other or to other disciplines and modes of thinking. If you're a literature lover, you may have also discovered the enormous fun of connecting the creative works you read to your own life. Good literature has a lot to teach us about our fellow humans and ourselves. All of these lines of inquiry are also useful to us in the context of studying creative writing. However, the ways in which we tend to read as writers are often more strategic. As a general rule, we tend to read less analytically and more as craftspeople, focusing on: *who* is writing (the author's background and its possible relevance on the text); *what* they are writing about (their subject matter); *where* they might be coming from, geographically, culturally, aesthetically; *why* they may be writing this piece in this way; and *how* they crafted this piece to produce a certain series of effects.

When considering the authors and texts to include in this text, I was faced with many difficult decisions, not only because there are so many great poems and stories to choose from to use as examples, but also because the lives of writers (and humans, generally) are not always as exemplary as we wish they could be. Rather than ignore biographical facts, my students these days prefer to discuss the lives of the authors we study and to grapple with whatever contradictions come up. This is one of the reasons that the current generation of students is my favorite to-date. I invite you to do the same. We writers are also likely to make evaluative judgments on whether we think something *worked* in the piece, fell flat, and why. All of these questions help us apply what we're reading to our own work: either directly (we may pick up a technique or be inspired to stretch ourselves in some way), or more indirectly, as influences over time. The reading we do informs our sense of what has been done or not yet attempted and our sense of what's possible.

Ultimately, by using this text as a guide, you're joining a long tradition of writers who have studied and learned from each other. But how will you reconcile that first burst of creative energy, that need to get it down on the page just the way you hear it or feel it, with the things you're learning? I suggest thinking of creative writing as a two-part process: first, there's the initial impulse, in which you can feel absolutely free to play, without worrying for a second about messing up. This may take the form of some notes or a list, a first draft of a piece in your notebook, or a voice recording on your phone. While you're creating this first *impression*, we could call it, don't let a critical voice (of this text, your instructor, or your own self-editor) interrupt your flow. If a self-critical voice comes up, which it inevitably will at some point, banish it immediately. Keep playing with words as a toddler plays in a sandbox: without care or concern for any kind of assessment or judgment.

Next, once you've had time to put that first draft aside for a while, pick it back up and start thinking about different ways you might develop it. This is where the work of revision comes in. This book will offer exercises, examples, and discussion on methods of revision throughout, and you'll likely discuss how to apply these methods in class, especially if you're engaged in workshopping each other's writing. But to start, it may be helpful to think of revision instead as *re-imagination*, for in going back to your work, you'll be doing much more than fixing a few typos or changing a word here and there. Instead, with some practice, you'll be able to use your first drafts to help generate many more pieces of creative writing, and to develop whole modes of writing you may not have thought possible. We won't be as focused on editing individual words or phrases (banish that red pen), as much as we'll be learning to question, add, combine, recombine, flex, generate, and grow.

It's probably best if you can think of your time spent with the exercises in this book as time for experimentation. Instead of putting pressure on yourself that every exercise you try, every draft you attempt, will immediately turn into a finished product, feel free to try out different methods to see which ones may fit your needs now, may help you acquire a new creative tool, or may be useful later. Every writer has to produce lots of unfinished work, lots of attempts or bits and pieces of things, sketches, impressions, or drafts, in order to produce a few complete, solid pieces. And this takes time. So, the less attached you are to the outcome of each individual piece, and the more detached you can be about ideas of success or failure, the more progress you'll make.

Maintaining this sense of *play* as you write is easier said than done, since we humans tend to be very attached to the results of our writing. At times, in this process of creative experimentation and growth, you may feel emotionally vulnerable. But again, this is part of the process for any writer at any stage. If we look at the draft material and journals of some of our favorite authors, we'll see just that: great struggle punctuated by creative breakthroughs. It's the effort that's most important: the will to keep going despite that nagging voice that says you can't. With an open mind and a willingness to try new things, to listen, and to learn, you'll grow as a writer—more than you may have ever imagined possible.

PART I | POETRY

introduction

basic elements and enduring mysteries

AN ANCIENT FORM THAT predates written text, poetry was originally recited or sung, often to tell stories or to pass down important information. Whether in Greece or Africa or China, almost every culture across human history has enjoyed a vibrant poetic tradition. And although many of us today have probably listened to more songs than poems, poetry still plays a central role in our digital (and post-digital) lives: whether we write it for ourselves, study it in school, or follow the latest Instagram or spoken word poets.

What is it about poetry that makes it endure? After all, for an art form to survive across time and space, it must serve some basic human need or function and yet be flexible enough to be adapted. When we look up the word *poetry* in the *Oxford English Dictionary* (you may be able to access this invaluable resource online through your library), we find that it dates back to the ninth century and has multiple origins—partly borrowing from the Latin *poēta*, closely related to the Greek word for making, *poiesis*, and partly borrowing from French *poétrie*. According to its many definitions, poetry is related to creation or making; to the life of the imagination; and to its particular qualities, including rhythm and sound. What is poetry to you? From its definitions and what we know experientially, we can start to generate a list of attributes: *Songlike. Visual. Communal.* Somehow *Magical.* Tied to *Creation* and *Emotion.*

This is a good start. However, this list of attributes doesn't exactly answer the questions of why we seem to need poetry or why it persists. In fact, poetry may be trickier to define than we first thought, and maybe this is part of its allure. We'll circle back on poetry's purposes and powers as we read and write from a wide variety of perspectives. For now, however, we can begin to get a better sense of what poetry does well by briefly discussing the genre's basic elements: elements that the following chapters will take up in greater detail.

Poetry's Basic Elements

- Lineation
- Images
- Sound and Rhythm
- Traditional Form
- Free Verse
- Theme
- Voice and Tone

How do you know that what you're reading or writing is a poem? The most obvious difference between poetry and other forms of writing is **lineation**; poems, like song lyrics, are generally broken into **lines** and **stanzas** (similar to paragraphs), unless they're **prose poems** (poems that resemble prose on the page). This fact is a reminder that poetry not only comes out of an oral tradition, but it is also most often musical in nature. In fact, many poets report composing aurally; they hear a line or lines in their head long before they know what the poem will be about or the precise shape it will take. Poems also tend to benefit from being read and heard aloud, and reading your own poetry aloud or having it read to you by a classmate or friend is one of the best ways to work on it; you'll hear the poem's **rhythm** or beat, which may help you catch places where you unintentionally stumbled.

In chapter 5, we'll work in-depth with lineation, by looking at what you've written so far, thinking about your natural inclinations, and experimenting with some of the many possibilities. However, it is important to know at the outset that lines can be short, long, or anywhere in between. They can be **regular**, meaning that each line is approximately the same length, or **irregular** (of varying line lengths). They can be **end-stopped**, so that the end of the line is also the end of the phrase or sentence. Take, for instance, the first stanza of "I wandered lonely as a cloud" by British Romantic poet William Wordsworth (1770–1850):

I wandered lonely as a Cloud
That floats on high o'er Vales and Hills,
When all at once I saw a crowd,
A host of golden Daffodils;
Beside the Lake, beneath the trees,
Fluttering and dancing in the breeze.

All but the first of Wordsworth's lines are marked with punctuation, indicating a stop or ending. And although the first line doesn't end with any punctuation, it is nonetheless a complete phrase.

On the other hand, poets can use **enjambment**, meaning that the phrase or sentence runs over the line-break without punctuation. The beginning of stanza three of Wordsworth's poem serves as a good example:

The waves beside them danced, but they
Out-did the sparkling waves in glee:—

See how the poet runs the sentence over the line-break? And here, there isn't punctuation at the end of the first line because it wouldn't make sense grammatically. Most often, contemporary poets use a mix of end-stopped and enjambed lines, and there are countless combinations and possibilities. Regardless, as a poet, lineation is an important tool to have at your disposal. As you revise and refine your poetry, you'll become more aware of the tension between the **syntax**, or sentence structure, of the poem and the unit of the line. And this awareness will help you control movement, pace, and meaning.

In addition, most poems make ample use of **sensory detail**: any detail capable of being perceived by the five senses (sight, hearing, touch, smell, and taste), especially **images** (a detail we can picture or see). Since these details are necessary to create an emotional as well as intellectual experience for your reader, we'll take them up early on, in chapter 2. This doesn't mean that all good poems involve piling on as much description as possible. But it does mean that we can often enliven a poem by transforming an **abstraction** (such as love, peace, or hatred) through the use of sensory detail and by letting images do much of the work for us: whether we're painting a picture or telling a story.

In some cases, we'll use **figurative language**, or language that suggests more than one meaning, to do this. For example, we may use **simile** (a comparison using *like* or *as*), **metaphor** (a comparison without *like* or *as*). Or we may use **symbolism** to suggest additional meaning. In any case, images used in poetry can either be quite concrete or they can suggest meanings and associations beyond the obvious. For example, a door key could be used in a poem to simply describe an object, action, or a scene, but it could also be used to symbolically suggest a range of meanings: entrance into the unknown, unlocking a secret, gaining knowledge, and so on. We'll only know how to read the image through the context of the poem: the other elements around it, how much space it takes up, and whether it's repeated. And we'll only know how we want to use sensory detail and figurative language in our own poems once we've tried out a range of possibilities.

We've already briefly discussed the importance of considering music in the process of crafting poems, but what about the particular sounds of your poetry, one of the topics of chapter 3 on sound and rhythm? Will you use rhyme, linking words through their sound, or will you write poetry that is primarily unrhymed? Will you use **sound devices**, including **alliteration** (the repetition of initial sounds)? And if you decide to use rhyme, how will you keep it subtle, so that it doesn't drown out the other aspects of the poem? Many poets start out with either an attachment to rhyme or an aversion to it. At some point, however, it might be helpful to try the opposite (and everything in between): to try out all kinds of sound patterns to see what makes your poems come alive. When they're well played, the sounds you use can energize your poems and create a powerful emotional experience for your reader.

Although there is an inherent beat or rhythm to most poetry, this too is an element you can tune and shape so that your poems truly pulse and ring. Basic means of establishing rhythm in poetry include the use of line-length, **repetition** and **anaphora** (the repetition of a word or phrase at the beginning of lines or sentences), the quirky but often helpful practice of **counting syllables**, and the process of using **meter**, a specific rhythmic pattern. Although many poets are initially wary of writing in a specific metrical pattern, once you become attuned to the language's innate metrical rhythms and begin to find organic ways to incorporate these patterns, you'll find that working with meter can be informative and satisfying. Whether or not they make it a lifelong pursuit, most poets have studied form at some point, in order to gain a deeper understanding of the way language works, rhythmically and sonically. Typically, to their surprise, about half of my creative writing students become addicted to writing in **traditional form** or set structure each semester.

In chapter 4, we'll look at a variety of forms and focus particular attention on two centuries-old ones, which are still popular today: the **sonnet** (from the Italian word *sonetto* or "little song"), a compact form that originated in thirteenth-century Italy and is written in fourteen lines with a set meter and rhyme scheme; and the **villanelle** (from the Italian word *villanella*, from *villano* or "peasant"), a dance-like form that originated in sixteenth-century France and is written in nineteen lines broken into five three-line stanzas and one four-line stanza, characterized by two repeating lines and two repeating rhymes. We'll also explore **invented** or **chance forms**, forms that you can make up yourself, based on a concept or on a random process of selection.

Although you'll be in good company as you explore the use of traditional form, the majority of poems being written today are written in **free verse**, meaning that they adhere to no set pattern. We'll explore the **typographical** (appearance on the page) and **auditory** (sonic) possibilities of free verse in chapter 5. In particular, poets experiment with the use of **white space**, or the area around the poem, not only by focusing on line length but also by using indentation or extra spaces within and between lines. When used effectively, such techniques can lend your work breathing room, visual shape, and multiple ways of reading. How poetry looks on the page is an essential aspect of the genre, especially given the enormous print culture thriving today: from traditional journals and books to e-readers, online publications, and social media outlets. Although some poems lend themselves either to the page or to live performance, most seem to occupy a space in between; to reach their audience, working poets tend to publish *and* do live readings, so we'll focus on both aspects of poetic production.

At this point in our discussion of poetry's basic elements, you may be wondering about the role of the poem's **subject matter** or topics: are there subjects that are off-limits or others on which you'll want to focus your attention? The short answer is: it's up to you. As you progress as a poet, you'll find the subjects that seem most uniquely tied to your experience: the stories that you have to tell. We'll explore ways of getting started with this process in chapter 1 and revisit the topic again in chapter 6 on **theme**: the "big idea" or part of the work that comments on human nature. Poets often liken the experience of developing their subject matter to finding an itch they must scratch; the questions that haunt you, the repeated themes of your lived experience offer rich areas for exploration. This process of growth involves learning to avoid **truism** or cliché to gradually uncover a more engaging and complex set of poetic subjects and themes.

Connected to subject and theme is the element of organization. Although free-verse poetry doesn't adhere to a set organizational structure, poets focus a great deal of attention on designing their poems. Whether the poem is **narrative**, containing the structure of a story; **lyrical**, relying on the sound of the lines and the intimacy of address; **dramatic**, in that it is spoken through a character or characters; or some combination of these modes, it is important to consider the order of your poem to create a dynamic experience for your reader. Therefore, in chapter 6, we'll not only focus on theme, but also on strategies of organization. We'll consider **poetic sequences** or **series**: groupings of individual poems meant to be read in a certain order. Once you've written a number of poems, it can be useful to begin to organize them in different orders, either to begin collecting them for a portfolio of completed works or simply to gain a clearer perspective on the styles and subjects that interest you.

Last in our list of poetic elements are **voice** and **tone**; voice generally refers to the speaker and style of the poem whereas tone refers to the poem's attitude or mood. Chapter 7 takes up these subtle yet crucial aspects of poetry by exploring various tones—including reflective, melancholy, and comic. We'll also consider poems that use irony and sarcasm to great effect, and think more about how **diction**, or word choice, contribute to the world of the poem. One way to directly engage these elements is to try writing **persona poems**: poems written by a narrator other than you. By speaking through a character, whether historical or fictional, you're trying on another voice, tone, and style. Not only can this be fun, many poets find this process liberating; by switching your point-of-view or by taking on a persona, you may be able to explore subjects that would otherwise feel too close for comfort.

How do all of these elements add up? When used well, they can make for one explosive little package. Consider the density, compression, or condensation involved; you're starting with a relatively short form (excluding **epics** or lengthy narratives), and whether or not you use all of the elements we've discussed, you're sure to use some of them. What this means for the poem is that those elements—the shifts in voice, the various sensory details, the elements of story—bump up against each other, creating layers of experience and resonance. Ultimately, your poem has the potential to deeply move your reader in a mere instant: so that the experience can feel alternately seamless, unconscious, physical, and even magical.

Ready to get started? Remember, this list of poetic elements shouldn't scare you off, burden you, or make the process of writing any less enchanting. Think of the knowledge you're acquiring, the vocabulary you're building, and the examples you're reading as nutrients that will fertilize the soil of your creative mind for new growth. Once your pen hits the paper, your finger starts typing into your phone, your voice starts recording, catch whatever may come out without judgment. Only look over these first thoughts later, when you've had time to digest and reflect. It's then that the equally creative process of crafting begins.

one getting started

the crafting of a poem

YOU'VE BOUGHT YOURSELF A notebook. You've tried recording your voice on one of your devices or practiced reading something you've written aloud. But *what* should you write about and *how* should you write it? Unless poems are already pouring out of you, which I hope they are, you may be wondering how to get started. With any writing project, beginning is often the most difficult part. Maybe this is because writing feeds on confidence; the more confidence you have in your writing ability, the more you tend to write. And it's easy to psyche yourself out before you've even begun. Know this: you have the ability to do great writing. Poetry is not for the select few. Though many people are shy when it comes to their writing, if you publish a journal or zine, participate in a community writing contest, or drop in on an open mic night at your local bookstore, you'll soon find out that almost everyone has tried writing poetry at some point. But few of us believe we're any good.

From an early age, we're taught that writing poetry, like doing artwork, is a rare talent, reserved for a gifted few. For years I visited a K-12 Catholic girls' school to teach poetry for a day each spring. My day began with the kindergarten class, and by the time I left in the afternoon I had visited through Grade 5. The teachers and girls were delightful across the board, and I loved watching the girls light up as they listened to poetry read aloud or tried their hand at a writing exercise. However, each year I noticed a disturbing phenomenon: a steep drop-off in enthusiasm at Grade 4. It wasn't that the girls weren't excited to see me; they all enjoyed spending some time on poetry. But whereas the younger children were eager to read their poems aloud, often raising their hands so high they were almost standing, the older girls practically cringed when I asked if any of them would like to read their work to the class. Rather than being proud, each one of the older girls seemed to feel that the act of writing poetry was somehow not for her.

You could easily explain this phenomenon by discussing developmental changes according to age group: by arguing that the steep drop-off in enthusiasm had nothing to do with poetry or creative expression and everything to do with a typical sense of self-consciousness, which generally presents in pre-teen years. However, if you'd been with me in those classrooms, year after year, I'm sure you'd agree that creativity was what was (and is) at stake. We start off feeling confident and sometimes even gleeful about our innate abilities, and we end up in early adulthood dead on arrival. If you think back to your own childhood, you may recall your first experiences with creative affirmation—or the lack thereof. Were you encouraged to pursue your creative passions, told that you had talent? Or did you receive the explicit or implicit message that creative expression, in general, and creative writing, in particular, was for someone else? I'm not suggesting that you dwell on this question, since, as adults, we get to determine for ourselves what we can and cannot achieve. But I am suggesting that if a little voice inside tells you that you *can't*, you probably picked up this misconception from others or from the culture at large. So, it's time to toss that self-negating idea to the trash heap for good. And if you already possess a healthy self-confidence, get ready to surprise even yourself with the ways in which you can grow as a writer.

Once you've gotten in the right mindset to write, you may still struggle with the questions of when to fit writing into your busy life and where you can find the necessary conditions to do so. If you've ever sat down to a computer with the sole purpose of composing a poem on the spot, you may have faced a rather daunting experience. The blank screen and that ever-annoying blinking cursor may as well be staring at you as if to say, *let's make a bet. I dare you to try writing a poem.* And if there's the added pressure of producing a poem within a certain time frame for class, the prospect can become uncomfortable enough to make you not want to write at all. This experience of expectation and sometimes even debilitating pressure is familiar to almost all poets, regardless of their level of experience. Most of us find that we have to trick ourselves into writing:

a process that usually involves simply taking notes or journaling, with no thought of the product until later.

And what about finding the right environment in which to generate material? Here too, the perfect silence of an uninhabited lake house can turn out to be not so perfect if you're feeling pressured. In fact, many writers start off scribbling notes for poems in between interruptions—on a grocery list or the back of an envelope, in between meetings or classes. And many of us are used to getting started in public places, rather than in solitude. Recently, while at a secluded arts residency, I met a well-established Portuguese novelist who was having difficulty writing in his serene woodland studio, since he was accustomed to composing in noisy Lisbon cafés. He ended up working half of the day in the residency's library to break up all of that solitude, if not silence. Although my first poetry teachers instructed us to refrain from listening to music while we wrote, I now find that having music in the background (especially if it's instrumental rather than vocal) often feeds my imagination, frees me up, and gets me writing. And many of my students report the same: that music helps to create a conducive environment.

The long and short of it is: there's no right way to do it. What's important is making yourself feel comfortable so that you'll *want* to write. To establish a productive routine (however unorthodox it may be) takes some trial and error. You may benefit from setting aside a certain time of day and a certain place in which to write. See what suits you. I often think of my writing life as a relationship I'm in; I need to know that there's a familiar routine I can count on, but I don't want it to get stale, to feel like a chore. I want to keep it joyful or at least pleasant, and in order to do this, I have to keep the pressure at a low simmer, unless, of course, I temporarily need to bring it to a brisk boil. So, keep it simple; do what feels good; keep trying.

Sources

As we've already discussed, there are really no off-limits topics for poetry. But if you're just beginning or want to generate new material, it may be useful to review sources for possible subject matter. If you've been writing for a while, maybe you can add some of your own tried-and-true sources to this brief list. I've drawn the first three from poet Kenneth Koch's landmark study, *Wishes, Lies, and Dreams: Teaching Children to Write Poetry.* Although Koch describes his method of teaching children, specifically, his ideas are easily adapted, and many working poets continue to use similar strategies.

- Wishes: Desire is generally a fertile ground for poetry. Are there specific relationships or experiences you'd like to have, places to which you'd like to travel? Maybe you've always wanted to walk the shores of Belize or see what it would be like to fly. Like poems, wishes need not be realistic, just specific.

- Dreams: Many poets keep a notebook beside their beds to record their dreams. And thinkers from Aristotle to Freud have explored the connection between sleeping, dreaming, and poetry. The French surrealist poet, Saint-Pol-Roux, reputedly hung a sign on his bedroom door that read, "*Le Poète Travaille*" ("Poet at Work"). Whether or not you end up using actual dream material in your poems, cultivating an awareness of your dream life will help you tap in to your unconscious mind for starting points and associations.

- Lies: This common "ice-breaker" exercise for the first day of class can also be useful for your writing. Try writing down two truths about yourself—and one lie. Then try making up some lies about the world around you. Similar to mining for material in your wishes and dreams, this process focuses your attention on the often-blurred line between reality and fantasy.

- Secrets: What would you say if you were completely unafraid of the response? We all have secrets: some big and some small. The revelation or partial revelation of secrets often provides poems with a necessary source of tension. Whether or not your poems end up being autobiographical, you can mine for material by thinking more about the secrets you carry.

- Mixed Emotions: Most of us find that writing a powerful poem grounded in a single emotion, such as happiness or anger, is difficult, if not impossible. And, as readers, we seem to crave poems that come out of a state of **ambivalence** or mixed emotions: love *and* resentment, joy *and* melancholy, the bittersweet. As you search for subjects, focus particular attention on experiences that feel complex or unresolved. Maybe you're still wondering why you and your sweetheart broke up, or why you hold mixed emotions in relation to a family member. The questions in our lives, the things with which we're wrestling, almost always provide useful fodder for poems.

- Sounds: Some poems simply begin with the sound of a line or **wordplay** (language used in an inventive way). And it's certainly not necessary to have a subject, topic, or theme in mind before you begin.

Are there words or combinations of words that draw your attention? Maybe you've seen a turn-of-phrase online, on a billboard, or in a newspaper. Feel free to incorporate this **found material** into a poem.

- Daily Observations: As poets, we're always observing the things around us: the way the moon looks on a particularly clear night, our mother crossing her smooth hands when she speaks about a painful topic, the smell of hot coffee filling the house on a cold morning. We're particularly tuned-in to how things look, hear, feel, smell, and taste. This kind of **sensory detail**, also the topic of the next chapter, makes up the bulk of our daily observations. And these observations are key to writing powerful poetry.

Active Reading

Equally important as finding sources of material is learning to read actively: that is, engaging with the reading you do in a way that will yield results for your own writing practice. In the following poem, notice the way that Serbian-born United States poet Charles Simic (b. 1938) uses carefully observed sensory detail to develop a basic comparison between **the speaker** (the voice behind the poem) and "a big shade tree." This first poem is annotated to model the process of active reading. If you can get in the habit of marking up poems—including memorable lines, questions, poetic elements that seem significant, and definitions—you'll not only be ready for class discussions, but you'll also be more likely to internalize and remember whatever is most significant for you personally. You may also want to keep an online dictionary, such as merriam-webster.com, close by as you read. Since poetry depends so highly on each word, it's helpful to review various definitions, even for words such as "enchanted," with which you may be familiar.

The World

As if I were a big old shade tree *simile—speaker & tree*
On a side street with a small café.
Neon beer sign with the word "cold" shining in it. *sense of sight and touch*
Summer dusk.

The solitary customer, who looks like my father, *why "like" his father?*
Is bent over a book with small print
Oblivious of the young waiter
Who is about to serve him a cup of black coffee. *sight and taste*

I have an incalculable number of leaves
Not one of which is moving. interesting paradox
It's because we are enchanted, I think. placed under a magic spell
We don't have a care in the world.

Craft Questions

- What details does Simic use to develop the comparison between the speaker and the shade tree? What feelings do you associate with these details?
- What is the role of the "solitary customer, who looks like [the speaker's] father" in the poem?
- What feelings do lines 9–10 evoke?
- In the last two lines, the poem switches to the plural, "we." How might this switch expand your understanding?
- Thematically, what is this poem about?

In discussion, you may have some difficulty agreeing on a single theme. (Though we can probably all agree that there are many things that this poem is *not* about: cats, serial killers, or race cars.) Rarely does a poem mean just one thing, especially when you ask multiple people. Simic has begun with a **simile** expressed in a hypothetical statement, has developed the comparison through concrete particulars, and has left us to draw our own conclusions. Notice how he doesn't have to *tell* us about emotion or about the human condition; he *shows* us those feelings through a series of carefully placed details. We'll take a closer look at the role of such details in the next chapter, but before we do, we'll discuss self-portraits and try some jump-starts to help us get started writing poems.

Self-Portraits

Underlying this chapter is the assumption that *you* are actually the richest source of material for your own poems. Like a tortoise who carries their home on their back, you contain all you need to write. Whether you end up writing historical poems, poems with a social conscience, poems that require some research (more on this later), or poems in which you adopt a persona, it's your unique perception of things, your heartaches and mysteries, your vision of the world that makes your work engaging to others. After all, you need to create buy-in; your readers need to believe that your story is authentic in some way, even if it's not literally true.

As we discussed, in the case of Simic's "The World," a great deal can be inferred by the extended comparison. However, we can't be sure whether the "I," the speaker of the poem, refers to the poet, Charles Simic, himself. And, in a sense, it doesn't really matter, if we trust the voice of the poem. In your own work, there are times that you may want to write more directly about your life, however. And especially as you're getting started, it may be useful to do just that.

To get you started thinking about ways to write about your own life, what follows is a folio of self-portraits: poems in which the poet takes up the subject of their own life more—or less—directly. After all, poems are always so wily! The folio begins with a poem by British Romantic poet, John Clare (1793–1864). Clare's life was challenging, and his work often reflects on this fact. Suffering from mental illness, poverty, and a relative lack of poetic recognition for most of his life, Clare nonetheless created a body of groundbreaking work, of which this gem is a part:

Lines: "I Am"

I am—yet what I am, none cares or knows;
My friends forsake me like a memory lost:
I am the self-consumer of my woes—
They rise and vanish in oblivious host
Like shadows in love-frenzied stifled throes—
And yet I am and live—like vapours tossed

Into the nothingness of scorn and noise,
Into the living sea of waking dreams
Where there is neither sense of life or joys
But the vast shipwreck of my life's esteems;
Even the dearest that I loved the best
Are strange—nay, rather, stranger than the rest.

I long for scenes where man hath never trod,
A place where woman never smiled or wept,
There to abide with my Creator, God,
And sleep as I in childhood sweetly slept,
Untroubling and untroubled where I lie,
The grass below—above, the vaulted sky.

Craft Questions

- What images does Clare use to describe himself?
- What contradictions and ambivalences does he explore?
- Can you tell that this poem was written in an earlier era? Which elements seem Romantic and which seem contemporary?
- Discuss the significance of place in this self-portrait.

Next in our chronological folio of self-portraits is a poem by twentieth-century United States poet, Laura (Riding) Jackson (1901–91). Jackson was a fiercely independent thinker and writer, whose poems often explored metaphysical questions, language itself, and gender roles. This self-portrait touches on some of these concerns:

Postponement of Self

I took another day,
I moved to another city,
I opened a new door to me.
Then again a last night came.
My bed said: 'To sleep and back again?'
I said: 'This time go forward.'

Arriving, arriving, not yet, not yet,
Yet yet arriving, till I am met.
For what would be her disappointment
Coming late ('She did not wait').
I wait. And meet my mother.
Such is accident.
She smiles: long afterwards.
I sulk: long before.
I grow to six.
At six little girls in love with fathers.
He lifts me up.
See. Is this Me?
Is this Me I think
In all the different ways till twenty.
At twenty I say She.
Her face is like a flower.
In a city we have no flower-names, forgive me.
But flower-names not necessary
To diary of identity.

Craft Questions

- How does Jackson describe the self?
- How is the poem organized?
- What is the role of gender in this coming of age story?
- Discuss the simile at the end of the poem.

Our third and most definitive self-portrait is by contemporary United States poet, Evie Shockley. Both formally experimental and lyrical in nature, Shockley's poems, like Clare's, are often interested in place. And like Jackson, Shockley frequently explores questions of subjectivity, perception, and identity.

canvas and mirror

self-portrait with cats, with purple, with stacks
  of half-read books adorning my desk, with coffee,

      with mug, with yesterday's mug. self-portrait
    with guilt, with fear, with thick-banded silver ring,

  painted toes, and no make-up on my face. self-
    portrait with twins, with giggles, with sister at

    last, with epistrophy, with crepuscule with nellie,
with my favorite things. self-portrait with hard

head, with soft light, with raised eyebrow. self-
  portrait voo-doo, self-portrait hijinks, self-portrait

    surprise. self-portrait with patience, with political
  protest, with poetry, with papers to grade. self-

  portrait as thaumaturgic lass, self-portrait as luna
  larva, self-portrait as your mama. self-portrait

    with self at sixteen. self-portrait with shit-kickers,
with hip-huggers, with crimson silk, with wild

mushroom risotto and a glass of malbec. self-
  portrait with partial disclosure, self-portrait with

    half-truths, self-portrait with demi-monde. self-
  portrait with a night at the beach, with a view

  overlooking the lake, with cancelled flight. self-
  portrait with a real future, with a slight chance of

    sours, with glasses, with cream, with fries, with
a way with words, with a propositional phrase.

Craft Questions

- Which images jump out at you?
- What do these images or objects reveal (or not reveal) about the poet's identity?
- Describe the poem's pace and rhythm.
- In what ways can the poem be read as "canvas" and in what ways as a "mirror"?

Notice how list-like Shockley's poem is. You may want to start working on your own self-portrait poem by simply listing a series of your attributes—along with the colors, objects, places, and music—that seems tied to you in some way. Once you've generated a list, you can circle the elements that seem most suggestive or evocative, and start working them into a poem. Or you can hold off for now, and use your initial list once we get to the "I'm Nobody! Who Are You?" exercise at the end of the next chapter.

In addition, after you've spent some time with the self-portraits by Clare, Jackson, and Shockley, you can consider their historical and chronological context in greater depth. Since the first is drawn from England in the nineteenth century, the second and third from the United States (twentieth and twenty-first centuries, respectively), we might expect differences in content, as well as style. Do you detect such differences? And what about similarities? In fact, this book will often place older poems next to newer ones, in order to generate a conversation on poetic traditions and innovations. Depending on your level of interest, you may even decide to do some quick research on the poets you're encountering here. At the very least, by reading poems from different periods side-by-side, you'll get a sense of the complex and often contested history of poetic practice.

To round out our discussion of the process of getting started writing poems, try a few (or all) of the following jump-starts. And feel free to jump around amongst them. These exercises and ones like them at the end of each chapter aren't homework. They're food for thought, ways of tapping into your own innate creativity and sense of invention. If you start one and find that it takes you in a different direction, follow your hunch.

Exercises

Jump-Starts: Use any of these jump-starts to generate material. Once you've completed an exercise, set it aside for at least a day, come back to it later, and try gradually turning your notes into a poem.

1. **Automatic Writing**: Time yourself. Write by hand for ten minutes without lifting your hand. Don't read back over what you've written, just keep going until the time is up.

2. **Ambivalence**: Recall a time in which you felt strongly mixed emotions: joy *and* grief, anger *and* empathy.... Write about the experience in prose without thinking about *how* your piece is written.

3. **I Remember**: United States poet Joe Brainard (1942–94) wrote a book-length prose-poem called "I Remember," an experimental, tongue-in-cheek memoir in which each entry begins with the phrase *I remember.* Here are a few lines:

   I remember the only time I ever saw my mother cry. I was eating apricot pie.

   I remember when my father would say "Keep your hands out from under the covers" as he said goodnight. But he said it in a nice way.

   I remember when I thought that if you did anything bad, policemen would put you in jail.

   Write your own list of memories, beginning each one with the words *I remember.* Your list, like Brainard's, can include a combination of the serious memories and those that may seem silly or random. Generate at least 10 entries.

4. **Found Speech**: Bring your notebook with you to a public place: a bookstore, café, bus stop, or store. Write down the first bit of speech you hear. Or else, wait until you hear a phrase that seems particularly evocative. Begin a poem with this bit of stolen language, and see where it takes you.

5. **Meditation on Place**: Observe the same scene each day for several days: the birds at your bird feeder, the homeless man who stands in front of your corner store. Record this scene in writing by noting both what has changed and what has remained the same.

6. **Dailies**: For one straight week, write a daily poem on whatever's on your mind that day. The only rule is that your daily poem's title should simply be the date. At the end of the week, you'll have seven dailies. Consider whether they can be read as a poetic sequence or series.

7. **Erasures:** Try an erasure poem. This experimental form of poetry involves erasing, crossing out, or whiting out portions of an existing text and creating a poem from the words that remain. You can either leave the marked page, so that readers can discover the poem by piecing together words that haven't been whited out or crossed out, or you can use the remaining words to create a new poem altogether.

two | images

the truth is in the details

As we consider the elements that make up any successful poem, it is impossible to overstate the role of sensory experience and concrete visual detail. Rather than telling us what they mean, poems show us where they want us to go. They take us on a journey, allowing us an opportunity to connect and reflect. And imagery is one of the main tools that poets use to create this experience.

To be precise, when we speak of **images** in poetry, we are referring to words that invoke any of the five senses: sight, sound, taste, smell, and touch. Is it a good idea to use all five senses in every poem you write? Not necessarily. However, by becoming more attuned to the role of the senses, you help to ensure that your poems will trigger a response in the mind of your reader.

Imagery also refers to the concrete *things* in the poem—the small café, newspaper, neon beer sign, and summer dusk—the places, objects, and other details—that populate it. By bringing the stuff of lived experience into the poem, you bring the poem itself to life.

And, as we'll explore in this chapter, images are often used as figures of speech, including similes, metaphors, and symbols. Without becoming preoccupied by the literary definitions, we can observe how figures of speech function to create layers of association and meaning. This heightened awareness will serve us well as we write and revise.

In contrast to image is **abstraction**, a concept without concrete, visual dimensions. As real as they are to us, concepts such as *love, depression, peace,* and *independence* are difficult to visualize. However, since it is nearly impossible to write poetry without having some abstractions in mind, it is the poet's job to translate such broad, conceptual thoughts into particular details.

As we explore the role of images, keep in mind that different poets fall on different ends of a continuum—between concreteness and abstraction. For instance, take a look at this poem by United States poet William Carlos Williams (1883–1963):

This Is Just to Say

I have eaten
the plums
that were in
the icebox

and which
you were probably
saving
for breakfast

Forgive me
they were delicious
so sweet
and so cold

Williams, who coined the phrase, "no ideas but in things," clearly wants us to experience the sensations of touching and tasting the "delicious," "sweet," "cold" plums he describes. The poem's title, which also serves as its first line, and its lack of punctuation, contribute to its casual offhandedness. Devoid of grandiose comparisons, "This Is Just to Say" falls on the concrete end of the spectrum. Could the speaker's playfully guilty tone and the description of the sensuous plums suggest ideas of truthfulness, fidelity, and desire? Sure. But it's fair to say that the poem mainly focuses our attention on the sensory experience of the central image itself.

Thing Poems

Poems that focus on concrete objects or experience are sometimes referred to as **thing poems**. Poets such as Frank O'Hara (1926–66) and his New York School contemporaries are known for writing their own kind of *thing* poem: the so-called *I did this, I did that* poem. Populated with the people, places, and things of everyday life, their poems tend to resist symbolic suggestion.

For example, O'Hara's elegy for jazz singer Billie Holiday (1915–59), or Lady Day, as she was called, describes the speaker's day leading up to hearing the news of Holiday's death:

❧ The Day Lady Died

It is 12:20 in New York a Friday
three days after Bastille day,[1] yes
it is 1959 and I go get a shoeshine
because I will get off the 4:19 in Easthampton[2]
at 7:15 and then go straight to dinner
and I don't know the people who will feed me

I walk up the muggy street beginning to sun
and have a hamburger and a malted and buy
an ugly NEW WORLD WRITING[3] to see what the poets
in Ghana are doing these days
                                                            I go on to the bank
and Miss Stillwagon (first name Linda I once heard)
doesn't even look up my balance for once in her life
and in the GOLDEN GRIFFIN[4] I get a little Verlaine
for Patsy with drawings by Bonnard although I do
think of Hesiod, trans. Richmond Lattimore or
Brendan Behan's new play or *Le Balcon* or *Les Nègres*
of Genet, but I don't, I stick with Verlaine
after practically going to sleep with quandariness

and for Mike I just stroll into the PARK LANE
Liquor Store and ask for a bottle of Strega and

1 The French national holiday of July 14 that marks the storming of the Bastille prison in 1789.

2 A town in eastern Long Island frequented by New York artists and writers.

3 A literary magazine published by New American Library between 1952 and 1959.

4 A bookshop close to the Museum of Modern Art, where O'Hara was a curator.

then I go back where I came from to 6th Avenue
and the tobacconist in the Ziegfeld Theatre and
casually ask for a carton of Gauloises and a carton
of Picayunes, and a NEW YORK POST with her face on it

and I am sweating a lot by now and thinking of
leaning on the john door in the 5 SPOT
while she whispered a song along the keyboard
to Mal Waldron and everyone and I stopped breathing

Craft Questions

- What mood or tone is established through O'Hara's inclusion of so many daily details?
- In what ways does O'Hara comment on issues of race? How might this content be different if the poem were written today?
- Are there places where the poem seems to speed up or slow down?
- What do we learn about the speaker's memory? About memory in general?

Although "The Day Lady Died" was written in 1959 and published in 1964, in many ways, it still feels fresh. O'Hara's decision to include details from everyday life in his poetry continues in the work of many of the contemporary poets collected in this book, including David Trinidad (in chapter 3) and Sandra Simonds (in chapter 4).

Simile and Metaphor

In contrast to "This Is Just to Say" and "The Day Lady Died," most poems use at least some **figurative language**: language that compares one thing to another, creating a new "figure" or meaning for the reader. The most common **figures of speech** are **simile** and **metaphor**. The simile uses *like* or *as* to create a comparison, whereas the metaphor simply implies it.

When William Wordsworth writes, "I wandered lonely as a cloud," he is using simile, whereas when Emily Dickinson writes, "My Life had stood—a Loaded Gun—", she is using metaphor. Notice how the simile gives us time to digest the comparison, whereas the metaphor subtly and powerfully implies an association.

Here are some additional examples of these common figures of speech:

Simile

- Your absence has gone through me
  Like thread through a needle.
  (W.S. Merwin, "Separation")

- My darling, the wind falls in like stones
  from the whitehearted water....
  (Anne Sexton, "The Truth the Dead Know")

- My clouded reflection eyes me
  like a bird of prey....
  (Yusef Komunyakaa, "Facing It")

Metaphor

- And I am here, the mermaid whose dark hair
  streams black....
  (Adrienne Rich, "Diving into the Wreck")

- Love's the obstinate boy, the ship,
  (Elizabeth Bishop, "Casabianca")

- Death was a past tense
  (Michael Burkard, "Envelope of Night")

Often there are multiple similes and metaphors at work within a single poem. However, when a single metaphor is developed throughout, we refer to it as a **controlling metaphor** or **extended metaphor**. To get a sense of how a controlling metaphor can work, let's read a poem by Louise Glück (b. 1943), organized around the central image of the bright, somewhat showy yellow dahlia. As you read, notice how the comparison between the speaker's sister and the flower is at first presented in a pair of similes, and then transforms into a subtle, controlling metaphor as the poem progresses.

Yellow Dahlia

My sister's like a sun, like a yellow dahlia.
Daggers of gold hair around the face.
Gray eyes, full of spirit.

I made an enemy of a flower:
now, I'm ashamed.

We were supposed to be opposites:
one fair, like daylight.
One different, negative.

If there are two things
then one must be better,
isn't that true? I know now
we both thought that, if what children do
can really be called thinking.

I look at my sister's daughter,
a child so like her,
and I'm ashamed: nothing justifies
the impulse to destroy
a smaller, a dependent life
I guess I knew that always.
That's why I had to hurt myself instead:
I believed in justice.

We were like day and night,
one act of creation.
I couldn't separate
the two halves,
one child from the other.

Craft Questions

- How and where in the poem is the yellow dahlia described?
- Why is the description of the dahlia not developed in greater detail throughout?
- How is the speaker defined in relation to her sister?
- How might the image of the dahlia be related to the poem's underlying theme of seemingly inescapable family roles or mythologies?

Other Figures of Speech

Although simile and metaphor are the most common figures of speech, there are several others that we are likely to use in crafting poems. The first is **personification**, in which something nonhuman is described in human terms. If we describe birds weeping, as Robert Frost does in "The Need of Being

Versed in Country Things," or death bragging, as does William Shakespeare in "Shall I compare thee to a summer's day" (see the end of this chapter), we are using personification. Notice how the thing described as human may be nonhuman (such as an animal) or abstract (such as death). In either case, personification brings the thing described closer to home by humanizing it.

Here are some additional examples of personification:

- High on the frozen branches I saw a squirrel jump and
  skid.
  Is this scary? He seemed to say and glanced

  down at me, clutching his branch as it bobbed
  (Anne Carson, "New Rule")

- The sky drank in sparrows making lucid the oaks.
  (Gillian Conoley, "The Sky Drank In")

- … the great sea yearns,
  (John Berryman, "Dream Song 14")

And here's a poem by a student of mine, Carly Ceo. As you read it, notice how the abstraction of *heartbreak* comes alive through Carly's fresh, sarcastic use of personification:

Ship She

I'm not sure why people call ships 'she.'
I'm not cool with personifying a boat to be a woman.
But heartbreak?
Heartbreak smokes a pack a day and
gives you a dirty look in the mirror.
Her hands run up your back like spindly spiders,
when you think you've finally distracted yourself.
Her eyelashes curl to you, like a newborn grasping reaching fingers.
Heartbreak leaves the oven on all night,
until you wake up to the smell of burnt frozen pizza cheese,
crumbs forever sealed to the bottom.
Heartbreak cries a lot.
She whines, nags, complains, breaks stuff,
and then she apologizes.
Heartbreak changes her mind.
And then she changes it again.
And then maybe once more.

She wants you back.
She wants you gone.
Heartbreak she's a beaut ain't she?
She's a killer, *she* is.

Another useful figure of speech, **hyperbole** involves purposeful exaggeration. When the speaker of Walt Whitman's "Song of Myself" (chapter 3) refers to himself as a "kosmos" later in the poem, he gets our attention. Instead of using everyday language to describe his degree of awareness, the speaker describes himself as an entire universe. Readers understand that the speaker is not literally a kosmos; however, on a figurative level, he embodies this almost incomprehensibly vast state of being.

Puns can also function as dynamic parts of a poem by drawing our attention to the multiple meanings of a word or to other words that sound similar to it. Through this process of association, puns unlock a serious pleasure at the heart of poetry: the joy of wordplay. After proclaiming his beloved "more lovely" than "a summer's day," and touting their immortality in the personified line on death noted above, Shakespeare ends "Shall I compare thee to a summer's day" with "When in eternal lines to time thou grow'st; / So long as men can breathe or eyes can see, / So long lives this and this gives life to thee." Although this ending has been the subject of debate, it is fair to say that the word "lines" contains at least two meanings: wrinkles and poetic lines. So, Shakespeare ends his sonnet by proclaiming that when his beloved grows old, his sonnet ("this") will continue to give them life, while also proclaiming that his poetic lines themselves are the vehicle that will continue to enliven. More recently, puns continue to abound, both in popular forms of entertainment, such as hip-hop, and in poetry.

Let's take a look at a prose poem by contemporary United States poet Harryette Mullen (b. 1953), to see how puns can function in a contemporary context. As you read, take note of the double-meanings of many of the words the speaker uses to personify the dictionary and to describe her relationship with it.

Sleeping with the Dictionary

I beg to dicker with my silver-tongued companion, whose lips are ready to read my shining gloss. A versatile partner, conversant and well-versed in the verbal art, the dictionary is not averse to the solitary habits of the curiously wide-awake reader. In the dark night's insomnia, the book is a stimulating sedative, awakening my tired imagination to the hypnagogic trance of language. Retiring to the canopy of the bedroom, turning on the bedside light, taking the big dictionary to bed, clutching the unabridged bulk, heavy with the weight of all the meanings between these covers, smoothing the thin sheets, thick with accented syllables—all are exercises in the conscious regimen of dreamers, who toss words on their tongues while turning illuminated pages. To go through all these motions and procedures, groping in the dark for an alluring word, is the poet's nocturnal mission. Aroused by myriad possibilities, we try out the most perverse positions in the practice of our nightly act, the penetration of the denotative body of the work. Any exit from the logic of language might be an entry in a symptomatic dictionary. The alphabetical order of this ample block of knowledge might render a dense lexicon of lucid hallucinations. Beside the bed, a pad lies open to record the meandering of migratory words. In the rapid eye movement of the poet's night vision, this dictum can be decoded, like the secret acrostic of a lover's name.

Craft Questions

- Which words carry more than one meaning?
- What do Mullen's puns suggest, thematically?
- What does this piece suggest about the life of a poet?

Puns can be serious or silly, depending on the context, degree of subtlety, and number of them you decide to use in a single poem. How you use parts of speech depends on the overall experience you want for your reader. Regardless, it's worth trying some of these techniques to see if you like the results. If used skillfully, they can create explosive new possibilities within the compressed space and time of a poem.

Symbolism

Symbols, or images that stand for more than they literally connote, can also be used to create additional layers of depth within a poem. We are all familiar with symbols that carry agreed upon meanings. For example, the symbol of the dove normally connotes peace; the Christian cross connotes Christ's crucifixion and Christianity generally; the Canadian flag represents Canada; a smiley face connotes happiness; and our phones' ever-growing lexicon of emoticons connote a series of meanings that can be quickly and easily communicated between friends. Similarly, poetry sometimes uses images to refer to familiar symbolic meanings. Rather than refer to an acknowledged, single definition, however, symbols in poetry call to mind a range of possible associations.

Unlike figures of speech, poetic symbols begin not by comparison, but by simply using images. Once we read the poem over several times, and think about the context of the images and their interconnections, we begin to see something deeper at work. It's important not to force symbolic meaning—by consciously adding the word *black* throughout a poem about death, for instance—since heavy-handedness will likely create a dull experience for your reader. Instead, as we write and revise, we can become attuned to possible symbolic suggestion, and learn to let a range of meanings emerge and coalesce.

To begin to explore the role of symbolism in poetry, let's take a look at this poem by twentieth-century United States poet James Wright (1927–80):

A Blessing

Just off the highway to Rochester, Minnesota,
Twilight bounds softly forth on the grass.
And the eyes of those two Indian ponies
Darken with kindness.
They have come gladly out of the willows
To welcome my friend and me.
We step over the barbed wire into the pasture
Where they have been grazing all day, alone.
They ripple tensely, they can hardly contain their happiness
That we have come.
They bow shyly as wet swans. They love each other.
There is no loneliness like theirs.
At home once more,
They begin munching the young tufts of spring in the darkness.
I would like to hold the slenderer one in my arms,
For she has walked over to me
And nuzzled my left hand.
She is black and white,
Her mane falls wild on her forehead,
And the light breeze moves me to caress her long ear
That is delicate as the skin over a girl's wrist.
Suddenly I realize
That if I stepped out of my body I would break
Into blossom.

Craft Questions

- Are there particular lines or images that stand out? What makes them memorable?
- How does Wright describe the ponies?
- What overall mood or feeling does the scene create?

- What is the relationship between the description of the ponies and the last two lines?
- What might the ponies symbolize?

Avoiding Cliché

By including plenty of concrete sensory detail in your poems, you will help to ensure that you are avoiding the use of **cliché**: a simile or metaphor that has been used so much in everyday speech that its original power has been lost. Also referred to as a **dead metaphor**, a cliché is an expression that no longer creates a clear mental picture for your reader.

However, before we "throw the baby out with the bathwater," to use a common cliché, it is worth thinking about why we use these phrases in everyday speech in the first place. For one, they represent a kind of shorthand that can be useful, instructive, or humorous. In addition, they usually get at some common truth, except when they have been dead so long that we no longer understand the derivation of the phrase or how it functions.

For instance, we may be familiar with the phrase "barking up the wrong tree." We could say *I thought it was the right job for me, but it turned out that I was barking up the wrong tree,* meaning that I was pursuing the wrong goal. However, have you ever stopped to consider the phrase's derivation, where it comes from, and what it actually suggests? Although we may visualize a dog literally barking up a tree, what does the "wrong tree" mean, exactly? Well, the phrase refers to the situation in which a dog may bark up a tree to pursue its prey, without realizing that the prey has actually leapt to another tree altogether. So, the phrase *does* refer to pursuing one's object in the wrong place or through the wrong means. Notice, however, that while the basic idea has remained intact, the visual image has partially blurred over time. The more the metaphor is used, the more it "dies" in our mind's eye, rendering it, and potentially our poem, less vivid.

Once you recognize them, there are several ways to deal with clichés in your poems. The first is to transform the cliché into a fresh, vivid metaphor or simile. The second is to get rid of the figure of speech entirely, and focus on an image that captures meaning. Third, you can play with the cliché in some way to render it fresh again. (After all, a cliché such as "barking up the wrong tree" can be enticing, especially if you're fond of dogs!) So, for instance, what if you transformed the cliché by saying something like "barking up the wrong pant leg" to suggest a misguided attraction to a potential love interest, or "barking up the wrong ATM," to suggest a thwarted attempt to make money? Depending on the context and tone of your poem, transformed clichés can add texture, humor, and depth.

Sometimes you will find in revision that while your poem is free of cliché, the language could be livelier. This is often due to the use of **hackneyed** or overused phrases. Hackneyed language can be more difficult to spot than an actual cliché, since phrases and words we use in our everyday lives naturally work their way into our poems. We may be accustomed to referring to unfortunate events, for instance, in the clichés "it was like a bad dream," or "it was a nightmare," but the hackneyed language of *tough times* is equally dead, due to its overuse.

If we find that we are using the same words whenever we write about a particular topic, it may be time to search for a new way of expressing what we mean. This process often involves rethinking the way we describe a common emotion. For instance, if we are accustomed to writing about suffering from "a broken heart," we can use concrete particulars and fresh figurative language to describe how this emotion tastes, feels, and sounds: *bitter as dark chocolate, cold as sleet, broken as the sound of a ukulele with one string.*

Image Types

Whether your images are concrete, figurative, or suggestive of symbolic meaning, you'll want to give some thought to the types of images you tend to use. Do the images in a particular poem originate from a specific place or time? Are they linked by visual type? Or are they varied, jumping around from one set of associations to another? Once you are able to identify the types of images in your poems, you will be more likely to avoid redundancy, and to push yourself to choose images that build upon each other in some way. By building up a series of related details through successive drafts of a poem, you will create a world for your reader to inhabit.

For practice in identifying **image types** or related details, take a look at this poem by twentieth-century United States poet George Oppen (1908–84):

❧ Solution

The puzzle assembled
At last in the box lid showing a green
Hillside, a house,
A barn and man
And wife and children,
All of it polychrome
Lucid, backed by the blue
Sky. The jigsaw of cracks

Crazes the landscape but there is no gap,
No actual edged hole
Nowhere the wooden texture of the table top
Glares out of scale in the picture,
Sordid as cellars, as bare foundations:
There is no piece missing. The puzzle is complete
Now in its red and green and brown.

Craft Questions

- Circle the most vivid images or details. How are they related?
- What does Oppen's choice to repeat "no" in such a short poem imply?
- What could the "solution" of the jigsaw puzzle symbolically suggest?

First Thought to Final Draft

This chapter is subtitled "The Truth Is in the Details" to suggest that good writing, writing that gets at some essential truth or truths, is comprised of many particular details that we can see, touch, hear, and, yes, sometimes even smell and taste. To move our readers, we must earn their trust and awaken their senses.

Further, if we assemble the details well, we can be confident that our readers will be able to do the rest: engage in the work, interpret it, and make connections. At first, this may seem like a lofty goal: to reach into the hearts and minds of others through our writing. But draft by draft, we are focusing and sharpening our work to do just that.

Where do inspiration and intuition fit into this picture, you may ask? For building a poem is not exactly like building an engine or fixing a lawnmower—other activities that require step by step attention to detail. Surely, the more-difficult-to-quantify attributes are as equally important as the practical ones. However, just as a living plant requires the right kind of soil, the right amount of sun and water, our sheer creativity requires certain conditions to thrive. As poets, we have to lay the groundwork for our ideas by identifying techniques in the work of others and by practicing them ourselves.

Ultimately, with the understanding of where, when, and how to apply the actual stuff of lived experience (the nutrients) to our love poem, our poem about loss, our political protest poem, we are growing our ability to powerfully speak in a voice that distinguishes us, in a voice that others will want to hear and read—again and again.

Readings

Jan Beatty (b. 1952)
Blue Dress

Blue dress, white
laced V crossing
my bodice, I loved
that dress. Selfish,
my mother said. Wrong
to care so much for
a dress. I didn't say
the color soothed
my questions. Deep blue,
fresh cotton on
my skin, blue pleasure
rubbing the dress
between my legs
folds into folds
after church
in my bedroom.
Blue dress.

Craft Questions

- What concrete sensory details do you remember after hearing the poem aloud or reading it to yourself?
- Out of the five senses, which is evoked most powerfully? How is this sense related to the subject of the poem?
- How does Beatty's choice to use short, heavily enjambed lines contribute to the overall experience of the poem?

Emily Dickinson (1830–86)
My Life had stood—a Loaded Gun (764)

My Life had stood—a Loaded Gun—
In Corners—till a Day
The Owner passed—identified—
And carried Me away—

And now We roam in Sovreign Woods—
And now We hunt the Doe—

And every time I speak for Him
The Mountains straight reply—

And do I smile, such cordial light
Opon the Valley glow—
It is as a Vesuvian face
Had let it's pleasure through—

And when at Night—Our good Day done—
I guard My Master's Head—
'Tis better than the Eider Duck's
Deep Pillow—to have shared—

To foe of His—I'm deadly foe—
None stir the second time—
On whom I lay a Yellow Eye—
Or an emphatic Thumb—

Though I than He—may longer live
He longer must—than I—
For I have but the power to kill,
Without—the power to die—

Craft Questions

- What details does Dickinson use to personify death?
- What does this personification imply about the nature of mortality?
- Is there a spiritual meaning in Dickinson's metaphors?

Robert Frost (1874–1963)

The Need of Being Versed in Country Things

The house had gone to bring again
To the midnight sky a sunset glow.
Now the chimney was all of the house that stood,
Like a pistil after the petals go.

The barn opposed across the way,
That would have joined the house in flame
Had it been the will of the wind, was left
To bear forsaken the place's name.

No more it opened with all one end
For teams that came by the stony road
To drum on the floor with scurrying hoofs
And brush the mow with the summer load.

The birds that came to it through the air
At broken windows flew out and in,
Their murmur more like the sigh we sigh
From too much dwelling on what has been.

Yet for them the lilac renewed its leaf,
And the aged elm, though touched with fire;
And the dry pump flung up an awkward arm;
And the fence post carried a strand of wire.

For them there was really nothing sad.
But though they rejoiced in the nest they kept,
One had to be versed in country things
Not to believe the phoebes wept.

Craft Questions

- How would you describe the types of images in this poem?
- What overall mood or tone does Frost's description set?
- How does Frost's use of personification add to the emotional effect of the poem?

Rainer Maria Rilke (1875–1926)
translated by Stephen Mitchell
[Rose, oh pure contradiction]

Rose, oh pure contradiction, joy
of being No-one's sleep under so many
Lids.

Craft Questions

- What figure of speech is used in this poem?
- Can you paraphrase the contradiction of the rose?

William Shakespeare (1564–1616)
Shall I compare thee to a summer's day

Shall I compare thee to a summer's day?
Thou art more lovely and more temperate:
Rough winds do shake the darling buds of May,
And summer's lease hath all too short a date:
Sometime too hot the eye of heaven shines,
And often is his gold complexion dimm'd;
And every fair from fair sometime declines,
By chance, or nature's changing course, untrimm'd;
But thy eternal summer shall not fade
Nor lose possession of that fair thou ow'st;
Nor shall Death brag thou wander'st in his shade,
When in eternal lines to time thou grow'st;
So long as men can breathe or eyes can see,
So long lives this, and this gives life to thee.

Craft Questions

- What type of images does Shakespeare use in this sonnet?
- How is the controlling metaphor developed as the poem progresses?

Exercises

Exercise 1: "I'm Nobody! Who Are You?"

Begin by creating a list of images, objects, colors, and details—in nature or human-made—that remind you of yourself. Select a detail that seems most unique and use it to begin a poem which:

- uses the first person I;
- uses *like* or *as* to compare yourself to something else; this could be something in nature such as a plant or animal or something human-made;
- makes the object or being (you) do something that further emphasizes a particular emotional state;
- uses at least one color and any other details you wish to create a scene and a mood.

Review Charles Simic's "The World" (in chapter 1) for an example.

Objective: To use concrete sensory detail to develop a self-portrait that may surprise even you!

Exercise 2: Mad Libs for Poets[1]

Fill in the blanks below, working quickly. Avoid overthinking. If you have no immediate response, move on to the following sentence.

1. A rainy day is like ______________________________
2. Her diamond was shining as brightly as ____________________
3. Now that I was older, I no longer had to ____________________
4. "Deliver me," she whispered to ______________________
5. Waves of __________ poured out of the ____________________
6. A dog's hot breath is like ______________________________
7. I stared down at my watch as if ______________________
8. The number of stars in the sky is as incalculable as __________
9. Cream is to milk as ________ is to ____________________
10. A lemon as yellow as ______________________________
11. That day came more slowly than ______________________
12. Time passed as quickly as ______________________________
13. "Who am I to myself," she asked, now that ______________
14. Disappointment fell on my shoulders like ____________________
15. He couldn't tell her, now that they were ____________________
16. As dry as a sandbox in ______________________________

1 Adapted from Linnea Johnson's exercise "As/Like/Finish the Sentence" in *The Practice of Poetry: Writing Exercises from Poets Who Teach*, edited by Robin Behn and Chase Twichell (New York: HarperCollins, 1992).

17. ______________________________ is like a broken wind-up toy

18. Riding the glass elevator reminded her of the time she ________

19. If it's really your ________, you should know better ___________

20. It was so green that spring that ___________________________

Read over your finished sentences, alone or to a group. Begin a poem by using the sentence you like the most. Develop details around this metaphor, simile, or analogy. Or try working some of these into a poem you have already begun.

Objective: To begin a poem or transform one through the use of fresh figures of speech.

Exercise 3: A Colorful Arrangement

First, choose a color, and create a quick list of things that you associate with it. Make sure that your list includes both recognizable examples and more personal ones. Also consider symbolic associations. For example, if your color is red, you could include on your list: *apple, my first composition notebook, heated discussion.*

Once you have assembled a list of at least one full notebook page, begin circling the items that feel most unique, alive, or suggestive. Gradually turn the circled items on your list into a poem. If possible, use the color in your title, and repeat the color as many times as you like in order to create rhythm.

Objective: To use the visual imagery of color to jump-start your imagination and connect disparate ideas.

three | sound and rhythm

some enchanted music

POEMS SING. THEY WHISPER. They shout. Poems chant. They stutter. They fly. Poems pause. They give us room to breathe. They take our breath away. As we touched upon in the introduction, a great deal of poetry's power lies in its musical and rhythmic capabilities. To harness this power, you'll want to become more closely acquainted with the many possibilities of **sound**, including types of **rhyme** and **non-rhyming sound linkages**, as well as the variety of **rhythm** or beats, available to you as a poet. Although we have an enormous print-culture today, poetry maintains its oral roots as evidenced in the undying tradition of poetry readings. And in terms of poetic process, poets often report that they compose aurally—somehow hearing the music of the poem before they even know the exact words. So, if we want to gain an understanding of what a poem *means*, we must first hear how and why the poem sounds the way that it does.

Have you ever heard a song and almost immediately memorized its lyrics and melody? You probably didn't think of this as memorization, since it didn't require any special effort; rather, that song just seemed to stick in your head. Sometimes referred to as *earworms*, these catchy lyrics can seem impossible to get rid of once they've implanted themselves. A poem you love can have that same impact, and if you're inclined to try memorizing a few lines, you'll find the process comes naturally once you've read your favorite poem over enough times. Some of my favorite lines come at the beginning of this poem by twentieth- and twenty-first-century United States poet W.S. Merwin (1927–2019):

✤ Late Spring

Coming into the high room again after years
after oceans and shadows of hills and the sounds of lies
after losses and feet on stairs

after looking and mistakes and forgetting
turning there thinking to find
no one except those I knew
finally I saw you
sitting in white
already waiting

you of whom I had heard
with my own ears since the beginning
for whom more than once
I have opened the door
believing you were not far

Generally considered a love poem to his wife, Paula, whom Merwin married later in life, "Late Spring" highlights the poet's ability to tune in to language's aural qualities: the way in which he *listens*. Forgoing punctuation and rhythmic in its phrasing, the poem cries out to be read aloud, held close to your breath and heart. Notice, for instance, the repetition of "after" in the first stanza; here Merwin uses **anaphora**, the repetition of a word or phrase at the beginning of lines or sentences, to emphasize the fact that so much time has passed: whole lifetimes, in a sense. This makes the appearance of the beloved in the lines "finally I saw you / sitting in white / already waiting" even more astonishing, both as a kind of miraculous apparition and as somehow preexisting, before or outside of linear time.

Try flipping through this book or other collections you're reading to find a poem that *you* particularly love. Read the poem silently multiple times and read it aloud too, until you've internalized it. Carry a copy of it with you for a few days; read it at breakfast, when you're waiting for the bus, in between shifts. See how it works on you. See how it becomes your own, the same way that the music you carry with you, your favorite music, shapes your experience in ways almost impossible to articulate. This is part of the mystery and beauty of poetry. It's written *in* and made up *of* words, but at its best it often reaches us in a way that is somehow *before* or *beyond* language. But in order for this magic to work on us as lovers and creators of poetry, we have to tune our poetic ears. And learning to slow down—to enter poetry musically before we begin to analyze, critique, revise, or reimagine—is a helpful way to start.

Rhyme

To rhyme or not to rhyme? You may be asking yourself this question. Maybe you've generally written poetry in rhyme and want to try limiting it. Or maybe you'd like to learn to use rhyme more effectively. For a period of time, many of us involved in the teaching of poetry dissuaded beginning writers from using rhyme. The thinking went something like this: if used without the necessary skill, rhyme renders poems clunky, singsong, greeting-card-like. Its repeated sounds limit the attention given to other elements. It's a throwback to a previous era; it's not contemporary. Although these objections to rhyme are well founded, since rhyme used unskillfully can, in fact, ruin a perfectly good poem, in recent years we've experienced an increasing appreciation of how rich rhyme can be when used well.

The most obvious kind of rhyme is **true rhyme** (also called perfect or full rhyme): rhyme in which the final vowel and all following consonants or syllables are identical, while the preceding consonants are different, for example, *bread, head; today, dismay.* In the case of **slant rhyme** (also called imperfect or eye rhyme), there is a close, but not exact, sound linkage, as in *beetle, juggle*; *sun, gone.* Here are some additional examples of these common types of rhyme, emphasized in boldface:

True Rhyme

The instructor said,

Go home and write
a page tonight.
And let that page come out of ***you***—
Then, it will be ***true****.*

I wonder if it's that simple?
I am twenty-two, colored, born in Winston-**Salem**.

I went to school there, then Durham, then here
to this college on the hill above **Harlem**.
(Langston Hughes, "Theme for English B")

From narrow provinces
of fish and bread and **tea**,
home of the long **tides**
where the bay leaves the **sea**
twice a day and takes
the herrings long **rides**,
(Elizabeth Bishop, "The Moose")

Slant Rhyme

Tell all the truth but tell it slant—
Success in Circuit **lies**
Too **bright** for our infirm **Delight**
The Truth's superb **surprise**
(Emily Dickinson, "Tell all the truth but tell it slant—[1263]")

The plump good-natured children play in the blue **pool**:
roll and plop, plop and **roll**;

slide and tumble, oiled, in the slippery **sun**
silent as otters, turning over and **in**,
(P.K. Page, "Motel Pool")

Everywhere there is a **cushion**
a spacing **invitation**
(Elizabeth Savage, "Path")

Notice how the boldfaced words fall at the end of lines? This is because we're currently focusing on **end rhyme**.

If you look carefully at the above examples, however, you'll discover other kinds of rhyme, including **internal rhyme**: when a sound from a middle of a line is linked with a sound at the end of that line or with a sound in the middle of the next, as in, "*Then, it will be **true**.* // I wonder if it's that simple? / I am twenty-**two** ..."; and **identical rhyme** or repeated words, as in "roll and plop, plop and roll."

Non-Rhyming Sound Linkages

Just as you have probably tried using some rhyme, you have also probably tried using non-rhyming sound linkages, maybe without even noticing. It's wonderful when you don't have to force it: when your poems are naturally rich with sound. However, by becoming more aware of some of the possibilities, you may be able to help this process along. Here are some of the most common types of linkages:

- **Alliteration**: the repetition of sounds (usually consonants) at the *beginning* of words within close proximity, for example, *lightly lifted, suddenly swollen*

- **Assonance**: the repetition of vowel sounds in words within close proximity, for example, *gun, sun*; *altered, perturbed* (not spelled the same, but containing similar sounds)

- **Consonance**: the repetition of consonant sounds in words within close proximity, for example, *propelled, spelled*; *fitted, gifted*

To see these non-rhyming sound linkages in action, let's take a look at "Pied Beauty" by nineteenth-century British poet and Jesuit priest Gerard Manley Hopkins (1844–89). This poem is one of Hopkins's shortened sonnets (more on sonnets in the next chapter, but you may notice that there is a set pattern to the end rhymes and a set beat to the lines). Whether or not you relate to Hopkins's religious faith, notice the sheer exuberance of this poem. And as you read, see if you can mark rhymes and non-rhyming sound linkages. Spoiler alert: there are a lot! Hopkins was a maximalist when it came to sound:

Glory be to God for dappled things –
  For skies of couple-colour as a brinded cow;
    For rose-moles all in stipple upon trout that swim;
Fresh-firecoal chestnut-falls; finches' wings;
  Landscape plotted and pieced – fold, fallow, and plough;
    And all trades, their gear and tackle and trim.

All things counter, original, spare, strange;
  Whatever is fickle, freckled (who knows how?)
    With swift, slow; sweet, sour; adazzle, dim;
He fathers-forth whose beauty is past change:
          Praise Him.

Craft Questions

- What do you notice about the pattern of sounds—rhymed and unrhymed?
- How does this list poem change in tone and focus mid-way through?
- Discuss the ways in which the poem's rhyme and non-rhyming sound linkages emphasize its meaning.
- How does the structure of prayer affect the poem's structure?

Next, let's take a look at a poem by twentieth-century United States poet, Gwendolyn Brooks (1917–2000). If you're in class or in a small group, you could start by having several people read this poem aloud, noticing how your readings invariably differ. Brooks often wrote about the types of people she encountered growing up in South Side Chicago, and this poem is no exception:

The Bean Eaters

They eat beans mostly, this old yellow pair.
Dinner is a casual affair.
Plain chipware on a plain and creaking wood,
Tin flatware.

Two who are Mostly Good.
Two who have lived their day,
But keep on putting on their clothes
And putting things away.

And remembering ...
Remembering, with twinklings and twinges,
As they lean over the beans in their rented back room that is full of beads
and receipts and dolls and cloths, tobacco crumbs, vases and
fringes.

Craft Questions

- Which words are linked in rhyme? How do these paired words emphasize meaning?
- What non-rhyming sound linkages do you hear in the poem and in the last stanza in particular?
- How might the change in sound and rhythm at the end of the poem be related to a change in perspective?

And finally, let's take a look by contemporary United States poet Danez Smith. Smith is a Black, queer poet who is known not only for their groundbreaking books, but also for their live poetry performances. Like Hopkins, Smith frames the following poem as a kind of prayer:

The 17-Year-Old & the Gay Bar

this gin-heavy heaven, blessed ground to think *gay* & mean *we*.
bless the fake id & the bouncer who knew
this need to be needed, to belong, to know how
a man taste full on vodka & free of sin. i know not which god to pray to.
i look to christ, i look to every mouth on the dance floor, i order
a whiskey coke, name it the blood of my new savior. he is just.
he begs me to dance, to marvel men with the
                                                            dash
of hips i brought, he deems my mouth in some stranger's mouth
        necessary.
bless that man's mouth, the song we sway sloppy to, the beat, the bridge,
        the length
of his hand on my thigh & back & i know not which country i am of.
i want to live on his tongue, build a home of gospel & gayety
i want to raise a city behind his teeth for all boys of choirs & closets to
        refuge in.
i want my new god to look at the mecca i built him & call it damn good
or maybe i'm just tipsy & free for the first time, willing to worship
        anything i can taste.

Craft Questions

- How does Smith establish a rhythm or beat in "The 17-Year-Old & the Gay Bar"?
- What rhyme and non-rhyming sound linkages do you hear in the poem? How might these sounds contribute to meaning?
- Discuss the mood or tone of the poem.
- Does Smith's poem contribute to your understanding of what it means to come of age as a queer adolescent?

Although they lived in different places and times, Hopkins, Brooks, and Smith all experiment with sound. And in each of these poems, sounds help set up a certain rhythm, beat, and pattern of breath—a pattern that is then strategically altered—making the experience of reading the poems physical as well as intellectual. In addition, all three poets seem to elevate ordinary, imperfect, and everyday reality through their representations: a radical statement in Victorian England, midcentury America, and today. What similarities and differences do *you* detect in the work of these historically distinct poets?

Rendering Rhyme Subtle

Hopkins, Brooks, and Smith manage to use rhyme without allowing it to take over. If your poems tend to rhyme, you may have encountered the struggle to keep rhyme from drowning out other elements, including meaning. One way of achieving this goal of rendering rhyme subtle is to use internal rhyme instead of (or in addition to) end rhyme. For instance, take a look at this poem by contemporary United States poet Donald Revell (b. 1954). As you read, focus particular attention on the opening lines:

Car Radio

An in-joke and the long days faltering
at the edge of fields just visible as we
drive on, the windows shuddering in twilight,
are parts of the songs. And we are traveling
faster all the time, no way to keep
up with them. Between ourselves and the night
coming on to uneasy towns like smoke
the songs are a commitment we do not make
that gets made for us. Our own words reshaped
into the reliable, broken speech of the next
town and all those after it. As we
drive on, we see each one of them escape
us, certain that it will reappear in the context
of another song, the in-joke of the whole country.

Notice how Revell strategically places the *ing* sound of gerunds to create a distinct yet partially muted or soft sound. The end rhyme of "faltering" and "traveling" is spaced four lines apart; "shuddering" is placed in the middle, instead of at the end, of line three; and "coming" begins line seven.

Another related method of rendering rhyme subtle is to use **enjambment**. Although line two of Revell's poem is the most dramatically enjambed, since the line breaks on "as we" and then runs on to the next line, "drive on," other lines are not end-stopped with punctuation, but run into the following lines as well. This keeps rhyme from weighing the poem down; the poem keeps moving, as does the car and its passengers, even as we hear the *ing* sounds reverberate. We could even say that the poem's use of enjambment *enacts* the ideas it explores: of personal and cultural transience, of memory's traces.

Rhythms in Everyday Life

As we're discovering, it's not just the sounds that you use in your poems that are important; equally important is their placement. Similarly, we can't understand how to work with rhythm without thinking about where and how it appears—both in our lives and in our poems. Right now, as I type, I hear the rhythm of a snoring dog: the inhalation and exhalation of a creature I love. And without really hearing it, I too am participating in the essential rhythm of breathing. My heart is beating (along with my furry friend's). The clock in my kitchen is ticking. The birds outside are chirping (not quite on beat, but almost). The list goes on. Stop for a moment and consider the rhythms of *your* daily life—or just of this particular moment. And if you're in a place that's noisy with many sounds, notice this cacophony; this too is a kind of (irregular) rhythm.

In fact, rhythm is with us throughout our entire life. Before we're even born, we're experiencing the rhythms of our mother's heart, and soon after, we may have been sung lullabies with simple, soothing rhythms. Do you remember the nursery rhymes and lullabies of Mother Goose? Although the author's actual identity remains unknown, most rhymes can be traced back to seventeenth-century France. Here's one that may sound familiar:

Hush little baby, don't say a word,
Papa's gonna buy you a mockingbird.

And if that mockingbird won't sing,
Papa's gonna buy you a diamond ring.

And if that diamond ring turns to brass,
Papa's gonna buy you a looking glass.

And if that looking glass gets broke,
Papa's gonna buy you a billy goat.

And if that billy goat won't pull,
Papa's gonna buy you a cart and bull.

And if that cart and bull turn over,
Papa's gonna buy you a dog named Rover.

And if that dog named Rover won't bark,
Papa's gonna buy you a horse and cart.

And if that horse and cart fall down,
You'll still be the sweetest little baby in town!

Craft Questions

- Describe the basic rhythm of this lullaby.
- How do the simple rhymes and rhythm complement the verse's meaning and purpose?
- Would you sing "Hush little baby" to a child? Why or why not?

Repetition and Line Length

If you want to build more of a sense of rhythm in your poems, you might begin by working with repetition and focusing on line length. To really get an idea of rhythmic potential of these two techniques, let's look at the work of two of North America's most oratorical poets, Walt Whitman (1819–92) and Allen Ginsberg (1926–98). Whitman's *Leaves of Grass*, first published 1855, broke out of nineteenth-century forms and conventions, establishing a socially and formally radical free-verse poetry, marked by long lines and establishing Whitman as an important voice in poetry of and about the United States. To a large extent, Beat poet Allen Ginsberg followed in Whitman's footsteps, publishing his own radical epic, *Howl*, in 1956, and performing to large audiences both live and on the page.

Walt Whitman
Excerpts from *Song of Myself* (1892 version)

1
I celebrate myself, and sing myself,
And what I assume you shall assume,
For every atom belonging to me as good belongs to you.

I loafe and invite my soul,
I lean and loafe at my ease observing a spear of summer grass.
My tongue, every atom of my blood, form'd from this soil, this air,
Born here of parents born here from parents the same, and their parents
        the same,
I, now thirty-seven years old in perfect health begin,
Hoping to cease not till death.

Creeds and schools in abeyance,
Retiring back a while sufficed at what they are, but never forgotten,
I harbor for good or bad, I permit to speak at every hazard,
Nature without check with original energy.

2

Houses and rooms are full of perfumes, the shelves are crowded with perfumes,
I breathe the fragrance myself and know it and like it,
The distillation would intoxicate me also, but I shall not let it.

The atmosphere is not a perfume, it has no taste of the distillation, it is odorless,
It is for my mouth forever, I am in love with it,
I will go to the bank by the wood and become undisguised and naked,
I am mad for it to be in contact with me.

The smoke of my own breath,
Echoes, ripples, buzz'd whispers, love-root, silk-thread, crotch and vine,
My respiration and inspiration, the beating of my heart, the passing of blood and air through my lungs,
The sniff of green leaves and dry leaves, and of the shore and dark-color'd sea-rocks, and of hay in the barn,
The sound of the belch'd words of my voice loos'd to the eddies of the wind,
A few light kisses, a few embraces, a reaching around of arms,
The play of shine and shade on the trees as the supple boughs wag,
The delight alone or in the rush of the streets, or along the fields and hill-sides,
The feeling of health, the full-noon trill, the song of me rising from bed and meeting the sun.

Have you reckon'd a thousand acres much? have you reckon'd the earth much?
Have you practis'd so long to learn to read?
Have you felt so proud to get at the meaning of poems?

Stop this day and night with me and you shall possess the origin of all poems,
You shall possess the good of the earth and sun, (there are millions of suns left,)
You shall no longer take things at second or third hand, nor look through the eyes of the dead, nor feed on the spectres in books,

You shall not look through my eyes either, nor take things from me,
You shall listen to all sides and filter them from your self.

...

Craft Questions

- What do you notice about the experience of reading or hearing the poem aloud?
- What elements help to establish the poem's rhythm?
- How do Whitman's multiple repetitions work to further the meaning or experience of the poem?
- Discuss how the poem's end-stopped lines might serve Whitman's needs as a list-maker, as a poet who tries to get the whole world into his poetry.

Allen Ginsberg
A Supermarket in California

What thoughts I have of you tonight, Walt Whitman, for I walked down the sidestreets under the trees with a headache self-conscious looking at the full moon.

In my hungry fatigue, and shopping for images, I went into the neon fruit supermarket, dreaming of your enumerations!

What peaches and what penumbras! Whole families shopping at night! Aisles full of husbands! Wives in the avocados, babies in the tomatoes!—and you, Garcia Lorca, what were you doing down by the watermelons?

I saw you, Walt Whitman, childless, lonely old grubber, poking among the meats in the refrigerator and eyeing the grocery boys.

I heard you asking questions of each: Who killed the pork chops? What price bananas? Are you my Angel?

I wandered in and out of the brilliant stacks of cans following you, and followed in my imagination by the store detective.

We strode down the open corridors together in our solitary fancy tasting artichokes, possessing every frozen delicacy, and never passing the cashier.

Where are we going, Walt Whitman? The doors close in an hour. Which way does your beard point tonight?

(I touch your book and dream of our odyssey in the supermarket and feel absurd.)

Will we walk all night through solitary streets? The trees add shade to shade, lights out in the houses, we'll both be lonely.

Will we stroll dreaming of the lost America of love past blue automobiles in driveways, home to our silent cottage?

Ah, dear father, graybeard, lonely old courage-teacher, what America did you have when Charon quit poling his ferry and you got out on a smoking bank and stood watching the boat disappear on the black waters of Lethe?

Craft Questions

- In what ways does Ginsberg's poem stylistically resemble the opening sections of Whitman's "Song of Myself"? Consider stanza breaks, line length, rhythm, and rhyme.
- In what ways does Ginsberg's poem thematically resemble Whitman's? Here, consider subject matter.
- Why do you think Ginsberg addresses Whitman? What role does Whitman serve in the poem?
- How does the tone change from the beginning of the poem to the end?

If we think of the unit of the line as an inhalation made possible by literally inspiring breath, it is no wonder that Whitman's and Ginsberg's extremely long lines seem connected not only to the body but also to the spirit. And in both cases, the use of anaphora seems to echo the language of the Bible or of oratory, generally. Of course, there are other ways that long lines can function, but for now, it might be helpful to experiment with various line lengths before settling on your poem's final form. (See exercise 2 at the end of this chapter.)

To further observe the impact of lineation on rhythm, let's look at a poem that uses relatively short lines by contemporary United States poet Alice Notley (b. 1945):

I the people

I the people
to the things that are were &
come to be.
We were once what we know
when we
make love When we go away
from each other because

we have been created
    at 10th & A, in winter &
of trees & of the history of houses
    we hope we are
notes of the musical scale of
    heaven—I the
people so repetitious, & my
    vision of
to hold the neighbors loose-
    ly here in
light of gel, my gel, my vision
    come out of
my eyes to hold you sur-
    round you in
gold & you don't know it
    ever. Everyone
we the people having our
    vision of
gold & silver & silken liquid
    light flowed
from our eyes & caressing
    all around all the
walls. I am a late Pre-
    in this dawn of
We the people
to the things that are & were
    & come to be
Once what we knew was only
    and numbers became
It is numbers & gold & at 10th
    & A you don't
have to know it ever. Opening
    words that show
Opening words that show that we
    were once
the first to recognize
    the immortality of numbered
bodies. And we are the masters
    of hearing & saying
at the double edge of body &
    breath
We the lovers & the eyes
All over, inside her
    when the wedding

is over, & the Park "lies cold &
    lifeless"
I the people, whatever is said
    by the first
one along, Angel-Agate. I wear
    your colors
I hear what we say & what
    we say … (and I
the people am still parted in
    two & would cry)

Craft Questions

- Read the poem aloud. How does Notley establish the poem's beat or rhythm?
- Describe the experience created by the poem's short, enjambed lines and indentations.
- What kind of democracy does Notley seem to espouse?

Like Whitman and Ginsberg, second-generation New York School poet, Notley often confronts conflicts between personal freedoms and social hierarchies, and she too often does this in longer, even epic poems. As a twenty-first-century poet, Notley experiments with and extends this tradition of social resistance. What similarities and differences do you detect between the three poets? Are you drawn to one more than the others?

Finding your own unique rhythms—the sounds, beats, and forms that make your poems tick—will often involve an intuitive process. But as this chapter has suggested, the more you tune into the sounds around you and the inspiring poetry of others, the more quickly your own poetic ear will develop. This involves trying on some things that *won't* fit too; you'll only know once you've tried. So instead of settling on line-length, rhyme, and rhythm right away, stay loose and experiment as long as you can! Keep your poem in progress instead of rushing it onto the computer. This is why that notebook or voice memo app may be so helpful. Before you type up a draft, keep playing with the poem every which way. Then, when you sit down to type, keep playing. After all, it only takes a few seconds to click return to see how a different form of lineation may alter the sound and sense of your poem. Similarly, with a little practice, the process of altering rhyme and working with repetition will come naturally too. Before you know it, you'll be trying multiple variations before settling on one you love. And not long after that, you'll begin to arrive at a style and voice that feels uniquely your own.

Readings

Gwendolyn Brooks (1917–2000)
"We Real Cool"

The Pool Players.
Seven at the Golden Shovel.

We real cool. We
Left school. We

Lurk late. We
Strike straight. We

Sing sin. We
Thin gin. We

Jazz June. We
Die soon.

Craft Questions

- After hearing several people read this poem aloud, what differences did you hear in the performances?
- What does the enjambment do to the rhyme of the poem?
- What kind of beat do you hear? Does it remind you of a song pattern or a common beat?
- Does the beat and rhythm seem to mirror the subject matter of the poem?

e.e. cummings (1894–1962)
67: "when faces called flowers float out of the ground"

when faces called flowers float out of the ground
and breathing is wishing and wishing is having —
but keeping is downward and doubting and never
— it's april(yes,april;my darling)it's spring!
yes the pretty birds frolic as spry as can fly
yes the little fish gambol as glad as can be
(yes the mountains are dancing together)

when every leaf opens without any sound
and wishing is having and having is giving —
but keeping is doting and nothing and nonsense
— alive;we're alive,dear:it's(kiss me now)spring!

now the pretty birds hover so she and so he
now the little fish quiver so you and so i
(now the mountains are dancing,the mountains)

when more than was lost has been found has been found
and having is giving and giving is living—
but keeping is darkness and winter and cringing
—it's spring(all our night becomes day)o,it's spring!
all the pretty birds dive to the heart of the sky
all the little fish climb through the mind of the sea
(all the mountains are dancing;are dancing)

Craft Questions

- What gives the poem its forward momentum?
- How do the multiple repetitions work to further the meaning or experience of the poem?
- How do you read the parenthetical refrain lines: as asides, in a different tone from the rest of the poem, in some other way?
- What do you notice about cummings's verbs?

David Trinidad (b. 1953)
Slicker

came in a pink,
orange and white
striped metal tube,
with a black curlicue
border and a splayed
gold base. It came
in any number of
mod shades: Nippy
Beige, Chelsea Pink,
Poppycock, Hot Nec-
taringo, Pinkadilly,
Dicey Peach. There
were several tubes in
my mother's makeup
drawer in the bath-
room five out of six
of us used (my father
had his own bathroom,
as forbidden as the
walk-in closet where

his *Playboys* were
hidden under a stack
of sweaters on the top
shelf). All the girls
at school had Slicker
in their purses; I
watched them apply
The London Look
at the beginning and
end of each class. I
marveled at what else
spilled out: compact,
mascara brush, eye
shadow, wallet, troll
doll, dyed rabbit's
foot, chewing gum,
tampon, pink plastic
comb. At home I
stared at myself in
the medicine cabinet
mirror and, as my
brother pounded
on the locked bath-
room door, twisted
a tube and rubbed,
ever so slightly,
Slicker on my lips.

Craft Questions

- How would this personal narrative's pace and tone be different if it were written in longer, end-stopped lines? (Try recopying a few lines to see.)
- What do we discover about the speaker's adolescence through the objects he describes?

Joy Harjo (b. 1951)

The Woman Hanging from the Thirteenth Floor Window

She is the woman hanging from the 13th floor
window. Her hands are pressed white against the
concrete moulding of the tenement building. She
hangs from the 13th floor window in east Chicago,
with a swirl of birds over her head. They could
be a halo, or a storm of glass waiting to crush her.

She thinks she will be set free.

The woman hanging from the 13th floor window
on the east side of Chicago is not alone.
She is a woman of children, of the baby, Carlos,
and of Margaret, and of Jimmy who is the oldest.
She is her mother's daughter and her father's son.
She is several pieces between the two husbands
she has had. She is all the women of the apartment
building who stand watching her, watching themselves.

When she was young she ate wild rice on scraped down
plates in warm wood rooms. It was in the farther
north and she was the baby then. They rocked her.

She sees Lake Michigan lapping at the shores of
herself. It is a dizzy hole of water and the rich
live in tall glass houses at the edge of it. In some
places Lake Michigan speaks softly, here, it just sputters
and butts itself against the asphalt. She sees
other buildings just like hers. She sees other
women hanging from many-floored windows
counting their lives in the palms of their hands
and in the palms of their children's hands.

She is the woman hanging from the 13th floor window
on the Indian side of town. Her belly is soft from
her children's births, her worn Levis swing down below
her waist, and then her feet, and then her heart.
She is dangling.

The woman hanging from the 13th floor hears voices.
They come to her in the night when the lights have gone
dim. Sometimes they are little cats mewing and scratching
at the door; sometimes they are her grandmother's voice,
and sometimes they are gigantic men of light whispering
to her to get up, to get up, to get up. That's when she wants
to have another child to hold onto in the night, to be able
to fall back into dreams.

And the woman hanging from the 13th floor window
hears other voices. Some of them scream out from below
for her to jump, they would push her over. Others cry softly
from the sidewalks, pull their children up like flowers and gather

them into their arms. They would help her, like themselves.
But she is the woman hanging from the 13th floor window,
and she knows she is hanging by her own fingers, her
own skin, her own thread of indecision.

She thinks of Carlos, of Margaret, of Jimmy.
She thinks of her father, and of her mother.
She thinks of all the women she has been, of all
the men. She thinks of the color of her skin, and
of Chicago streets, and of waterfalls and pines.
She thinks of moonlight nights, and of cool spring storms.
Her mind chatters like neon and northside bars.
She thinks of the 4 A.M. lonelinesses that have folded
her up like death, discordant, without logical and
beautiful conclusion. Her teeth break off at the edges.
She would speak.

The woman hangs from the 13th floor window crying for
the lost beauty of her own life. She sees the
sun falling west over the grey plane of Chicago.
She thinks she remembers listening to her own life
break loose, as she falls from the 13th floor
window on the east side of Chicago, or as she
climbs back up to claim herself again.

Craft Questions

- Which words and phrases are repeated in Harjo's poem?
- Does Harjo's poetic use of repetition remind you of other genres (such as sermons or songs)?
- How do the poem's repetitions impact the narrative?

John Ashbery (1927–2017)
Street Musicians

One died, and the soul was wrenched out
Of the other in life, who, walking the streets
Wrapped in an identity like a coat, sees on and on
The same corners, volumetrics, shadows
Under trees. Farther than anyone was ever
Called, through increasingly suburban airs
And ways, with autumn falling over everything:

The plush leaves the chattels in barrels
Of an obscure family being evicted
Into the way it was, and is. The other beached
Glimpses of what the other was up to:
Revelations at last. So they grew to hate and forget each other.

So I cradle this average violin that knows
Only forgotten showtunes, but argues
The possibility of free declamation anchored
To a dull refrain, the year turning over on itself
In November, with the spaces among the days
More literal, the meat more visible on the bone.
Our question of a place of origin hangs
Like smoke: how we picnicked in pine forests,
In coves with the water always seeping up, and left
Our trash, sperm and excrement everywhere, smeared
On the landscape, to make of us what we could.

Craft Questions

- How would you describe the sound and pace of "Street Musicians"?
- Keeping in mind that not all poems have to have a clear, easily paraphrased meaning, what feelings or moods do you associate with this poem?

Exercises

Exercise 1: Lyrical Re-Do

For a few days, collect favorite song lyrics from a number of different songs, copying them into your notebook or creating voice recordings on your phone. Use brief snippets from each song (1–4 lines).

Once you have collected at least ten samples, type them all up into one file as a single poem. Next, think about order, shuffling and recombining lines however you see fit, considering both sound and meaning. Add some additional lines of your own for "connective tissue" if you think the poem needs it.

Objective: To create a poem out of found material. By combining and recombining others' voices, you'll eventually arrive at your own original sound.

Exercise 2: Long Lines, Short Lines

Find some poems you love in different rhythms, including some poems in long lines and some in short lines, to determine their potential effects. Next, look at some of your own poems. How would you characterize their rhythms? Or did you mix up rhythms in the same poem?

Once you determine a pattern (or patterns), write a new poem that breaks your default. Try to choose a pattern that enhances your poem. For example, try couplets for a love poem or short lines for a poem that benefits from a clipped, staccato beat.

Objective: To focus your attention on the rhythm of poetry and the importance of line length. By becoming more conscious of your own natural instincts, you will then be freed up to experiment with various rhythmic variations.

Exercise 3: Repetition and Difference

Find a phrase or line that you feel like repeating. This phrase might be something you overhear or see, or it might pop into your head out of thin air. In any case, don't overthink it.

Use your repeated or refrain line to create rhythm in a new poem or in a poem with which you're currently struggling. Read aloud to determine how to revise. Are you currently repeating your phrase or line too often? Not often enough? Try varying your phrase or sentence and moving it around within the poem to create more rhythmic interest. Also think about the various meanings these differences may suggest.

Objective: To train your ear in the beat or rhythm of poetry. To warm-up for villanelles (in the next chapter).

four | traditional form

rules are made to be broken

So far, we've mostly been concerned with **free verse** or poetry written in no fixed form. But you may have noticed that many of the free verse poems we've discussed do, in fact, contain *some* elements of form—whether we're looking at the altered rhyme schemes in Brooks's "The Bean Eaters" and "We Real Cool" or the **quatrains** (four-line stanzas) of Simic's "The World" in chapter 1. Through these and multiple other examples, we can see that accomplished free verse poets possess knowledge of what has come before them, in terms of the **traditional form** or set patterns of poetry, and this knowledge informs much of what they do, subtly or explicitly. Many poets today continue to draw from the formal tradition, adapting it to suit their own purposes; this process represents a vital part of their practice.

Rather than being a burden, form can actually free you as a poet, if you find ways to make it your own. And a lot of the fun comes in breaking the rules, once we know what they are. This is true for other kinds of artists too. Have you ever heard a local band cover one of your favorite songs? Or a popular band cover a song by someone else? If so, you may have noticed that their versions were different: often intentionally so. If you're a jazz fan, you may be familiar with jazz standards: important songs in most jazz musicians' repertoire. Songs such as "Night and Day" or "My Funny Valentine" have been played by so many musicians and in so many different ways that the original represents only one version. And in some cases, a musician may riff on the original to such an extent that the song becomes altogether new. As we'll soon see, contemporary poets are often up to something similar. If you're not already trying your hand at adopting and adapting forms, this chapter invites you to do so. You'll find a veritable treasure trove of possibilities.

Stanza Patterns

Similar to a prose paragraph, the unit of the **stanza** is most often used to contain a set of thoughts or feelings. In free verse poetry, stanzas can be any length, and are often **irregular**, meaning that they do not contain a fixed number of lines. However, many free verse poets also choose to use stanzas of consistent length. Such patterns were originally used in syllabic and metered poetry (more on that later). Here are some of the most common stanza patterns:

Couplets: two-line stanzas. In the seventeenth and eighteenth centuries, poets such as Alexander Pope (1688–1744) wrote poems in rhymed couplets. Here's a poem by contemporary Canadian poet Sina Queyras (b. 1963) that takes this traditional form and runs with it:

The Couriers

Words from a leaf on the shell of a snail?
Tendency as reciprocity etched in shale.

Cider vinegar wrapped in sealskin?
Accept it, so little is genuine.

A box on a meteor compelled by earth?
Lies, emptiness, grief: it's not a first.

Frost on the dock at Penetanguishene?
Tears from Lake Huron, Erie, and Michigan.

Not a moment to yourself?
Don't let love put you on a shelf.

A preponderance of errors?
The soft one sucks her rivers.

Love, love, needs no reason.
Yes, yes, yes, is my season.

In the case of Queyras's whimsical, inventive poem, the traditional rhymed, end-stopped couplets are used to juxtapose her voice with the voice of twentieth-century United States poet Sylvia Plath (1932–63).

Rarely rhymed or end-stopped today, couplets nonetheless maintain their popularity. For examples of unrhymed, enjambed couplets, take another look at Evie Shockley's "canvas and mirror" in chapter 1 and Dean Rader's "Cartography: or American Allegory I" later in this chapter. When enjambed, the multiple stanza breaks created by couplets can create a sense of surprise, suspense, and a multiplicity of meaning.

Tercets (also called **triplets**): three-line stanzas. Whether rhymed or unrhymed, tercets generally provide variety and movement. For example, take a look at this short unrhymed poem, comprised of two tercets, by contemporary United States poet Anne Marie Macari (b. 1955):

From the Plane

It is a soft thing, it has been sifted
from the sieve of space and seems
asleep there under the moths of light.

Cluster of dust and fire, from up here
you are a stranger and I am dropping
through the funnel of air to meet you.

For another example of tercets, see Elizabeth Bishop's "One Art" later in this chapter.

Quatrains: four-line stanzas, often used for narratives. Rhyme schemes of traditional quatrains include ABAC or ABCB (ballad form); AABB; ABAB; ABBA; and AABA. However, once again, contemporary poets often invent their own rules, so rhymes vary, and many quatrains don't rhyme at all. See if you can mark the rhyme scheme in each of the six quatrains of this poem by twentieth-century United States writer Ursula K. Le Guin (1929–2018).

Six Quatrains

AUTUMN

gold of amber
red of ember
brown of umber
all September

MCCOY CREEK

Over the bright shallows
now no flights of swallows.
Leaves of the sheltering willow
dangle thin and yellow.

OCTOBER

At four in the morning the west wind
moved in the leaves of the beech tree
with a long rush and patter of water,
first wave of the dark tide coming in.

SOLSTICE

On the longest night of all the year
in the forests up the hill,
the little owl spoke soft and clear
to bid the night be longer still.

THE WINDS OF MAY

are soft and restless
in their leafy garments
that rustle and sway
making every moment movement.

HAIL

The dogwood cowered under the thunder
and the lilacs burned like light itself
against the storm-black sky until the hail
whitened the grass with petals.

For other examples of quatrains, see Emily Dickinson's "My Life had stood—a Loaded Gun—" in chapter 2 and Gwendolyn Brooks's "The Bean Eaters" in chapter 3.

Counting Syllables

In the last chapter, we discussed natural rhythms or beats, and we explored methods of establishing or enhancing rhythm in your poems. In fact, if we think about it further, what we mean by rhythm is often a pattern in the syllables themselves. We all know what a syllable is; the word *po-et-ry* has three syllables, the word *be-come* two, and the word *fall* has one.

Syllabic poetry, which creates a pattern based on the number of syllables per line, is pretty rare these days. However, the idea of counting syllables to see how long lines actually are rhythmically (as opposed to how they appear on the page) is never a bad idea. And some forms that persist today *do* involve the counting of syllables. The most obvious example is the **haiku**. Originating in the ancient Japanese *hokku*, the beginning of a longer poem, this short form contains just three lines, consisting of five syllables, seven syllables, and five syllables, respectively. Haiku are usually set in the present tense, concerned with time and place, and contain some reference to nature and the seasons. Early practitioners include Japanese poets Basho (1644–94), Yosa Buson (1716–84), and Kobayashi Issa (1763–1828).

Haiku were popularized in the West in the early twentieth century, and many contemporary poets, including Robert Hass (included at the end of this chapter), have translated or created versions of earlier haiku. Twentieth-century poets have also continued to craft their own haiku. Here's a series written by United States poet Etheridge Knight (1931–91), who served eight years in an Indiana State Prison:

Haiku

1
Eastern guard tower
glints in sunset; convicts rest
like lizards on rocks.

2
The piano man
is stingy, at 3 A.M.
his songs drop like plum.

3
Morning sun slants cell.
Drunks stagger like cripple flies
On jailhouse floor.

4
To write a blues song
is to regiment riots
and pluck gems from graves.

5
A bare pecan tree
slips a pencil shadow down
a moonlit snow slope.

6
The falling snow flakes
Cannot blunt the hard aches nor
Match the steel stillness.

7
Under moon shadows
A tall boy flashes knife and
Slices star bright ice.

8
In the August grass
Struck by the last rays of sun
The cracked teacup screams.

9
Making jazz swing in
Seventeen syllables AIN'T
No square poet's job.

Craft Questions

- What elements are emphasized by the short form of haiku?
- Is the order of haiku important here? Why or why not?
- How does the poem address the form itself?
- Discuss the ways in which Knight makes the form his own.

Meter

In haiku, we're mainly concerned with the number of syllables per line. But, as we know, in the English language, certain syllables are actually stressed or emphasized. For example, we don't say sylLAble, but SYLlable. (We emphasize the first syllable, not the second.) To become better attuned to how this pattern of stressed and unstressed syllables works, try reading aloud to hear what's loudest. If you're having difficulty, begin by just listening to the rise and fall of the English language. For practice, let's start by rereading the first line of Emily Dickinson's "My Life had stood—a Loaded Gun—" from chapter 2:

My Life had stood—a Loaded Gun—

Where do you hear stress? Don't get frustrated if you can't hear it at first. In fact, there are many subtle gradations, but you may begin to hear the line as:

my LIFE had STOOD a LOADed GUN

This process takes practice: practice that's invaluable in training your ear as a poet.

Once you begin to hear these rhythms, you're ready to tune in to **meter**, the pattern of stressed and unstressed syllables, and to practice metrical **scansion**: the process of applying symbols to illustrate this pattern. The most basic metrical unit is a **foot**, which is typically made up of one stressed syllable and one or two unstressed syllables. The following chart contains the most common types of feet. A (◡) represents an unstressed syllable and a (ˏ) represents a stressed one.

Foot	Adjective	Pattern	Examples
iamb	iambic	da-DUM: ◡ ˏ	my life; between
trochee	trochaic	DUM-da: ˏ ◡	loaded; stillness
anapest	anapestic	da-da-DUM: ◡ ◡ ˏ	understand; to surprise
dactyl	dactylic	DUM-da-da: ˏ ◡ ◡	compromise; stare at it
spondee	spondaic	DUM-DUM: ˏ ˏ	heartbreak; fateful
pyrrhic	pyrrhic	da-da: ◡ ◡	to the; out of

Although metrical poems normally include some variation or **metrical substitutions**, the pattern is usually established at the outset of the poem. The most common line in English is **iambic pentameter** or five iambs. Lines of four feet (**tetrameter**) are the most common after pentameter. Here's a brief list of metered line lengths:

monometer: one foot per line
dimeter: two feet per line
trimeter: three feet per line
tetrameter: four feet per line
pentameter: five feet per line
hexameter: six feet per line
heptameter: seven feet per line
octometer: eight feet per line

At this point, you may want to run in the other direction to escape this seemingly rigid system of metrical poetry. Or, on the other hand, you may be tempted to try your hand at a particularly difficult form (say pyrrhic dimeter). For now, just keep reading, listening, and learning. Though if you'd like to try writing a few lines in a comparably natural pattern, such as iambic tetrameter, go for it. Later in the chapter, you'll have a chance to try writing in meter and form. By the way, can you identify the form of Emily Dickinson's "My Life had stood—a Loaded Gun" (above and in chapter 2)?

In order to practice metrical scansion, let's read a poem by radical English poet and artist, William Blake (1757–1827), who, incidentally, was an important influence on Allen Ginsberg, whom we discussed in the last chapter. Published as part of his collection *Songs of Innocence and Experience* in 1794, "The Tyger" is the sister poem to "The Lamb," a reflection of similar ideas from a different perspective. As you read, try marking up the poem's metrical feet. The first line has been completed as an example.

The Tyger

´ ˘ | ´ ˘ | ´ ˘ | ´
Tyger Tyger, burning bright,

In the forests of the night;

What immortal hand or eye,

Could frame thy fearful symmetry?

In what distant deeps or skies.
Burnt the fire of thine eyes?
On what wings dare he aspire?
What the hand, dare seize the fire?

And what shoulder, & what art,
Could twist the sinews of thy heart?
And when thy heart began to beat,
What dread hand? & what dread feet?

What the hammer? what the chain,
In what furnace was thy brain?
What the anvil? what dread grasp,
Dare its deadly terrors clasp!

When the stars threw down their spears
And water'd heaven with their tears:
Did he smile his work to see?
Did he who made the Lamb make thee?

Tyger Tyger burning bright,
In the forests of the night:
What immortal hand or eye,
Dare frame thy fearful symmetry?

Craft Questions

- How many syllables are there per line?
- What is the poem's meter?
- Does the poem's use of fixed rhyme and meter imply that its ideas are narrowly defined as well? Discuss the relationship between the poem's form and its various meanings.

Note: you may have noticed that there is an absence of a syllable in the final foot of each line. This absence is called a **catelexis**.

Traditional Forms

Now that we've familiarized ourselves with common stanza patterns, syllables, and meter in poetry, we're ready to explore some of the most widely practiced traditional forms (beyond haiku). If you're struggling with the endless possibilities of writing free verse, it may be helpful to try writing in one or more of these fixed forms. Or you may have a poem already in progress that would benefit from applying the right pattern. In fact, rather than beginning with a form in mind, many poets find a form that fits as a poem progresses. Whatever the case, having some knowledge of the unique properties and possibilities of various forms will no doubt inform your poetry in meaningful ways. And you'll get a chance to try out some of the moves that countless others have used—a chance to participate in a living tradition.

Sonnet

One of the oldest forms of poetry in English, the sonnet or "little song" originated in Italy and was introduced to England in the early sixteenth century. Traditionally composed of fourteen lines of iambic pentameter, linked by a rhyme scheme, the sonnet's compact form and orderly structure make it ideal for developing a single thought, theme, or emotion. Sonnets often begin with an idea or **conceit** (extended metaphor), develop it, and then conclude.

There are two basic types of sonnets: the Italian or **Petrarchan**, named after the fourteenth-century Italian poet, Petrarch (1304–74); and the English or **Shakespearean**, made famous by Renaissance playwright, actor, and poet William Shakespeare (1564–1616). Here are the patterns of these two types:

Type	Rhyme Scheme	Stanzas
Italian or Petrarchan	abab abab cde cde	two rhyming quatrains and two rhyming tercets
English or Shakespearean	abab cdcd efef gg	three rhyming quatrains and a rhyming couplet

As you can see from this diagram, the Shakespearean sonnet contains more variation in rhymed sounds and is characterized by a final rhymed couplet, whereas the Petrarchan sonnet repeats sounds in the first two quatrains. Both the Shakespearean and Petrarchan sonnet include a **volta** (Italian for "turn"). As we'll see in the following examples, this is often where the poet deepens their point or takes the poem in a slightly different direction.

To see these patterns in action, let's take a look at a Shakespearean sonnet by Shakespeare himself and a Petrarchan one by twentieth-century United States poet Edna St. Vincent Millay (1892–1950). Both sonnets are double-spaced so that you can mark up the rhyme scheme, identify the volta, and scan the meter. The first few lines are already marked, as an example.

William Shakespeare
"My mistress' eyes are nothing like the sun"

˘ ´ | ˘ ´ | ˘ ´ | ˘ ´ | ˘ ´ |
My mistress' eyes are nothing like the sun; **A**
´ ˘ | ˘ ´ | ˘ ´ | ˘ ´ | ˘ ´ |
Coral is far more red than her lips' red; **B**
˘ ´ | ˘ ´ | ˘ ´ | ˘ ´ | ˘ ´ |
If snow be white, why then her breasts are dun; **A**

If hairs be wires, black wires grow on her head.

I have seen roses damasked, red and white,

But no such roses see I in her cheeks;

And in some perfumes is there more delight

Than in the breath that from my mistress reeks.

I love to hear her speak, yet well I know

That music hath a far more pleasing sound;
I grant I never saw a goddess go;
My mistress, when she walks, treads on the ground.
  And yet, by heaven, I think my love as rare
  As any she belied with false compare.

Craft Questions

- How does Shakespeare develop his controlling comparison or conceit as the sonnet progresses?
- Translate the final couplet into ordinary, contemporary speech. What is Shakespeare saying here?

Edna St. Vincent Millay

"What lips my lips have kissed, and where, and why"

What lips my lips have kissed, and where, and why,
I have forgotten, and what arms have lain
Under my head till morning; but the rain
Is full of ghosts tonight, that tap and sigh
Upon the glass and listen for reply,
And in my heart there stirs a quiet pain
For unremembered lads that not again
Will turn to me at midnight with a cry.
Thus in the winter stands the lonely tree,
Nor knows what birds have vanished one by one,
Yet knows its boughs more silent than before:

I cannot say what loves have come and gone,

I only know that summer sang in me

A little while, that in me sings no more.

Craft Questions

- Paraphrase the poem in contemporary speech. Why might the Petrarchan form suit the subject of this sonnet?
- Did you find a spot where Millay breaks out of the Petrarchan rhyme scheme, using what's called a reversal? How might this reversal emphasize meaning?
- How does Millay keep rhyme and meter subtle?

Although sonnets were often used for love poems during the Renaissance, as you can see from these examples, from early in their history, the form was adapted to suit poets' individual interests. In fact, Shakespeare's ironic, unconventional praise of the beloved responds to earlier poems by Petrarch and others, which exalted the beloved by listing her classically beautiful attributes. And Millay employs the repetitions of the Petrarchan form to emphasize the speaker's attempts to remember her numerous past lovers: a racy subject for a poem written by a woman in 1923.

Speaking of adaptation, let's take a look at a radical leap by contemporary poet Sandra Simonds. You won't find either the Shakespearean or Petrarchan form here, but Simonds's sonnet proclaims its identity as such by appearing in her 2014 collection *The Sonnets*, and it does capture the spirit of the form:

Red Wand

Sometimes I try to make poetry but mostly
    I try to earn a living. There's something still living
  in every urn, I am sure of it. The ash moves
  around inside the vase like the magnetic filings that make
the moustache of Wooly Willy.[1] Maybe a new face counts
    as reincarnation. The wand says, "I'll be your ostrich,
  if you'll be my swan." In this life, what did I do wrong?
I think my heart is a magnet too. It attracts anything
  that attracts joy like the summer grasses the swans track through.

1 A toy in which metal pieces are moved with a magnetic wand in order to add features onto a cartoon face. The toy was launched in 1955.

OMG, how in love I am with joy and with yours—how I know
that adding to it would only take it further off course,
off its precarious center, so for once, I won't touch it.
I will stand wand-length away—let it
glide stupidly on its weightless line, without me.

Craft Questions

- What formal elements does Simonds employ? What elements does she adapt or discard?
- Is this a love poem? Why or why not?
- Compare the meaning of the word "line" in Simonds's poem to the word "lines" in Shakespeare's "Shall I compare thee to a summer's day" at the end of chapter 2.
- In what ways might "Red Wand" pose a challenge to our understanding of the role of poetry and the poetic tradition?

The ongoing tradition of adopting and adapting the sonnet form is rich, so we'll look at a couple of additional examples at the end of this chapter. Suffice it to say, you'll definitely want to try writing a sonnet or two of your own, whether they're true to form or loosely adapted.

Villanelle

Another widely practiced form, the **villanelle**, evolved from Renaissance Spanish and Italian folk dance songs and took hold as a fixed form in the late nineteenth century. Originally a French syllabic form, the villanelle never gained widespread popularity in France, but instead became popular among English-language poets. Sometimes written in iambic pentameter, but often written in other metrical patterns or in no fixed meter at all, the form consists of five tercets and a final quatrain, with the first and third lines of the first stanza repeating alternately in the following stanzas.

The villanelle's two refrain lines form the final couplet in the quatrain, and are particularly significant, since they repeat often. Therefore, when you craft a villanelle, it is important that the refrain lines contribute in some way to the poem's central concerns. Rather than just repeat in their entirety, refrain lines often change slightly as the poem moves along, creating both a sense of forward momentum and a return or echo. For this reason, poems that deal with issues of memory are often well suited to this form. Here's a chart of the form, with the rhyme scheme in parentheses:

Stanza 1
Refrain line 1 (a)
(b)
Refrain line 2 (a)

Stanza 2
(a)
(b)
R 1 (a)

Stanza 3
(a)
(b)
R 2 (a)

Stanza 4
(a)
(b)
R 1 (a)

Stanza 5
(a)
(b)
R 2 (a)

Stanza 6
(a)
(b)
R 1 (a)
R 2 (b)

Feeling overwhelmed by the intricacy of the form? One way of demystifying the process is to start by coming up with a couple of rhymed refrain lines, and go from there. You'll find that the form maintains its roots in dance; you can almost envision the weaving motion of figures as you begin to craft your own villanelle.

To bring the above chart to life, try marking up the refrains and rhyme scheme of the following villanelle by twentieth-century American poet, Elizabeth Bishop (1911–79). The first stanza is already marked, as an example:

One Art

The art of losing isn't hard to master; R1 a
so many things seem filled with the intent b
to be lost that their loss is no disaster. R2 a

Lose something every day. Accept the fluster
of lost door keys, the hour badly spent.
The art of losing isn't hard to master.

Then practice losing farther, losing faster:
places, and names, and where it was you meant
to travel. None of these will bring disaster.

I lost my mother's watch. And look! my last, or
next-to-last, of three loved houses went.
The art of losing isn't hard to master.

I lost two cities, lovely ones. And, vaster,
some realms I owned, two rivers, a continent.
I miss them, but it wasn't a disaster.

—Even losing you (the joking voice, a gesture
I love) I shan't have lied. It's evident
the art of losing's not too hard to master
though it may look like (*Write* it!) like disaster.

Craft Questions

- What types of loss does Bishop describe? Discuss the progression of losses from the beginning to the end of the poem.
- In what ways might this progression be emphasized by Bishop's use of refrain lines?
- How is rhyme rendered subtle?
- In what ways does the final stanza resolve or complicate the poem's dynamic between mastery and disaster?

Sestina

Another form with Italian and French roots, the **sestina** forgoes rhyme, instead creating an intricate pattern through the repetition of lines' end words. The form consists of six, six-line stanzas, and a final tercet as the **envoi** (concluding remarks). Here's a chart of the form:

Stanza 1	Stanza 2	Stanza 3	Stanza 4	Stanza 5	Stanza 6
A	F	C	E	D	B
B	A	F	C	E	D
C	E	D	B	A	F
D	B	A	F	C	E
E	D	B	A	F	C
F	C	E	D	B	A

Envoi
E
C
A

Since the form of the sestina is admittedly somewhat forced, sestinas can be quite difficult to pull off. In fact, some of the most successful sestinas parody the form or engage the issue of artifice. This sestina by contemporary United States poet, Sandra Beasley (b. 1980), is no exception; playfully covering serious terrain, Beasley's poem comments on the history of poetic form itself. As you read, mark the last word in each stanza; the first two stanzas are already marked as an example.

Let Me Count the Waves

We must not look for poetry in poems.
—Donald Revell

You must not skirt the issue wearing skirts. A
You must not duck the bullet using ducks. B
You must not face the music with your face. C
Headbutting, don't use your head. Or your butt. D
You must not use a house to build a home, E
and never look for poetry in poems. F

In fact, inject giraffes into your poems. F
Let loose the circus monkeys in their skirts. A
Explain the nest of wood is not a home E
at all, but a blind for shooting wild ducks. B
Grab the shotgun by its metrical butt; D
aim at your Muse's quacking, Pringled face. C

It's good we're talking like this, face to face.
There should be more headbutting over poems.
Citing an 80s brand has its cost but

honors the teenage me, always in skirts,
showing my sister how to Be the Duck
with a potato-chip beak. Take me home,

Mr. Revell. Or make yourself at home
in my postbellum, Reconstruction face—
my gray eyes, my rebel ears, all my ducks
in the row of a defeated mouth. Poems
were once civil. But war has torn my skirts
off at the first ruffle, baring my butt

or as termed in verse, my luminous butt.
Whitman once made a hospital his home.
Emily built a prison of her skirts.
Tigers roamed the sad veldt of Stevens's face.
That was the old landscape. All the new poems
map the two dimensions of cartoon ducks.

We're young and green. We're braces of mallards,
not barrels of fish. Shoot if you must but
Donald, we're with you. Trying to save poems,
we settle and frame their ramshackle homes.
What is form? Turning art to artifice,
trading pelts for a more durable skirt.

Even urban ducklings deserve a home.
Make way. In the modern: *Make way, Buttface.*
A poem is coming through, lifting her skirt.

Craft Questions

- What do you notice about the words Beasley chooses to repeat?
- How does Beasley keep the form's repetitions from overwhelming the poem?
- How does the form itself harmonize with the poem's subject?

Ghazal

Common to Arabic, Persian, Turkish, Uzbek, Pashto, and Urdu literature, the ghazal became popular in English in the twentieth century and continues to enjoy widespread popularity today. The form comprises self-contained couplets of similar length, which end on the same word or phrase (the *radif*), and are preceded by the couplet's rhyming word (the *qafia*, appearing twice in the first couplet). After the twelfth century, poets started to include their names in the final couplet. Contemporary ghazals in English tend to break one or more of these rules. In terms of subject matter, this melancholy form often deals with romantic attachment, loss, and longing.

Here's a relatively long ghazal by contemporary United States poet Dean Rader (b. 1967), in which the poet reflects on his upbringing in Oklahoma, among other things.

Cartography; or American Allegory I

after Bruce Snider

Once upon a time in Oklahoma,
there was no such thing as Oklahoma.

When I look out off the east coast of California,
I am standing on our farm in Hinton, Oklahoma.

Answer: Because Texas sucks and Kansas blows.
Question: Why is it so windy in Oklahoma?

All roads might lead to Rome,
but all trails take you to Oklahoma.

The stars dragged along in their wagons of dust,
the moon on its cot, the last long light of Oklahoma.

Pawhuska, Nuyaka, Wewoka, Taloga, Oologah,
Okemah, Eufaula. O, the missing map of Oklahoma.

Knife wind, ice wind, blind wind, hatchet wind, stone wind,
skin wind, dust wind, and must wind all whisper *Oklahoma*.

I think of Bruce Snider floating above the corn of Indiana.
Is he waving at Jesus rising above the wheat of Oklahoma?

I have often wondered if there is more oil
or blood beneath the soil of Tulsa, Oklahoma.

My second baptism was the First Baptist Church.
My first was in the summer rains of Oklahoma.

State amphibian: bullfrog. State beverage: milk. State soil:
Port Silt Loam. State mammal: bison. State song: "Oklahoma."

The first dead body I saw was my friend Kevin Wright's.
I was six years old in a funeral home in Weatherford, Oklahoma.

It's time to talk about the scent of Denise Barker's cautious
skin. It was like mist on a summer sidewalk in Oklahoma.

Recently uncovered manuscript from Ovid in
which the gods learn to play football in Oklahoma.

Where are you, Rhonda Harder, first girl to kiss me?
I'm sorry your name became a joke for the boys of Oklahoma.

Put down your pen, Lord Death. The names of
my parents are not yet on your list for Oklahoma.

If you ask me what one is to do with this world,
I will tell you that the answer is not to be found in Oklahoma.

Poem of the open prairie, couplet of the spread-out sky,
metaphor of mistletoe and milkweed: who will write Oklahoma?

God has bequeathed himself to the grape leaves of Sonoma
and the fog of San Francisco. Is his next gift to Oklahoma?

My grandfather and my son share the name Dean Rader. This morning my
son sinks into our bright bed, my grandfather into the dark dirt of
Oklahoma.

Craft Questions

- How do the form's signature repetitions add to your experience of Rader's poem?
- In terms of the poem's narrative, how are couplets ordered?
- Describe the various tones of the poem.

Pantoum

Like the villanelle, the pantoum's signature is its repetition of lines. The form began as a short folk poem, typically made up of two rhyming couplets that were recited or sung in fifteenth-century Malaysia. As the form spread and was adapted, these rules loosened. The contemporary pantoum is composed of any number of quatrains. The second and fourth lines of each stanza typically serve as the first and third lines of the next, and the last line is often identical to the first. As you read the following pantoum by contemporary United States poet A.E. Stallings (b. 1968), notice the ways in which the form's pattern of rhyme and repetition creates a subtle sense of reverberation:

Another Lullaby for Insomniacs

Sleep, she will not linger:
She turns her moon-cold shoulder.
With no ring on her finger,
You cannot hope to hold her.

She turns her moon-cold shoulder
And tosses off the cover.
You cannot hope to hold her:
She has another lover.

She tosses off the cover
And lays the darkness bare.
She has another lover.
Her heart is otherwhere.

She lays the darkness bare.
You slowly realize
Her heart is otherwhere.
There's distance in her eyes.

You slowly realize
That she will never linger,
With distance in her eyes
And no ring on her finger.

Craft Questions

- How do the form's shifting, repeated lines contribute to the poem's meaning?
- Describe the mood and tone of Stallings's "lullaby."
- Why personify sleep?

Cinquain

Otherwise known as the **quintain** or **quintet**, the cinquain, a form that originated in medieval French poetry, is any poem or stanza of five lines. The most common cinquains in English follow the rhyme scheme of *ababb*, *abaab*, or *abccb*, though not all cinquains rhyme. Early twentieth-century United States poet, Adelaide Crapsey (1878–1914), used a form of 22 syllables in five lines in a 2, 4, 6, 8, and 2 pattern, respectively. Here's one of Crapsey's cinquains:

Amaze

I know
Not these my hands
And yet I think there was
A woman like me once had hands
Like these.

Craft Questions

- Can you see yourself adopting Crapsey's form? Why or why not?
- What subject(s) might work well for this short, syllabic form?

Ode

A poem of lyric address, often performed with song and dance in Ancient Greece, and later popular with the Romantic poets, the ode has enjoyed a long history in various forms. The three types of ode include: the **Pindaric**, named after ancient Greek poet, Pindar, who invented the form, and often composed to celebrate athletic victories; **Horatian**, named for Roman poet, Horace, and generally less formal; and **Irregular**, which varies in form. Though it almost always functions as a form of praise, the contemporary ode can take on a surprising degree of depth and dimension as it meditates on various aspects of a person, place, or event. Here's such an ode by one of the great twentieth-century practitioners of the form, Chilean poet Pablo Neruda (1904–73), translated by Margaret Sayers Peden:

Ode to Tomatoes

The street
filled with tomatoes,
midday,
summer,
light is
halved

like
a
tomato,
its juice
runs
through the streets.
In December,
unabated,
the tomato
invades
the kitchen,
it enters at lunchtime,
takes
its ease
on countertops,
among glasses,
butter dishes,
blue saltcellars.
It sheds
its own light,
benign majesty.
Unfortunately, we must
murder it:
the knife
sinks
into living flesh,
red
viscera,
a cool
sun,
profound,
inexhaustible,
populates the salads
of Chile,
happily, it is wed
to the clear onion,
and to celebrate the union
we
pour
oil,
essential
child of the olive,
onto its halved hemispheres,

pepper
adds
its fragrance,
salt, its magnetism;
it is the wedding
of the day,
parsley
hoists
its flag,
potatoes
bubble vigorously,
the aroma
of the roast
knocks
at the door,
it's time!
come on!
and, on
the table, at the midpoint
of summer,
the tomato,
star of earth,
recurrent
and fertile
star,
displays
its convolutions,
its canals,
its remarkable amplitude
and abundance,
no pit,
no husk,
no leaves or thorns,
the tomato offers
its gift
of fiery color
and cool completeness.

Craft Questions

- How does Neruda's ode elevate the ordinary object of the tomato?
- What various states of being does the tomato come to represent?
- How do the short lines contribute to your experience of the poem?

Hopefully, by engaging with some of the most popular forms (there are many more to explore!), you're developing a desire to try out some of the possibilities, either in new work or for poems already in progress. And if you're currently developing a body of work—either for class, your own satisfaction, or possible publication (more on this process in appendix B)—poems in fixed forms can add depth and variety to your collection.

Should you follow the form exactly or play it loose, adapting or breaking the rules where you see fit? That's up to you (and possibly your instructor). There's a lot to be said for both practices. Following the rules of form can provide you with a stimulating challenge, making you more attuned to the way the language works, stretching your lexicon, and training your ear. Breaking the rules can often lead to poems that more quickly feel like your own; rather than hamstringing yourself, you are using just what the poem needs and ignoring what it doesn't. Say, for example, you're working on a poem on a certain childhood memory, and the idea of repeating a line or two feels right. Try using refrain lines to create a villanelle. Then decide whether to also use rhyme and meter or to alter the sound and rhythm. The poem may benefit from the mandates of the form or it may feel forced. Ultimately, you'll need to be the judge. The poems that follow represent a spectrum; some are true to the traditional form, some slightly adapted, and some use the form as a very loose framework. As you read, see if you can identify the form and the extent to which it's been adapted.

Readings

Robert Hass (b. 1941)
Selected Haiku by Issa

Don't worry, spiders,
I keep house
  casually.

  New Year's Day—
everything is in blossom!
  I feel about average.

  The snow is melting
and the village is flooded
  with children.

  Goes out,
comes back—
  the love life of a cat.

Mosquito at my ear—
does he think
I'm deaf?

Under the evening moon
the snail
is stripped to the waist.

Even with insects—
some can sing,
some can't.

All the time I pray to Buddha
I keep on
killing mosquitoes.

Napped half the day;
no one
punished me!

Craft Questions

- How do Issa (and Hass) create suspense and surprise in this short form?
- Discuss the element of nature in these haiku.
- Discuss the passage of time.

Terrance Hayes (b. 1971)
American Sonnet for My Past and Future Assassin

I lock you in an American sonnet that is part prison,
Part panic closet, a little room in a house set aflame.
I lock you in a form that is part music box, part meat
Grinder to separate the song of the bird from the bone.
I lock your persona in a dream-inducing sleeper hold
While your better selves watch from the bleachers.
I make you both gym & crow here. As the crow
You undergo a beautiful catharsis trapped one night
In the shadows of the gym. As the gym, the feel of crow-
Shit dropping to your floors is not unlike the stars
Falling from the pep rally posters on your walls.
I make you a box of darkness with a bird in its heart.
Voltas of acoustics, instinct & metaphor. It is not enough
To love you. It is not enough to want you destroyed.

Craft Questions

- In what ways does Hayes interrogate the sonnet form?
- How are African American experience and the sonnet form explicitly linked in Hayes's poem?
- Discuss Hayes's use of wordplay.

Sylvia Plath (1932–63)
Mad Girl's Love Song

I shut my eyes and all the world drops dead;
I lift my lids and all is born again.
(I think I made you up inside my head.)

The stars go waltzing out in blue and red,
And arbitrary blackness gallops in:
I shut my eyes and all the world drops dead.

I dreamed that you bewitched me into bed
And sung me moon-struck, kissed me quite insane.
(I think I made you up inside my head.)

God topples from the sky, hell's fires fade:
Exit seraphim and Satan's men:
I shut my eyes and all the world drops dead.

I fancied you'd return the way you said,
But I grow old and I forget your name.
(I think I made you up inside my head.)

I should have loved a thunderbird instead;
At least when spring comes they roar back again.
I shut my eyes and all the world drops dead.
(I think I made you up inside my head.)

Craft Questions

- In what ways does the form of Plath's poem enact a kind of madness?
- Discuss the use of parentheticals.

Elizabeth Bishop (1911–79)
Sestina

September rain falls on the house.
In the failing light, the old grandmother
sits in the kitchen with the child
beside the Little Marvel Stove,
reading the jokes from the almanac,
laughing and talking to hide her tears.

She thinks that her equinoctial tears
and the rain that beats on the roof of the house
were both foretold by the almanac,
but only known to a grandmother.
The iron kettle sings on the stove.
She cuts some bread and says to the child,

It's time for tea now; but the child
is watching the teakettle's small hard tears
dance like mad on the hot black stove,
the way the rain must dance on the house.
Tidying up, the old grandmother
hangs up the clever almanac

on its string. Birdlike, the almanac
hovers half open above the child,
hovers above the old grandmother
and her teacup full of dark brown tears.
She shivers and says she thinks the house
feels chilly, and puts more wood in the stove.

It was to be, says the Marvel Stove.
I know what I know, says the almanac.
With crayons the child draws a rigid house
and a winding pathway. Then the child
puts in a man with buttons like tears
and shows it proudly to the grandmother.

But secretly, while the grandmother
busies herself about the stove,
the little moons fall down like tears
from between the pages of the almanac
into the flower bed the child
has carefully placed in the front of the house.

Time to plant tears, says the almanac.
The grandmother sings to the marvelous stove
and the child draws another inscrutable house.

Craft Questions

- Discuss the words Bishop chooses to repeat. What kind of mood or tone do they create?
- How does Bishop keep form subtle?
- Discuss the poem's story. What do we know about the grandmother and the child? What remains mysterious?

John Yau (b. 1950)

Overnight

In Memory of Paul Violi (1944–2011)

I did not realize that you were fading from sight
I don't believe I could have helped with the transition

You most likely would have made a joke of it
Did you hear about the two donkeys stuck in an airshaft

I don't believe I could have helped with the transition
The doorway leading to the valleys of dust is always open

Did you hear about the two donkeys stuck in an airshaft
You might call this the first of many red herrings

The doorway leading to the valleys of dust is always open
The window overlooking the sea is part of the dream

You might call this the first of many red herrings
The shield you were given as a child did not protect you

The window overlooking the sea is part of the dream
One by one the words leave you, even this one

The shield you were given as a child did not protect you
The sword is made of air before you knew it

One by one the words leave you, even this one
I did not realize that you were fading from sight

The sword is made of air before you knew it
You most likely would have made a joke of it

Craft Questions

- Discuss "Overnight" as an elegy or poem of remembrance.
- How do the elegiac couplets and the pantoum form contribute to the poem's impact?

Kevin Young (b. 1970)
Ode to the Hotel Near the Children's Hospital

Praise the restless beds
Praise the beds that do not adjust
  that won't lift the head to feed
  or lower for shots
  or blood
  or raise to watch the tinny TV
Praise the hotel TV that won't quit
  its murmur & holler
Praise the room service
  that doesn't exist
  just the slow delivery to the front desk
  of cooling pizzas
  & brown bags leaky
  greasy & clear
Praise the vending machines
Praise the change
Praise the hot water
& the heat
  or the loud cool
  that helps the helpless sleep.

Praise the front desk
  who knows to wake
  Rm 120 when the hospital rings
Praise the silent phone
Praise the dark drawn
  by thick daytime curtains
  after long nights of waiting,
  awake.

Praise the waiting & then praise the nothing
  that's better than bad news

Praise the wakeup call
  at 6 am
Praise the sleeping in
Praise the card hung on the door
  like a whisper
  lips pressed silent
Praise the stranger's hands
  that change the sweat of sheets
Praise the checking out

Praise the going home
  to beds unmade
  for days
Beds that won't resurrect
  or rise
that lie there like a child should
  sleeping, tubeless
Praise this mess
  that can be left

Craft Questions

- In what ways does Young's poem make use of formal tradition?
- In what ways does the poem stand as a challenge to that same tradition?
- How might the poem's use of indentation emphasize its rhythm and meaning?

Exercises

Exercise 1: Writing the Sonnet

Write a sonnet. Choose to use either the Petrarchan or the Shakespearean model. In either case, follow the form exactly. Get started by looking over the chapter and read some additional sonnets online or elsewhere. It may also be helpful if you define your subject before you start.

Try to follow the rhyme scheme and form of the sonnet exactly. For some writers, it's easier to start out by getting the heartbeat of iambic pentameter (u/|u/|u/|u/|u/|) in mind as they begin. For others, it's easier to begin drafting and rework lines to fit the meter later.

Once you've completed a solid draft, consider lessening some of the restraints of form in places that seem forced. Adapt the form as much or as little as you please, in order to produce a poem you like.

Objective: To try your hand at writing in a specific fixed form. You'll gain experience in the use of a set rhyme, rhythm, and meter.

Exercise 2: Writing the Villanelle

Write a villanelle. In this case, begin by allowing yourself some liberties with regard to the form, but be sure to employ the two repeating refrain lines as described earlier in the chapter. Choose whether to use an existing draft of a poem as your starting point or whether to begin an entirely new poem. Use the villanelle form for a poem that deals with reoccurrence, memory, haunting, echoes, and the like.

Objective: To meaningfully adapt a form to suit your own purposes. You'll gain experience in using form (instead of it using you).

Exercise 3: OULIPO and Other Chance Operations

Ouvroir de litterature potentielle (OULIPO) or Workshop of Potential Literature, was created by a group led by French mathematician François Le Lionnais and writer Raymond Queneau in 1960. This playful technique explores writing under certain arbitrary constraints. A popular formula is "N+7," in which the writer substitutes each noun of an existing poem with a noun that is seven nouns ahead in the dictionary. In the "avalanche" exercise, the first line of a new poem is one word long; the second is two words long, and so on. Other groups, such as FLARF, use Google as a means of finding language for poems, and deliberately create "bad" poetry full of clichés, swear words, and the like.

Write a poem using a chance operation. Decide on the rules ahead of time, and consider inviting a friend or classmate to collaborate with you on the poem.

Objective: To use found material and/or arbitrary constraints to help free your imagination.

five | free verse

without a net

Now that you've internalized some specific rhyme schemes and metrical patterns and have tried your hand at writing poems in set form, you're in a better position to further develop your own unique way of doing things. Did you find the ghazal difficult, but enjoy writing in couplets? Did iambic pentameter come naturally to you once you began to hear it as a heartbeat? Did you find the sestina maddening? (Almost everyone does.) Moving forward, you're free to choose which elements to keep working with and which to leave on the shelf. Although you're likely returning to reading and writing **free verse**—poetry that doesn't use a set rhyme scheme, metrical pattern, line length, stanzaic pattern, or visual appearance—you're returning with a more trained ear and eye.

Free verse has its roots in the seventeenth-century French *vers libéré* or poetry liberated from metrical form. In English, free verse became popular around 1900, but if we look back on our discussion of Walt Whitman in chapter 3, we can recall that his *Leaves of Grass* broke the mold even earlier, beginning in 1855. Like much of the poetry that followed, Whitman's free verse employed unique **auditory** (sound based) and **visual** (relating to how the poem looks on the page) qualities. In

Whitman's case, the extremely long lines, use of anaphora, and listing techniques are some of the many elements that give his ground-breaking poem its own unique sense of form: its personality. Free verse doesn't so much dispense with the rules as it brings with it a myriad of possibilities for how a poem can sound, look, move, and make meaning.

And there's more gray area between forms and free verse than poets themselves sometimes admit. Twentieth-century poet Robert Frost famously declared that writing free verse was like playing tennis without a net, implying that working without structured form made little sense to him. And if we read Frost's poems, we can see the subtle but strong influence of formal structure on his seemingly casual rhythms. In a sense, Frost's comment can be read ironically, however, given the fact that his own work often seamlessly merges form with the speech patterns of everyday life. In fact, form informs the free verse of twentieth-century poets like Frost and much of the poetry being written today.

White Space and Typography

Poems don't just sing; they also exhibit or display. They're visual as well as auditory, and for most poems, how they look on the page is significant; layout contributes to motion, emotion, experience, and meaning. Although we've begun to explore various line lengths and stanza patterns, so far, our discussion has mostly focused on poems in which each line begins at the left margin. And although we've touched on the breathing room or suspense created by the extra white space of a poem written in couplets, we haven't yet discussed the myriad possibilities for how a poem can be placed on a page.

In the two-dimensional visual arts, it's widely agreed upon that the white space or negative space is often equally (or sometimes even *more*) significant than the image itself. Not only does this space give our eye a place to rest, depending on how much or how little of it there is and where exactly it's placed, it exerts a specified amount of pressure on the image itself: highlighting certain areas, downplaying others, and so on. The combination of positive and negative space determines the piece's overall composition.

Similarly, poetry is made up not only of words, lines, and stanzas on a page, but it's also made up of the white space that surrounds those marks. For many poets, using extra white space to surround lines, stanzas, or sections enacts experience and creates meaning. For instance, take a look at the following poem by contemporary United States poet Solmaz Sharif (b. 1983). As you read, keep in mind that the poem references the graveyard of dissidents executed by the Islamic regime in Iran.

❧ Ground Visibility

this mangy plot where

by now
only mothers still come,

only mothers guard the nameless dead

•

and then sparingly

•

these graves: the Place of the Damned

the prison: History's Dumping Ground

•

Peepholes burnt through the metal doors

of their solitary cells,

•

just large enough
for three fingers to curl out
for a lemon to pass through
for an ear to be held against
for one eye then the other
to regard the hallway
to regard the cell and inmate

•

peepholes without a lens

so when the GUARD comes to inspect me,
I inspect him.

Touch me, you said.

•

And through that opening

I did.

Craft Questions

- After reading the poem aloud several times, are there places where the poem slows down, speeds up, or grinds to a halt?
- What is the emotional impact of these movements?
- Could the white space of the poem indicate a kind of erasure? If so, how might this relate to the poem's central concerns?
- Discuss the poem as an act of political witness. In what ways does Sharif's poem pay homage to the executed? What does Sharif suggest about her own (and our) involvement?

Similarly, contemporary United States poet Ocean Vuong (b. 1988), uses white space in "Aubade with Burning City" to emphasize the poem's central concerns. Keep in mind that the French word **aubade** can be literally translated as "dawn serenade." And the **epigraph**, or text set before the poem, introduces the historical event depicted in the poem, while cluing us in that most of the italicized lines of the poem are drawn from Berlin's iconic song, "White Christmas":

Aubade with Burning City

South Vietnam, April 29, 1975: Armed Forces Radio played Irving Berlin's "White Christmas" as a code to begin Operation Frequent Wind, the ultimate evacuation of American civilians and Vietnamese refugees by helicopter during the fall of Saigon.

Milkflower petals on the street
like pieces of a girl's dress.

May your days be merry and bright…

He fills a teacup with champagne, brings it to her lips.
Open, he says.
She opens.
Outside, a soldier spits out
his cigarette as footsteps
fill the square like stones fallen from the sky. *May all*
your Christmases be white as the traffic guard
unstraps his holster.

His hand running the hem
of her white dress.

His black eyes.
Her black hair.
A single candle.
Their shadows: two wicks.

A military truck speeds through the intersection, the sound of children
shrieking inside. A bicycle hurled
through a store window. When the dust rises, a black dog
lies in the road, panting. Its hind legs
crushed into the shine
of a white Christmas.

On the nightstand, a sprig of magnolia expands like a secret heard
for the first time.

The treetops glisten and children listen, the chief of police
facedown in a pool of Coca-Cola.
A palm-sized photo of his father soaking
beside his left ear.

The song moving through the city like a widow.
A white ... A white ... I'm dreaming of a curtain of snow

falling from her shoulders.

Snow crackling against the window. Snow shredded

with gunfire. Red sky.
Snow on the tanks rolling over the city walls.
A helicopter lifting the living just out of reach.

The city so white it is ready for ink.

The radio saying run run run.
Milkflower petals on a black dog
like pieces of a girl's dress.

May your days be merry and bright. She is saying
something neither of them can hear. The hotel rocks
beneath them. The bed a field of ice
cracking.

Don't worry, he says, as the first bomb brightens
their faces, *my brothers have won the war*

and tomorrow...
The lights go out.

I'm dreaming. I'm dreaming...
to hear sleigh bells in the snow...

In the square below: a nun, on fire,
runs silently toward her god—

Open, he says.
She opens.

Craft Questions

- How do particular images and lines dramatize the contrasting experience of soldiers and civilians?
- How do the interspersed song lyrics heighten the tension in this scene of violence?
- If white space, in part, calls our attention to what's missing, who or what might be missing in the United States narrative about the Vietnam War?

If you look back over Sharif's and Vuong's poems, you'll see that not only do they use white space, by walking the lines across and down the page, but they also use **typography**, or the style of print, to emphasize meaning. In Sharif's case, take a minute to look at the poem's use of bullet points between fragments of text, and in Vuong's, think more about the choice to italicize song lyrics, break them up, and, in some cases, to run them in with standard Roman typeface.

Contemporary United States poet, Brenda Hillman (b. 1951) also often incorporates typography, white space, and image, and like Sharif and Vuong, she is concerned with issues of social justice. Here's one of her recent poems:

Describing Tattoos to a Cop

After Ed Sanders

We'd been squatting   near the worms
in the White House lawn, protesting
the Keystone Pipeline =$=$=$=$=$=>>;
i could sense   the dear worms
through   the grillwork fence,
twists & coils   of flexi-script, remaking
the soil   by resisting it ...
After the ride in the police van

telling jokes, our ziplocked handcuffs
pretty tight,
when the presiding officer asked:

—*Do you have any tattoos?*
—Yes, officer, i have two.
—*What are they?*
—Well, i have a black heart on my inner thigh &
an alchemical sign on my ankle.
—*Please spell that?*
—Alchemical. A-L-C-H-E-M-I-C-A-L.
—*What is that?*
—It's basically a moon, a lily, a star & a flame.

He started printing in the little square

MOON, LILY, STAR

Young white guy, seemed scared. One blurry
tattoo on his inner wrist ... i should have asked
about his, but couldn't
cross that chasm. Outside, Ash
Wednesday in our nation's capital. Dead
grass, spring trees
about to burst, two officers
beside the newish van. Inside,
alchemical notes for the next time—

Craft Questions

- What conflict does the poem present? What questions does it raise?
- How would you characterize the overall mood or tone of the poem?
- Part of Hillman's poem consists of a dialogue between the speaker and the police officer. How does the poet bring this dialogue to life?
- Try rewriting Hillman's poem without indentations, symbols, and other typographical innovations. How does the experience of the poem change?
- Would you consider using similar typographical elements in your poetry? Why or why not?

Whatever your conclusions, keep in mind that white space and typography provide useful opportunities for you as a poet. As you can see from the previous examples, these elements, when used well, are not arbitrary. At the end of this chapter, you're invited to try using white space more explicitly in your poems. And although editors tend to discourage the use of fancy fonts for their own sake, there are certainly typographical considerations and options that will present themselves as you progress in your craft.

Concrete Poetry

Originally termed **shaped poetry** or **pattern** poetry, and dating back to premodern times, what has become known as **concrete poetry** is verse in which the letters, lines, or words are shaped into objects: often those they are describing. Although much of the concrete poetry written today is easily passed off as amateurish, there are many notable exceptions: from the seventeenth century when the form was especially popular through today. Following are two such examples. The first is "Easter Wings" by British poet and clergyman, George Herbert (1593–1633), and the second is "Fingers Remember" by contemporary United States poet, Marilyn Nelson (b. 1946). As you read, notice elements that differ—between this seventeenth-century poem and the twenty-first-century one—including subject matter and diction, while also noting the elements that endure.

Easter Wings

Lord, who createdst man in wealth and store,
Though foolishly he lost the same,
Decaying more and more,
Till he became
Most poore:
With thee
O let me rise
As larks, harmoniously,
And sing this day thy victories:
Then shall the fall further the flight in me.

My tender age in sorrow did beginne
And still with sicknesses and shame.
Thou didst so punish sinne,
That I became
Most thinne.
With thee
Let me combine,
And feel thy victorie:
For, if I imp my wing on thine,
Affliction shall advance the flight in me.

Craft Questions

- What does Herbert's poem suggest about the role of Christ in the speaker's life?
- What is the flight to which Herbert refers?
- How does the shape of the poem reinforce this idea or theme?
- How would the poem be different if it were not shaped?

Fingers Remember

long fing- ers, how
signals flow up them
from tip and finger-
print all the way
up the arm and
the neck to what
ever magic light takes
flame so touch ignites
as the palm smooths warm
from one person to another, passes
sunlight one skin has taken in, which
the other receives like thirsty soil gulps
rain and infinite generations of ancestors
yawn awake asking if it's time for the line
to miracle up a new life. They were so young,
and innocence is a birth gift intended all along
to be opened with love, promises, and blessing
as you enter the future that only exists if you live
into it. His name was John. His moving muscles
formed shapes she had not met before. Green
time laid its fragranced landscape before them.
So they entered. Married. Irene came soon.
At eighteen, Gussie was widowed, with a
toddler older than her youngest siblings.
The family's hand opened and closed
in welcome. But fingers remember.

Craft Questions

- What story does Nelson tell in this poem?
- Consider the title and reflect on the significance of the hands described in the poem. How does the hand imagery contribute to the poem's meaning?
- How would Nelson's poem be different if it were not shaped?
- Does Nelson's poem, like Herbert's prayer, contain spiritual elements?

Whether or not you decide to try *your* hand at writing serious concrete poetry, it might be fun to try shaping a poem in progress or to doodle a concrete poem or two in your notebook. And if you are particularly visually inclined, this form could serve as a great starting point for a piece of artwork that incorporates words. You'll be in good company. Emily Dickinson wrote poems on envelopes (de-facto shaped poems), the Dadaists and Surrealists of the early twentieth century often incorporated words into their playful, political artworks, and contemporary poet, Alice Notley, has long incorporated typographical elements and shaped works as part of her repertoire, while simultaneously creating beautifully decorated fans with words.

Lineation and Syntax

As we discussed in the introduction, lines of poetry can be **end-stopped**, so that the end of the line is also the end of the phrase or sentence, or **enjambed**, so that the phrase or sentence runs over the line-break without punctuation. But how can we make full use of the myriad possibilities of both syntax, the order in which words appear to create sentences, and **lineation**, the arrangement of lines? Whereas some poems rely more on the unit of the line and some more on the unit of the sentence, most make use of the tension between the two to create rhythmic variation and to emphasize meaning.

If we check, when we're beginning to write poetry, most of us have an unconscious default setting when it comes to the use of line breaks. Our lines tend to be short, medium, or long, and we tend to either use enjambment frequently or not much at all. Similarly, we may or may not tend to use stanza breaks, and those breaks may or may not fall in a regular pattern. The same is true for punctuation; we may use it as we would in prose, use it sparingly, or not use it at all. As we become more experienced readers and writers, however, it's useful to experiment with lineation and syntax in order to tune up our poetic ear and eye. At the end of this chapter, I invite you to consciously break your default setting and to try out more than one possibility for crafting lines. To get started thinking more about the possibilities, let's engage in a tried and true exercise. This works best for a class or group, but if you're on your own, you can still benefit from it.

Below is a block of text, which I've copied word for word, without stanza or line breaks, from a well-known poem.

> Sundays too my father got up early and put his clothes on in the blueblack cold, then with cracked hands that ached from labor in the weekday weather made banked fires blaze. No one ever thanked

him. I'd wake and hear the cold splintering, breaking. When the rooms were warm, he'd call, and slowly I would rise and dress, fearing the chronic angers of that house, Speaking indifferently to him, who had driven out the cold and polished my good shoes as well. What did I know, what did I know of love's austere and lonely offices?

Take out a piece of paper and recopy the poem, creating stanza breaks and line breaks as you see fit. Don't overthink this, and don't change any of the words or punctuation. When you're done, compare your versions by putting them on the whiteboard (if you're in a classroom), exchanging with a friend, or creating more than one version yourself. Read the various versions aloud, noticing the pacing and rhythm. Then read silently and think more about emphasis and meaning. You'll find that you, individually or collectively, actually have created more than one poem; that's because lineation has a much more significant impact on our poems than we often expect.

After you're done with this first part of the exercise, take a look at the original poem by twentieth-century United States poet Robert Hayden (1913–80):

Those Winter Sundays

Sundays too my father got up early
and put his clothes on in the blueblack cold,
then with cracked hands that ached
from labor in the weekday weather made
banked fires blaze. No one ever thanked him.

I'd wake and hear the cold splintering, breaking.
When the rooms were warm, he'd call,
and slowly I would rise and dress,
fearing the chronic angers of that house,

Speaking indifferently to him,
who had driven out the cold
and polished my good shoes as well.
What did I know, what did I know
of love's austere and lonely offices?

Craft Questions

- Note lines that are enjambed, with particular focus on line 4. How do these lines impact the pace of the poem? Which actions do they emphasize?
- Note the inclusion of an entire sentence in line 5. Again, consider the impact on pace and meaning.
- What does this narrative poem suggest about how the speaker felt about his father as a child? How he feels as an adult?
- How is the story organized in stanzas?

After completing this lineation exercise and discussing the poem, it's always fun to compare your version to the "actual" poem. In some cases, you probably came pretty close to the intended lineation, which may be a sign that the poem indicates syntactical breaks and rhythmic patterns by other means. The simplest way that the language of the poem, itself, may indicate order is through its punctuation; punctuation gives us a sense of where to slow down, pause, and stop. But the cadence of the lines, the rise and fall of language implied by the poem's syntax and meter, also communicates this information, as does the unfolding of the poem itself: the story it has to tell or the order of its associations. In a powerful poem such as Robert Hayden's, all of these elements—lineation, punctuation, rhythm, sound, order, and meaning—work together to deliver an emotional experience for us as readers: an experience that *appears* seamless and immediate. Kind of magical, right?

All things considered, Hayden's poem is written in a fairly natural way, meaning that lines are mostly broken according to where one would breathe or pause in speech, or according to **breath unit**. That's why lines four and five stand out: because we probably wouldn't pause there. As you can see from flipping through this book, there are many examples of poems that use far less natural lineation to achieve a certain sense of movement, rhythm, and meaning. As you develop your craft, you'll be making all sorts of decisions about lineation. And eventually, your adventures in experimentation will help you arrive at a new go-to method or default: one that will better serve you since it will be more well-informed. Your new line lengths will also be more flexible: you'll be able to stretch them or depart from them when the need arises.

Prose Poetry

At some point in your experimentation with the unit of the line, you may become frustrated, finding that no options seem to work well for a particular poem, or you may have an idea or story in mind that seems to lend itself more to sentences than lines. This is an excellent time to try writing some prose poetry.

Dating back to the nineteenth century in its most well-known examples, and arising most notably in the works of French poets such as Charles Baudelaire (1821–67) and Arthur Rimbaud (1854–91), the origins of this hybrid form can actually be traced back to earlier forms, including prose passages from *Lyrical Ballads* by British Romantic poets William Wordsworth (1770–1850) and Samuel Taylor Coleridge (1772–1834), folktales, and even poetic prose passages from the Bible. In any case, the form gained traction in the nineteenth century and continues in its popularity today.

Written either in standard paragraphs, with no regard to line breaks, or in long lines that resemble prose, prose poems often include some element of narrative, as well as a compression or density of image, thought, and feeling. When sound and rhythm are major elements, prose poems can alternately be described as **poetic prose** or **lyrical prose**. And some very short forms of fiction, called **flash fiction** or **short-shorts**, are almost indistinguishable from prose poetry. The hybridity of the form makes prose poetry inherently experimental in nature, and there are many contemporary writers who work in the intersection between genres.

To begin to get a sense of some of the form's possibilities, let's take a look at a prose poem by Rimbaud, translated by Louise Varèse:

Ruts

To the right the summer dawn wakes the leaves and the mists and the noises in this corner of the park, and the left-hand banks hold in their violet shadows the thousand swift ruts of the wet road. Wonderland procession! Yes, truly: floats covered with animals of gilded wood, poles and bright bunting, to the furious gallop of twenty dappled circus horses, and children and men on their most fantastic beasts; —twenty rotund vehicles, decorated with flags and flowers like the coaches of old or in fairy tales, full of children all dressed up for a suburban pastorale. Even coffins under their somber canopies lifting aloft their jet-black plumes, bowling along to the trot of huge mares, blue and black.

Craft Questions

- Read the poem aloud. How would you describe its pace?
- Which images stand out in your mind?
- How might the poem be different if it were lineated?
- How does the form of the poem impact your experience of it?

Whereas Rimbaud's prose poem centers more on movement, image, and sensation, many contemporary prose poems tell stories, and some read almost as essays. Again, the lines between genres can become blurred when it comes to these hybrids, which you should take as an invitation for exploration. Are there poems you have in progress that would benefit from the lack of lineation, the run-together quality that the prose poem affords? Are there story ideas or even essay-like topics that lend themselves to being told in a compressed form?

As an example of the latter, take a look at this poem by contemporary United States poet Mary Ruefle (b. 1952):

Recollections of My Christmas Tree

I have always been vulnerable when confronted with Christmas decorations, and I am sitting in my living room staring at them. The lights on the tree are blinking on and off and I'm mesmerized. I have never been to a hypnotist but maybe mesmerization is the last state you enter before going over the edge into hypnosis. Maybe being mesmerized is the last thing you remember. It does seem to be a state all its own. When I was a child I did the same thing—watched the lights blink on and off, alone in the living room at night. The only difference is I know a lot more about Christmas now than I did then. I knew practically nothing then. My mother put an electric candle in each window, they were ivory-colored plastic, and at the end of each taper, near the bulb, fake drips of wax were molded; I loved the drips the most, it meant that the candles looked real to people inside the house, not just to people looking at them from the outside. What I didn't know then was that these decorations evolved from the Jewish menorah, the Hebrew festival of lights. I don't think my mother knew that either, but if she did she never mentioned it. And I certainly never contemplated the resemblance of a sleigh to a cradle. A sleigh is basically a very large cradle. The runners of the sleigh are what makes the cradle rock. Once there was a very eccentric man, in the nineteenth century in upstate New York, and when he was in his fifties he had a carpenter build him a cradle. I saw it in a museum, the biggest cradle ever made, and every night he slept in it, and when he entered his last illness he stayed in the cradle day and night, feeling the sensual throes of the cradle while somebody nursed and rocked him. I mean in the sense of caring for him. He died in his cradle, and the card on the wall of the museum said he was happy at the end. When I was a child one of my ornaments was a little red velveteen sleigh. I used to put a tiny doll in it, but now it is empty. I don't even like it anymore and when I was decorating the tree I thought about throwing it away but then I remembered the man in the cradle and decided to keep it. My mother and father also decorated the outside of our house with lights. We lived in a different house every year, so it wasn't easy—the length of the light strings kept changing. People who live in the same house every year don't think about things like that, their dimensions stay the same, there's no need to adjust anything, ever. After the lights were up on the outside of the house, my father would put us in the car and drive around the neighborhood, looking at the lights on the other houses. Sometimes he made disparaging remarks and sometimes in silence admired them. When he admired them he would make changes in his own lights the following year, but as we were by then in a new house none of the neighbors knew we were copycats. The most beautiful yard we ever saw had a snow scene with a frozen pond in the middle and life-sized figure skaters who floated across the pond wearing muffs. This was in Southern California, so everything was fake—the snow, the frozen pond, even the skaters were fake, and when they moved you could hear a slight whir under the ice—I guess it came from a motor. My father couldn't copy that—I could tell from his face that he was defeated. In those days everyone had lights. Not a single house was without them. That's one thing that has certainly changed. Today, only poor people have lights, and the poorest people of all have the most of them. At least this is true of the town I live in. There is one street that has the poorest people of all and at Christmas it is ablaze with lights, there are electric deer on the lawns and huge inflatable Santas, the roofs have more Santas descending in sleighs with reindeer, that kind of thing. The rich people think it is ugly, they don't bother anymore and they worry about the electric bill. They try to live calm, natural lives. They bake all their own bread, they make cookies and cakes and pies from scratch, they make their own beer and their own wine and liquors and they grow their own food in the summer—and come winter, when they want a Christmas tree or some holly, they just walk out on their land and cut it. Poor people have to use money, they have to go to the store and buy food, especially the kind that is already made. It didn't used to be that way. When I was a kid, it was understood that poor people had to make everything themselves while rich people got to buy things. My mother bought whole cakes at the grocery store and said we were lucky, not to have to make them ourselves. Now everything is reversed. If my mother and father were still alive they would be very confused. I think we would all become confused, eventually, if we didn't die. Maybe death prevents a major confusion that would, if it were allowed to go on, eventually kill us all. When I was little, one Christmas ritual majorly confused me. My mother had a little ceramic sleigh that sat on the table. It was driven by a ceramic Santa and pulled by ceramic reindeer. Every year I had to wrap empty matchboxes so they looked like tiny presents. Then we piled them in the sleigh; they were the presents Santa was hauling. But they were empty, and it made me sad. My mother would sit at the table smoking, watching me wrap the matchboxes. Can't we put anything in them? I asked. No, she said, they're fake. Couldn't we pretend? I said. That's what we're doing, she said. I mean *real pretend*, I said, but she just stared off into space and I knew the conversation had ended. One thing is for certain—I wouldn't want to be a Christmas tree. It would be nice to be the center of attention, to be so decorated and lit that people stared at you in wonder, and made a fuss over you, and were mesmerized. That would be nice. But then you'd start dropping your needles and people would become bored with you and say you weren't looking so good, and then they'd take off all your jewelry, and haul you off to the curb where you would be picked up and crushed and eventually burned. That's the terrible part. Maybe that's why so many people today have fake trees. They are quite popular. Their limbs come apart and you can put them in boxes and store them. You can have one of these trees until you die and you can pass it on to your children. They may not be real but when you look at them you can't tell the difference. That always makes people happy—not being able to tell the difference. And happiness, to want to be happy, is the most natural thing of all. That man in his big cradle was happy, though I never understood why, when he died, they didn't just saw the runners off and use it as his coffin. I don't think anyone would have noticed; in the end, the difference between a cradle and a coffin is hardly worth mentioning, though then again I wouldn't have seen the cradle later, in the museum, and if that hadn't happened I wouldn't have kept my red velveteen sleigh, I would have just thrown it away. No, never! When it comes to Christmas, when Christmas comes, I sit firmly on the lap of Charles Dickens, and repeat after him: Welcome, Everything! At this well-remembered time, when Everything is capable, with the greatest of ease, of being changed into Anything. On this day we shut out Nothing!

Craft Questions

- Which poetic elements do you spot in Ruefle's piece? Prose elements?
- How would the piece be different if it were broken into paragraphs?
- What themes stand out in Ruefle's Christmas story and how does the piece differ from other Christmas stories you've read, heard, or seen?
- How does the piece's form help to emphasize its various themes?

Ultimately, the best means of arriving at free-verse forms that work well for you is to keep reading contemporary poetry. Appendix B contains a list of online resources for finding new work, and visiting your local bookstore or library to peruse literary journals and new books are also still vital means of discovery. One of the most exciting things that happens in almost every poet's life is to discover poets you've not yet read and to find that their work opens up a new way of doing things that you'd not yet considered: a treasure-chest of aesthetic ideas and approaches. It's as if you've been given the go-ahead to set off in an interesting new direction. The poems that follow offer more chances for this to happen. Dive in.

Readings

C.D. Wright (1949–2016)
Flame

the breath	the trees	the bridge
the road	the rain	the sheen
the breath	the line	the skin
the vineyard	the fences	the leg
the water	the breath	the shift
the hair	the wheels	the shoulder
the breath	the lane	the streak
the lining	the hour	the reasons
the name	the distance	the breath

the scent	the dogs	the blear
the lungs	the breath	the glove
the signal	the turn	the need
the steps	the lights	the door
the mouth	the tongue	the eyes
the burn	the burned	the burning

Craft Questions

- Read the poem aloud. Which way do you read it?
- How does the spacing affect the poem's pace and rhythm?
- Note the poem's repetitions. How do they work to further meaning and sensation?
- How would you describe the state of consciousness the poem creates? Does it remind you of your own thought process at any given time?

Gerald Stern (b. 1925)
Galaxy Love

There's too little time left to measure
the space between us for that was
long ago—that time—so just lie
under the dark blue quilt and put
the fat pillows with the blue slips
on the great windowsill so we can
look over them and down to the
small figures hurrying by
in total silence and think of the heat
up here and the cold down there
while I turn the light off with the right
hand and gather you in close with the wrong.

Craft Questions

- Read the poem aloud. What do you notice about your breathing as you read?
- How does the lineation and syntax of the poem work together to create this experience?
- How do they work together to emphasize the poem's perception of time?

Exercises

Exercise 1: Walking the Poem

Keeping in mind that white space is generally read as a pause, and the amount of white space denotes the interval of silence, take a poem in progress that's aligned flush left, and try "walking" it across the page by using indentations. As you proceed, reconsider line breaks, on the basis of movement and meaning. Read the poem aloud to see how the spacing changes not only the look of the poem, but also its rhythm. White space will feel necessary instead of gimmicky if it emphasizes the poem's movements and meaning without being too obvious. If need be, return some lines to flush left to render your experiment subtler.

Objective: To transform a poem visually and aurally by experimenting with line breaks and white space.

Exercise 2: Writing It Backwards

Take a poem in progress and rewrite it backwards, starting with the last line, proceeding to the penultimate line, and so on. This will probably result in a poem that doesn't make much sense, so spend some time writing new lines to create "connective tissue," where necessary, and rearrange or cut lines where you see fit. Keep working on the poem by reading it aloud.

Objective: To shake up a poem that has become stuck: to see the lines, images, and other individual elements of the poem with fresh eyes and ears.

Exercise 3: Prose Poems

Try a free writing activity, where you write a brief narrative, rich with association (e.g., a self-portrait, an embarrassing or pivotal moment, a scene from childhood) in a page or less. Begin shaping your narrative into a prose poem by centering on images, figurative language, sounds, and rhythms that seem most evocative. Tighten up your piece by taking out all unnecessary words. For example, reconsider articles such as *a* and *the* and prepositions such as *of* and *from*. Decide whether to set your poem left justified (as a prose paragraph) or left and right justified (as a block of text).

Alternately, take a lineated poem in progress and try it as a prose poem by getting rid of existing line breaks.

Objective: To free yourself from the consideration of lineation.

six | theme

what's my poem about?

ALTHOUGH YOU'VE NO DOUBT given thought to the subject matter and themes of your poems and the poems of others, this guide has held off on addressing this important element directly until now since it's often helpful to begin writing individual poems without a specific **theme** or central concern in mind. This may sound odd, given that so many contemporary poets are addressing timely, relevant topics in their work—from questions of identity to issues of social justice and on. In most cases, however, this subject matter emerges from an authentic place of connection and emotion, between the subject and the poet, rather than emerging as a topic to write about per se. Further, many of the poets whose work we're studying have arrived at their subject matter after years of exploration. Finding your subject matter, the story that you are uniquely positioned to tell, or the story told in a way that only you can tell it, is often a matter of scratching an itch over and over (if you'll excuse the metaphor). What are the questions that keep you up at night? What themes seem to emerge repeatedly in your own life: Questions of power? Intimacy in relationships? Memories and the passage of time? Family dynamics?

When you have a handful of poems in draft form, it's a great time to take a look at them, and to ask yourself what they're about, individually and collectively. It's also useful to ask the same question of your classmates and friends, if you haven't already. If there's a disconnect between your perception and theirs, that, in itself, can be telling. Is there an idea you hope to express, a sensation you hope to create, or a story you hope to tell that isn't yet being clearly communicated in your work? If so, you'll need to decide whether you want to clarify or expand. If you're happy with the ways in which your work is being read, however, you may want to let go of your earlier intention: to let the poem breathe life on its own by developing it in new directions. Either way, focusing on your subject matter and themes is bound to be fruitful.

In order to think more about theme or central concern, we need to start by distinguishing it from **truism**: a claim or statement so obvious that it doesn't really need to be made, such as "you can't win them all." The tricky thing about a truism is that it may actually sound wise at first. And, like cliché, it does contain some kernel of truth. However, if we think about them further, truisms really don't offer us anything new to think about. And like clichés, truisms have been used so much that they offer very little space for questioning or reflection.

So, instead of crafting your poem around a moral, message, or truism, it's more useful to think of the less prescriptive idea of theme. Examples of themes in poetry include family dynamics, gender and sexuality, social justice, nature, and so on. As you can see, these categories leave plenty of room for all kinds of poems. And, of course, poems often contain more than one theme.

A Study in Subject and Theme: The Female Body

Most of the poems we'll look at in this chapter are narratives, or poems that tell stories. And in order to explore a variety of approaches in terms of theme, we'll look at poems that all focus on similar subject matter involving the female body. As you read and discuss, think about your own poetry. Are there particular subjects or themes you've been writing about lately? Are there ideas, concerns, or questions you seem to come back to in your notebook, journal, or in discussions? Once you've begun to identify some of your current subject matter, it's a good idea to search for poems that deal with similar topics or concerns to see what others are up to. The following readings and craft questions should serve as an example for your individualized exploration. Maybe your professor, classmates, or friends can offer suggestions on what to read next, according to your interests. And don't forget appendix B's list of online resources. In particular, the websites of The Academy of American Poets and The Poetry Foundation are searchable by theme.

The first poem we'll take a look at is written by twentieth-century United States poet Anne Sexton (1928–74). Widely regarded as a central figure in the so-called **Confessional School** of poetry of the mid-twentieth century, Sexton wrote about personal topics: those often previously considered taboo, including depression, sexuality, gender, and the female body. Here's one such poem:

In Celebration of My Uterus

Everyone in me is a bird.
I am beating all my wings.
They wanted to cut you out
but they will not.
They said you were immeasurably empty
but you are not.
They said you were sick unto dying
but they were wrong.
You are singing like a school girl.
You are not torn.

Sweet weight,
in celebration of the woman I am
and of the soul of the woman I am
and of the central creature and its delight
I sing for you. I dare to live.
Hello, spirit. Hello, cup.
Fasten, cover. Cover that does contain.
Hello to the soil of the fields.
Welcome, roots.

Each cell has a life.
There is enough here to please a nation.
It is enough that the populace own these goods.
Any person, any commonwealth would say of it,
"It is good this year that we may plant again
and think forward to a harvest.
A blight had been forecast and has been cast out."
Many women are singing together of this:
one is in a shoe factory cursing the machine,
one is at the aquarium tending a seal,
one is dull at the wheel of her Ford,
one is at the toll gate collecting,
one is tying the cord of a calf in Arizona,
one is straddling a cello in Russia,
one is shifting pots on the stove in Egypt,

one is painting her bedroom walls moon color,
one is dying but remembering a breakfast,
one is stretching on her mat in Thailand,
one is wiping the ass of her child,
one is staring out the window of a train
in the middle of Wyoming and one is
anywhere and some are everywhere and all
seem to be singing, although some can not
sing a note.

Sweet weight,
in celebration of the woman I am
let me carry a ten-foot scarf,
let me drum for the nineteen-year-olds,
let me carry bowls for the offering
(if that is my part).
Let me study the cardiovascular tissue,
let me examine the angular distance of meteors,
let me suck on the stems of flowers
(if that is my part).
Let me make certain tribal figures
(if that is my part).
For this thing the body needs
let me sing
for the supper,
for the kissing,
for the correct
yes.

Craft Questions

- What words or phrases of praise does Sexton use to describe her uterus?
- Who are "they" at the beginning of the poem?
- What attitudes, taboos, and actions does Sexton's poem challenge?
- How do stanzas two and three develop the idea of celebration?

Next, take a look at this poem by contemporary Canadian poet, Elizabeth Bachinsky (b. 1976), which bravely takes on the subject matter of a brutal kidnapping. Bachinsky wrote this poem in response to the poem "Wolf Lake" by Matt Rader. In Rader's poem two men witness a man pulling a woman's body out of a car's trunk. Bachinsky changes the point of view to the woman in the trunk.

❧ Wolf Lake

It was down that road he brought me, still
in the trunk of his car. I won't say it felt right,
but it did feel expected. The way you know
your blood can spring like a hydrant.
That September, the horseflies were murder
in the valley. I'd come home to visit the family,
get in a couple of weeks of free food, hooked up
with a guy I'd known when I was a kid and things
went bad. When he cut me, I remember
looking down, my blood surprising as paper
snakes leaping from a tin. He danced me
around his basement apartment, dumped me
on the chesterfield, sat down beside me, and lit
a smoke. He seemed a black bear in the gloam,
shoulders rounded under his clothes,
so I tried to remember everything I knew
about black bears: *whistle while you walk... carry bells...*
if you don't bother them, they won't bother you...
play dead. Everything slowed. I'll tell you a secret.
It's hard to kill a girl. You've got to cut her bad
and you've got to cut her right, and the boy had done neither,
Pain rose along the side of my body, like light.
I lay very still while he smoked beside me: this boy
I'd camped with every summer since we were twelve,
the lake so quiet you could hear the sound
of a heron skim the water at dusk, or the sound
of a boy's breathing. I came-to in the trunk of his car,
gravel kicking up against the frame, dust coming in
through the cracks. It was dark. I was thirsty.
I couldn't move my hands or legs,
The pain was still around. I think I was tied.
We drove that way for a long time before
the Chrysler finally slowed, then stopped. Sound
of gravel crunching under tires. I could smell the lake,
a place where, as kids, we'd come to swim
and know we'd never be seen. Logs grew
up from that lakebed. All those black bones
rising from black water. I remember,
we'd always smelled of lake water and of sex
by the end of the day, and there was a tape of Patsy
Cline we always liked to sing to on our way out —

which is what I thought we'd be doing that September
afternoon. That, or smoking up in his garage.

You know, you hear about the Body
all the time: *They found the Body…*
the Body was found… and then you are one.
Someone once told me the place had been
a valley, before the dam, before the town.
But that was a long time ago. When the engine stopped,
I heard the silver sound of keys in the lock
and then I was up on his shoulders, tasting blood.
I think he said my name. I think he walked
toward the woods.

Craft Questions

- Who is the speaker in this poem?
- What does Bachinsky's poem expose about the nature of violence, in general, and violence against women, in particular?
- Compare the bodily sensations described in the first stanza to the depiction of "the Body" in stanza two.
- How would you describe the voice and tone of the poem?

Although both poems deal with the subject matter of the oppression of women, there is certainly a leap from Sexton's affirmation of women's bodies to Bachinsky's inhabitation of the voice of the brutalized. However, this range begins to suggest a variety of possible approaches. If you look over your poems and discover that you're circling around a theme or set of themes, you may find that you can build on your existing work, in revision or in additional poems, by coming at the theme from different angles and perspectives.

Poetic Sequences and Series

In some cases, the poems you write on similar themes, ideas, or stories begin to suggest a **poetic sequence** or **linked series**: poems intended to be read together in a certain order as a whole. Or you may decide to break up a single poem into sections or to create a longer poem out of short sections you've already written. If you're taking a creative writing class, you may have been asked to complete a portfolio at the end of the unit or semester, consisting of finished poems. And, in many cases, you may be asked to create a series of interrelated poems.

The poetic sequence, which took root in the early twentieth century, is generally associated with the emotions and associations of lyric poetry, whereas the linked series, as in Shakespeare's sonnets, is more often connected by theme. These days, however, the terms **poetic sequence**, **linked series**, **series**, and **serial poem** are often used interchangeably. Here's a serial poem, or a poem in sections, by contemporary United States poet Stephanie Brown (b. 1961):

Feminine Intuition

I. Little Red Riding Hood

Astrid comes from upstate New York.
She comes from distress.
She's enthusiastic about it.
She doesn't belong, but she tries hard.
Her husband hurts her, but they have a drug-free life.
They roller skate and take up fads enthusiastically,
Neon clothing and the like.
He's an air traffic controller, so they move constantly.
This time it's California. After the picnic
I said, "She reminds me of Little Red Riding Hood."
My husband said, "Yeah."
We were doing the dishes.
I can't say some other things, so I say this.

II. Plastic Surgery, Skipped Dessert

That simple woman thought I was simple, but I was not.
I was never simple.
Not trees, stars, plot.
She smoked her fingers down to the yellow.
She had the harsh hearty laughter
Of the women who believe the men will leave them.
All the mothers I knew went nuts.
Hair the color of a screwdriver.
It's a cliché, but it's an altar.
Cotton candy spun into a knot.
Especially rich women, with art.
Kimono, muumuu.
Ice cubes.
But I was never simple. I was never simple.
The way I was raised, the men never leave a woman.
She was a woman: I could not trust her.

III. A Woman Clothed with the Sun

Imagine, all over America, women are losing bone mass.
Brittle old ladies: we create them.
Coiffured movie sirens lounging around the pool transmogrify
into brittle old sea hags.
(They don't know anything: they just nag.)
Let's let them swim out to sea.
Let's give them a spiny seahorse to ride on.
"Good-bye brittle old ladies, beautiful ones—
Ride out against the horizon and the orange sun!"

Craft Questions

- How would you describe the relationship between the speaker and the woman in each section?
- What do all three characters—Astrid, the rich woman, and the old lady—have in common? Why do you think they're presented in this order?
- Discuss the change in point of view in the last section. How might it up the stakes of the poem's central concern?
- Taking the title into consideration, how does the tone of the poem contribute to its theme?

One of the decisions you'll be making when you assemble a poetic series is whether to number, title, or insert a symbol to demarcate sections. Brown's triptych of interrelated portraits seems to lend itself to Roman numerals; there's something archetypal about the three women she depicts.

Finally, let's take a look at excerpts from the groundbreaking book, *Citizen: An American Lyric*, in which contemporary United States poet Claudia Rankine incorporates poems, prose poems, and images, without titles to separate them (sometimes using slash marks to indicate breaks). The poem takes up the ongoing history of aggression perpetrated against African Americans. Here's part of a section:

From *Citizen*, "Some years there exists a wanting to escape ..."

Some years there exists a wanting to escape—

you, floating above your certain ache—

still the ache coexists.

Call that the immanent you—

You are you even before you

grow into understanding you

are not anyone, worthless,

not worth you.

Even as your own weight insists
you are here, fighting off
the weight of nonexistence.

And still this life parts your lids, you see
you seeing your extending hand
as a falling wave—

/

I they he she we you turn
only to discover
the encounter

to be alien to this place.

Wait.

The patience is in the living. Time opens out to you.

The opening, between you and you, occupied,
zoned for an encounter,

given the histories of you and you—

And always, who is this you?

The start of you, each day,
a presence already—

Hey you—

/

Slipping down burying the you buried within. You are everywhere and you are nowhere in the day.

The outside comes in—

Then you, hey you—

Overheard in the moonlight.

Overcome in the moonlight.

Soon you are sitting around, publicly listening, when you hear this—what happens to you doesn't belong to you, only half concerns you He is speaking of the legionnaires in Claire Denis's film *Beau Travail and* you are pulled back into the body of you receiving the nothing gaze—

The world out there insisting on this only half concerns you. What happens to you doesn't belong to you, only half concerns you. It's not yours. Not yours only.

/

And still a world begins its furious erasure—

Who do you think you are, saying I to me?

You nothing.

You nobody.

You.

A body in the world drowns in it—

Hey you—

All our fevered history won't instill insight,
won't turn a body conscious,
won't make that look
in the eyes say yes, though there is nothing

to solve

even as each moment is an answer.

/

Don't say I if it means so little,
holds the little forming no one.

You are not sick, you are injured—

you ache for the rest of life.

How to care for the injured body,

the kind of body that can't hold
the content it is living?

And where is the safest place when that place
must be someplace other than in the body?

Even now your voice entangles this mouth
whose words are here as pulse, strumming
shut out, shut in, shut up—

You cannot say—

A body translates its you—

you there, hey you

/

even as it loses the location of its mouth.

When you lay your body in the body

entered as if skin and bone were public places,

when you lay your body in the body
entered as if you're the ground you walk on,

you know no memory should live
in these memories

becoming the body of you.

You slow all existence down with your call
detectable only as sky. The night's yawn
absorbs you as you lie down at the wrong angle

to the sun ready already to let go of your hand.

Wait with me
though the waiting, wait up,

might take until nothing whatsoever was done.

/

To be left, not alone, the only wish—

to call you out, to call out you.

Who shouted, you? You

shouted you, you the murmur in the air, you sometimes
sounding like you, you sometimes saying you,

go nowhere,

be no one but you first—

Nobody notices, only you've known,

you're not sick, not crazy,
not angry, not sad—

It's just this, you're injured.

/

Everything shaded everything darkened everything
shadowed

is the stripped is the struck—

is the trace
is the aftertaste.
I they he she we you were too concluded yesterday to
know whatever was done could also be done, was also
done, was never done—

The worst injury is feeling you don't belong so much
to you—

Craft Questions

- How does Rankine describe the experience of the body? Compare and contrast her treatment of this subject with the other selections in this chapter.
- How is the individual body connected with the body politic, or social sphere, in this piece?
- How does Rankine's use of form, including the use of white space and section marks, affect your emotional experience as you read? What themes does the form emphasize?

The selections we've read in this chapter are in no way exhaustive; they simply indicate interesting directions within a broad set of questions and concerns. As you begin to identify subjects and themes that are important to you, it may be comforting and eye opening to know some of what has come before and some of what is being written around you. And, at some point, you'll hopefully be able to connect with others working on some of the same subjects, either through your work, online, or in person. This can lead to exchange, critique, and collaboration. Ultimately, our poetry isn't meant to be written in a vacuum. The work we do can help to shape a conversation.

Readings

Adrienne Rich (1929–2012)
Diving into the Wreck

First having read the book of myths,
and loaded the camera,
and checked the edge of the knife-blade,
I put on
the body-armor of black rubber
the absurd flippers
the grave and awkward mask.
I am having to do this
not like Cousteau with his
assiduous team
aboard the sun-flooded schooner
but here alone.

There is a ladder.
The ladder is always there
hanging innocently
close to the side of the schooner.
We know what it is for,
we who have used it.
Otherwise
it is a piece of maritime floss
some sundry equipment.

I go down.
Rung after rung and still
the oxygen immerses me
the blue light
the clear atoms
of our human air.
I go down.
My flippers cripple me,
I crawl like an insect down the ladder
and there is no one
to tell me when the ocean
will begin.

First the air is blue and then
it is bluer and then green and then

black I am blacking out and yet
my mask is powerful
it pumps my blood with power
the sea is another story
the sea is not a question of power
I have to learn alone
to turn my body without force
in the deep element.

And now: it is easy to forget
what I came for
among so many who have always
lived here
swaying their crenellated fans
between the reefs
and besides
you breathe differently down here.

I came to explore the wreck.
The words are purposes.
The words are maps.
I came to see the damage that was done
and the treasures that prevail.
I stroke the beam of my lamp
slowly along the flank
of something more permanent
than fish or weed

the thing I came for:
the wreck and not the story of the wreck
the thing itself and not the myth
the drowned face always staring
toward the sun
the evidence of damages
worn by salt and sway into this threadbare beauty
the ribs of the disaster
curving their assertion
among the tentative haunters.

This is the place.
And I am here, the mermaid whose dark hair
streams black, the merman in his armored body.
We circle silently

about the wreck
we dive into the hold.
I am she: I am he

whose drowned face sleeps with open eyes
whose breasts still bear the stress
whose silver, copper, vermeil cargo lies
obscurely inside barrels
half-wedged and left to rot
we are the half-destroyed instruments
that once held to a course
the water-eaten log
the fouled compass

We are, I am, you are
by cowardice or courage
the one who find our way
back to this scene
carrying a knife, a camera
a book of myths
in which
our names do not appear.

Craft Questions

- If we read Rich's poem as an extended metaphor, what might the dive, the book, the camera, and the knife imply?
- How does the speaker describe their body? In what ways does the poem complicate our notions of gender identity?
- Note the poem's movement from singular to plural. The identity of the speaker is ultimately both one and many. Why?

Lynn Melnick
Twelve

When I was your age I went to a banquet.
When I was your age I went to a barroom

and bought cigarettes with quarters
lifted from the laundry money. Last night

I did all your laundry. I don't know why
I thought this love could be pure. It's enough

that it's infinite. I kiss your cheek when you sleep
and wonder if you feel it.

It's the same cheek I've kissed from the beginning.
You don't have to like me.

You just have to let me
keep your body yours. It's mine.

When I was your age I went to a banquet
and a man in a tux pinched my cheeks.

When I was your age I went to a barroom
and a man in a band shirt pinched my ass.

There is so much I don't know about you.
Last night I skipped a banquet

so I could stay home and do your laundry
and drink wine from my grandmother's glass.

When I was your age boys traded quarters
for a claw at my carcass on a pleather bench

while I missed the first few seconds of a song
I'd hoped to record on my backseat boombox.

When I was your age I enjoyed a hook.
You think I know nothing of metamorphosis

but when I was your age I invented a key change.
You don't have to know what I know.

Craft Questions

- What hopes, fears, desires, and dreams does the speaker have for her twelve-year-old daughter?
- How does the speaker describe her own adolescence?
- How does Melnick's use of couplets emphasize the poem's themes?

Alessandra Lynch

Admission

1.
In the bleeding berries on the nettle-hill
where pond was a ruse for calm
I gave voice
to what deadened the field what ended its green
said the word *assault*, prettier than *r____*.

Violets whitened.
The thing shrank from its essence.

The words took breath to say this pushing air away
(*dislodge it from the skin dislodge his breath from your face his voice*)

breath lost in one swift pull of winter.

After I said what I said said the word
assault was prettier. Assault was less
invasive. R____ would mean admission and surrender.

The words took breath.
(*Hush, hush. Come, forgiveness.*)

2.
It took seconds for him
to push me down then he was done—

I was supine. Perpendicular, the tree. That night
we made a kind of staggering diagram in the parking lot.
How had he risen from me? Jerked out, rolled
off.
        Crude knuckles scuffed by fatigue and dust, the roots
of the tree inches from my face. Had he gripped
my wrist, pressed a knife at my neck?

For decades I've walked in a daze
        through insect-amputees who are not dead
but don't have the gut or grip to shield their good
remaining legs. They're scuttle-dry and yellow-gray
        as storm-gripped sky.
For decades I've walked
        In a daze through this day's recitations.

Low crawl of red through leaves.

I pulled myself up. Parallel, the tree. That night
we made a kind of shuddering frame for the air.
How had he gotten me down? Had he seized
my arm or waist...I don't remember the least.

Craft Questions

- Discuss the progression of Lynch's visceral recollection in sections one and two of "Admission." In what ways does the speaker grapple with giving voice to the brutality she experienced?
- How do Lynch's images of nature contribute to the poem?
- Discuss the role of italics, white space, and typographical marks. How do these elements contribute to the various degrees of proximity or distance the speaker experiences with regard to her trauma? How do they contribute to your understanding?

Exercises

Exercise 1: Earn Your Statement

The following short poem by twentieth-century United States poet, James Wright (1927–80), overtly announces its subject in the last line, leading up to it through concrete sensory description. It's only after we've read the poem straight through that we can consider the possibility of metaphorical suggestion or foreshadowing leading up to the ending.

Lying in a Hammock at William Duffy's Farm in Pine Island, Minnesota

Over my head, I see the bronze butterfly,
Asleep on the black trunk,
Blowing like a leaf in green shadow.
Down the ravine behind the empty house,
The cowbells follow one another
Into the distances of the afternoon.
To my right,
In a field of sunlight between two pines,
The droppings of last year's horses
Blaze up into golden stones.
I lean back, as the evening darkens and comes on.
A chicken hawk floats over, looking for home.
I have wasted my life.

Using Wright's poem as a model for organization, try writing a poem in which you "earn the right" to make a direct statement on subject or theme by first engaging in concrete sensory description. You can write your statement first, and then lead up to it, or vice versa.

Objective: To explore a new balance between description and overt statement. You'll gain insight into ways of hinting at theme as well as stating it.

Exercise 2: What's My Poem About?

Take one of your finished poems, and complete the following sentence: "This poem is about...." Have friends or classmates read your piece and have them complete the same sentence. It is not important that all the answers be the same, of course, but if they are wildly disparate, try revising your poem so that its central concerns are more apparent.

Objective: To revise according to subject, theme, or central concern.

Exercise 3: Poetic Sequencing

Take a look at the poems you've written so far. Do you consider them a series, in terms of subject matter and theme? If so, think about the order in which you would present the work. Would you create a narrative arc, by introducing a topic or question early on and leading up to a climax or crescendo? Would you arrange poems in terms of length, varying short and long poems? Are there other forms of organization you can think of using?

Alternately, consider knitting several short poems or fragments together into a single poem in sections.

Objective: To see whether your poems begin to speak to each other when arranged in a series or in a poem with individual sections. By considering ordering your poems, you'll gain insight into the themes, forms, and strategies that reoccur across your work.

seven | voice and tone

dear reader

As you develop the subject matter of your poems, you'll want to consider **voice**, or who is speaking, as well as **tone**: the speaker's attitude. Poetic meaning depends on these elements. Just as it matters greatly *how* we say what we say, or the inflection that we use when we speak, the way in which a poem is delivered and received is vital to its power. The difference is that in poetry, the tone has to be implied within the words themselves, rather than being made clear by the situation or inflection. For example, if we say *please, sit down*, we can say it in a welcoming tone or a hostile one; whereas in a poem, we'd have to infer the tone of this utterance from the narrative or other clues around it. And as we're reading and writing, we may have to read a poem aloud more than once before we really hear its voice and tone: for it to fully come alive.

Poems can be reflective, melancholic, comedic, ironic, sarcastic, or wise. The list goes on. And often there's a mix of various tones within the same poem. In terms of voice, we often begin with the assumption that the speaker of a poem is the poet. Although this is sometimes true, we need evidence to prove it, for poets often take on the voice of others, either explicitly or implicitly in their work. Just as tone can take some time to pick up on or adjust, voice can be more mutable than we may at first assume. To gain a better understanding of the way these elements work in tandem, let's start with a poem by contemporary United States poet, Yusef Komunyakaa (b. 1947):

Facing It

My black face fades,
hiding inside the black granite.
I said I wouldn't
dammit: No tears.
I'm stone. I'm flesh.
My clouded reflection eyes me
like a bird of prey, the profile of night
slanted against morning. I turn
this way—the stone lets me go.
I turn that way—I'm inside
the Vietnam Veterans Memorial
again, depending on the light
to make a difference.
I go down the 58,022 names,
half-expecting to find
my own in letters like smoke.
I touch the name Andrew Johnson;
I see the booby trap's white flash.
Names shimmer on a woman's blouse
but when she walks away
the names stay on the wall.
Brushstrokes flash, a red bird's
wings cutting across my stare.
The sky. A plane in the sky.
A white vet's image floats
closer to me, then his pale eyes
look through mine. I'm a window.
He's lost his right arm
inside the stone. In the black mirror
a woman's trying to erase names:
No, she's brushing a boy's hair.

Craft Questions

- How does the speaker's perspective of the Vietnam memorial change as the poem progresses?
- How does tone of the poem shift to accompany these changes? Pick out individual phrases to discuss tone.
- What is the speaker's perspective on the Vietnam War itself? What details in the poem support this interpretation?

If you look up Komunyakaa's biography, you'll find that he is a Vietnam veteran, and given the poem's first-person narration, it's safe to assume that the speaker is, in fact, closely aligned with the poet himself. Knowing this information may deepen your experience of the poem. However, it's entirely possible to read, understand, and be moved by the poem without knowing Komunyakaa's background.

Another poem with a first-person narrator and subtly shifting tone is "Persimmons" by contemporary United States poet Li-Young Lee (b. 1957). Take a look:

Persimmons

In sixth grade Mrs. Walker
slapped the back of my head
and made me stand in the corner
for not knowing the difference
between *persimmon* and *precision*.
How to choose

persimmons. This is precision.
Ripe ones are soft and brown-spotted.
Sniff the bottoms. The sweet one
will be fragrant. How to eat:
put the knife away, lay down newspaper.
Peel the skin tenderly, not to tear the meat.
Chew the skin, suck it,
and swallow. Now, eat
the meat of the fruit,
so sweet,
all of it, to the heart.

Donna undresses, her stomach is white.
In the yard, dewy and shivering

with crickets, we lie naked,
face-up, face-down.
I teach her Chinese.
Crickets: *chiu chiu*. Dew: I've forgotten.
Naked: I've forgotten.
Ni, wo: you and me.
I part her legs,
remember to tell her
she is beautiful as the moon.

Other words
that got me into trouble were
fight and *fright*, *wren* and *yarn*.
Fight was what I did when I was frightened,
Fright was what I felt when I was fighting.
Wrens are small, plain birds,
yarn is what one knits with.
Wrens are soft as yarn.
My mother made birds out of yarn.
I loved to watch her tie the stuff;
a bird, a rabbit, a wee man.

Mrs. Walker brought a persimmon to class
and cut it up
so everyone could taste
a *Chinese apple*. Knowing
it wasn't ripe or sweet, I didn't eat
but watched the other faces.

My mother said every persimmon has a sun
inside, something golden, glowing,
warm as my face.

Once, in the cellar, I found two wrapped in newspaper,
forgotten and not yet ripe.
I took them and set both on my bedroom windowsill,
where each morning a cardinal
sang, *The sun, the sun*.

Finally understanding
he was going blind,
my father sat up all one night
waiting for a song, a ghost.

I gave him the persimmons,
swelled, heavy as sadness,
and sweet as love.

This year, in the muddy lighting
of my parents' cellar, I rummage, looking
for something I lost.
My father sits on the tired, wooden stairs,
black cane between his knees,
hand over hand, gripping the handle.
He's so happy that I've come home.
I ask how his eyes are, a stupid question.
All gone, he answers.

Under some blankets, I find a box.
Inside the box I find three scrolls.
I sit beside him and untie
three paintings by my father:
Hibiscus leaf and a white flower.
Two cats preening.
Two persimmons, so full they want to drop from the cloth.

He raises both hands to touch the cloth,
asks, *Which is this?*

This is persimmons, Father.

Oh, the feel of the wolftail on the silk,
the strength, the tense
precision in the wrist.
I painted them hundreds of times
eyes closed. These I painted blind.
Some things never leave a person:
scent of the hair of one you love,
the texture of persimmons,
in your palm, the ripe weight.

Craft Questions

- How does the tone shift as the poem progresses?
- How does the description of persimmons change to help signal these tonal shifts?
- In what ways do the poem's tones work in tandem with its themes?

Both Komunyakaa's and Lee's poems are inherently meditative, in that they contain a single speaking subject contemplating an object—the Vietnam memorial, persimmons—as a means of recollection, connection, and transformation. If you haven't already done so, try a similar exercise. Is there an object that sparks memory for you? Quickly list some of your associations, and gradually work them into a poem. See if your poem takes on multiple registers of thought, feeling, and tone, as you ruminate on your object of contemplation.

Satire

When we first start exploring the world of poetry, we may carry the assumption that it's serious stuff. And, in a sense, we're right; it often seems easier to write from a place of questioning, of ambivalence or mixed emotions, and sometimes even from a place of turmoil. However, if we think of the breadth of our emotional experience as humans, there is a wide range, and that range includes states of **satire**: including **irony** (involving some reversal), exaggeration, and humor. So, why shouldn't poetry work in these registers as well? The short answer is that it can and does! In fact, many of the most beloved poets of our time use various satiric tones to great effect.

Consider this prose poem by twentieth-century United States poet, James Tate (1943–2015), for instance. As we discussed in chapter 5, prose poems often lend themselves to narrative compression and surreal, unexpected turns. As you read Tate's poem, notice, in particular, the poem's abrupt shifts in perspective and tone.

❧ Distance from Loved Ones

After her husband died, Zita decided to get the face-lift
she had always wanted. Half-way through the operation
her blood pressure started to drop, and they had to stop.
When Zita tried to fasten her seat-belt for her sad drive
home, she threw-out her shoulder. Back at the hospital
the doctor examined her and found cancer run rampant
throughout her shoulder and arm and elsewhere. Radiation
followed. And, now, Zita just sits there in her beauty parlor,
bald, crying and crying.

My mother tells me all this on the phone, and I say:
Mother, who is Zita?

And my mother says, I am Zita. All my life I have been
Zita, bald and crying. And you, my son, who should have known
me best, thought I was nothing but your mother.

But, Mother, I say, I am dying ...

Craft Questions

- How do the perspectival shifts in the poem affect your experience of the story?
- Are there moments of absurdity, irony, sarcasm, or even humor? Alternately, are there sad moments that make you embarrassed or even ashamed to laugh?
- Consider Tate's title (which is also the title of the collection in which the poem first appeared). In what ways do the perspectival shifts and shifts in tone emphasize this theme?

For another example of irony and sarcasm, as well as the use of characters, look back on Stephanie Brown's poem, "Feminine Intuition" in chapter 6. Think more about the speaker's position with regard to the poem's female characters. To what extent does she reject them? To what extent does she resemble them?

Persona Poems

As we've discussed, we can't necessarily assume that the speaker of a first-person poem represents the poet. As a poet, you get to choose how much of yourself to reveal and how much to invent. In fact, instead of using first-person perspective, you may instead decide to use second (*you*) or third person (*she/he/they*). And, as you can begin to see in Tate's and Brown's poems, you have additional options, including the use of a character or **persona**. Poems are specifically referred to as **persona poems** when a character other than the poet is the speaker. In some cases, the persona is invented, and in others it is based on an actual person, historical or contemporary.

In 1842 British poet Robert Browning (1812–89) published the collection *Dramatic Monologues*, which still stands as an important precursor of the contemporary persona poem. As Browning's title suggests, his book consisted of poems in which the speaker is a character, as in a play. One of the most famous of Browning's monologues, "My Last Duchess" takes an actual historical figure, the Duke of Ferrara, Alfonso II d'Este, who, in 1558, married the daughter of the duke of Florence. She died under a cloud of suspicion three years into the marriage. Take a look:

My Last Duchess

Ferarra

That's my last Duchess painted on the wall,
Looking as if she were alive. I call
That piece a wonder, now; Fra Pandolf's hands
Worked busily a day, and there she stands.
Will't please you sit and look at her? I said
"Fra Pandolf" by design, for never read
Strangers like you that pictured countenance,
The depth and passion of its earnest glance,
But to myself they turned (since none puts by
The curtain I have drawn for you, but I)
And seemed as they would ask me, if they durst,
How such a glance came there; so, not the first
Are you to turn and ask thus. Sir, 'twas not
Her husband's presence only, called that spot
Of joy into the Duchess' cheek; perhaps
Fra Pandolf chanced to say, "Her mantle laps
Over my lady's wrist too much," or "Paint
Must never hope to reproduce the faint
Half-flush that dies along her throat." Such stuff
Was courtesy, she thought, and cause enough
For calling up that spot of joy. She had
A heart—how shall I say?—too soon made glad,
Too easily impressed; she liked whate'er
She looked on, and her looks went everywhere.
Sir, 'twas all one! My favour at her breast,
The dropping of the daylight in the West,
The bough of cherries some officious fool
Broke in the orchard for her, the white mule
She rode with round the terrace—all and each
Would draw from her alike the approving speech,
Or blush, at least. She thanked men—good! But thanked
Somehow—I know not how—as if she ranked
My gift of a nine-hundred-years-old name
With anybody's gift. Who'd stoop to blame
This sort of trifling? Even had you skill
In speech—which I have not—to make your will
Quite clear to such an one, and say, "Just this
Or that in you disgusts me; here you miss,
Or there exceed the mark"—and if she let

Herself be lessoned so, nor plainly set
Her wits to yours, forsooth, and made excuse—
E'en then would be some stooping; and I choose
Never to stoop. Oh, sir, she smiled, no doubt,
Whene'er I passed her; but who passed without
Much the same smile? This grew; I gave commands;
Then all smiles stopped together. There she stands
As if alive. Will't please you rise? We'll meet
The company below, then. I repeat,
The Count your master's known munificence
Is ample warrant that no just pretense
Of mine for dowry will be disallowed;
Though his fair daughter's self, as I avowed
At starting, is my object. Nay, we'll go
Together down, sir. Notice Neptune, though,
Taming a sea-horse, thought a rarity,
Which Claus of Innsbruck cast in bronze for me!

Craft Questions

- How would you describe the speaker? What do his descriptions of the painting and statue tell you about him, specifically?
- Compare the speaker's perceptions of his former wife with your own perceptions. How does Browning build dramatic irony as the poem progresses?
- What cultural attitudes or norms does the form of the dramatic monologue allow Browning to explore?

Although Browning's poem is set in sixteenth-century Italy, it tells us a lot about norms and attitudes in Victorian England. To what extent do you think Browning is critiquing the values of his own time by taking on the controversial Duke as his speaker?

Jumping forward in time, next take a look at this persona poem by contemporary United States poet, Tyehimba Jess (b. 1965):

Sissieretta Jones

Ad libitum
I sing this body *ad libitum*, Europe scraped raw between my teeth until,
presto, "Ave Maria" floats to the surface from a Tituba tributary of
"Swanee." Until I'm a *legato* darkling whole note, my voice shimmering
up from the Atlantic's hold; until I'm a coda of sail song whipped in salted
wind; until my chorus swells like a lynched tongue; until the nocturnes

boiling beneath the roof of my mouth extinguish each burning cross. I sing this life in testimony to *tempo rubato*, to time stolen body by body by body by body from one passage to another; I sing tremolo to the opus of loss. I sing this story *staccato* and *stretto*, a fugue of blackface and blued-up arias. I sing with one hand smoldering in the steely canon, the other *lento*, slow, languorous: lingered in the fields of "Babylon's Falling" …

Note:
Sissieretta Jones was the first African American opera singer to perform at Carnegie Hall.

Craft Questions

- In what ways does Jess's poem, itself, read as a song?
- How does Jess's speaker affect our understanding and experience of Jones's story, in particular, and African American history, in general?
- How does the form of the poem impact your experience of it? How might the poem be different if it were lineated?

Although Browning's and Jess's poems come from different places and times, a similar question can be applied: to what extent can Jess's poem be read as a critique or protest of social injustice and violence? It may be useful to spend some time comparing the two poems.

In terms of your own poetry, you'll likely find that writing persona poems frees you up to say any number of things that have been difficult to voice directly. And who's to say a persona poem has to use a human speaker? For example, take a look at this poem by contemporary United States poet, Amy Gerstler (b. 1956):

Advice From a Caterpillar

Chew your way into a new world.
Munch leaves. Molt. Rest. Molt
again. Self-reinvention is *everything*.
Spin many nests. Cultivate stinging
bristles. Don't get sentimental
about your discarded skins. Grow
quickly. Develop a yen for nettles.
Alternate crumpling and climbing. Rely
on your antennae. Sequester poisons
in your body for use at a later date.
When threatened, emit foul odors

in self-defense. Behave cryptically
to confuse predators: change colors, spit,
or feign death. If all else fails, taste terrible.

Craft Questions

- How would you characterize the voice of the caterpillar?
- How does the form of advice help affect the poem's tone?
- Note Gerstler's use of enjambment. How does the poem's pacing contribute to its voice, tone, and meaning?
- What might the poem suggest about human life, albeit humorously?

Looking back on Gerstler's poem, notice the **diction** or word choice. Because the speaker is as specific and quirky as an advice-giving caterpillar, the world of the poem naturally becomes inhabited by words such as *molt, cultivate, bristles, skins, crumpling, climbing nettles, antennae, poisons,* and *predators.* By choosing your voice, tone, and situation carefully, you may unlock or discover a whole new lexicon from which to draw inspiration.

Considering Your Audience

As we've touched upon in previous chapters, most contemporary poets are primarily working in lyric and narrative modes, whereas Browning's monologues and persona poems are generally considered dramatic. These terms quickly become complicated, however, since there are so many possible combinations and exceptions. As you craft your own poems, it may be helpful to think about the implied contract between speaker and reader. If you're using a lyric structure of *I/you,* for instance, do you have a sense of who the *I* actually is? And what's the relationship between that *I* and *you*? Is the *you* the beloved, an unnamed reader, all of us? And what's the occasion of speech? What prompts the poem? These questions may be difficult to answer, and that's ok. The important point is to become more aware of the relative intimacy or distance between your speaker and reader.

One way to engage this dynamic directly is to read and write some poems in various modes of lyric address. Examples include poems of advice or instruction, such as Gerstler's; elegies, such as John Yau's "Overnight" (in chapter 4); and odes, such as Kevin Young's "Ode to the Hotel Near the Children's Hospital" (in chapter 4). Last, consider writing an **epistolary** or letter poem. Dating back to ancient Greek and Roman poets, including, most notably, Horace (65 BCE–8 BCE), the letter poem has gradually evolved from a poem written in form to one now commonly written in free verse. For instance, take a look at this free-verse letter poem by contemporary United States poet, Christopher Bursk (1943–2021):

Letter to a Great-great-grandson

Dear child-I-can-only-imagine,
there are advantages to being unborn:
no colic, no mushy peas to be tricked into eating,
no tug of war over potty training, or spelling tests,
no fractions to learn or girls to stammer in front of.
Your feet don't yet smell, nor your palms sweat.
No words stick in your throat.
You don't have to mope around the house
wondering if you'll ever get your driver's license
or manage the mechanics of making love.
Child, by the time you're born, I'll likely be long dead
but, if lucky, a ghost
who'd give anything for nocturnal emissions or a door to bang.
Will the seas have risen and taken back
what was theirs in the first place?
Will the price of gas be $30 a gallon?
Will there be pharmaceutical riots,
drugs doled out in church basements instead of soup?
Are the Cubs still trying to trade for a starting pitcher
to get them at last to the World Series?
Does spring still forget to arrive on time?
Or am I just another of those poets
who can't imagine being silenced,
egomaniac enough to insist on being heard
even after reduced to ashes? My verses
like the scribble of dew on the leaves this morning,
messages that'll vanish before anyone deciphers them?
Seed of a seed, if I can imagine you,
I can imagine a life to come.
This letter lets me do just that, each word
presupposing a future: the time in which it is written
implying a time afterwards in which it is read.

Craft Questions

- How does the speaker's address to the as-yet unborn manage to create a sense of intimacy?
- What themes and emotions does the form emphasize?
- Discuss the end of the poem. Ultimately, what does the letter form allow the poet to do?
- How would you describe the overall tone of the poem?

Aside from writing in modes of lyric address, in order to work with tone, it's helpful to continually ask yourself what your own attitude toward the subject of your poem truly is. Readers tend to be moved by a sense of authentic feeling and honesty, even if you've made up many of the details along the way. Keep pushing yourself beyond cliché, truism, sentimentality, as well as melodrama, to try to get at your real feelings, which are usually messy and mixed. And see what others have to say. Are they picking up on the mood, attitude, and tone of your poem? As we've discovered, tone carries so much meaning. So, tuning into it is essential.

Readings

Lorna Crozier (b. 1948)
Onions

The onion loves the onion.
It hugs its many layers,
saying, O, O, O,
each vowel smaller
than the last.

Some say it has no heart.
It doesn't need one.
It surrounds itself,
feels whole. Primordial.
First among vegetables.

If Eve had bitten it
instead of the apple,
how different
Paradise.

Craft Questions

- Describe the tone or tones of the poem.
- Which words or phrases help to establish tone?
- Do you consider "Onions" an ode? Why or why not?

C.D. Wright (1949–2016)
✤ Clockmaker with Bad Eyes

I close the shop at six. Welcome wind,
weekend with two suns, night with a travel book,
the dog-eared sheets of a bed
I will not see again.

I not of time, lost in time
learned from watches—
a second is a killing thing.

Live your life. Your eyes go. Take your body
out for walks along the waters
of a cold and loco planet.

Love whatever flows. Cooking smoke, woman's blood,
tears. Do you hear what I'm telling you?

Craft Questions

- Compare the tone in the first half of the poem with the tone of the second.
- What does Wright's turn to the mode of instruction or advice add to the poem?
- How would you describe the tone of the question at the end?

✤ Susan Stewart (b. 1952)
from Lessons From Television

You must laugh at yourself, laugh and laugh.
Music swells the emotions;
music exists to punctuate seeing.
Emotion, therefore, is punctuation.

Formless, freedom resembles abasement.
Abasement is as infinite as desire.
You must laugh at yourself, laugh and laugh.

Those who are not demons are saints.
You are not a demon or a saint.

Women are small and want something,
so laugh at yourself, laugh and laugh.

Beds are sites of abasement.
The news is about the news.

Faces in close-up are always in anguish.
Hair and teeth are clues to class.

Clothes are changing,
hanging up or down
And change itself is a laugh.

Cause can't be figured
and consequence is yet to come.

You're either awake or asleep
and that, too, is a clue to class.

Children are never with groups of children
unless they are singing in chorus.

Their mothers cannot do enough,
though there's always room for improvement.

And improvement lies in progress,
though collapsing is good for a laugh.

Saints will turn to the worse.
Demons die if they can be found.

Nature is combat, weather is sublime.
Even weather can make you laugh.

People you don't know are louder than you are,
but what is far away cannot harm you—

Books are objects, families are inspiring.
Animals protect their young;
the young come with the territory.

English is the only language.
Reading is an occasion for interruption,
and interruption is a kind of laugh.

Something is bound to get better.
And there is a pill with your name on it.

When indoors, stick with your own race—
that way you'll feel free to laugh.

Strangers are paying attention to your smell.
A camera will light like a moth on disaster.
Pity will turn to irony.

The street is a dark and frightful place.
Fires are daily.

Your car is your face.
You must laugh at yourself, laugh and laugh.

Craft Questions

- Who is speaking to whom in the poem?
- How would you characterize the tone or attitude of the speaker?
- What is *your* attitude toward the speaker's statements and instructions?
- How do these two attitudes work together?

Exercises

Exercise 1: First to Third Person

Take a look at the voice in your poems so far. If you've mostly used first person (*I*), try writing a poem in third (*he/she/they*), and vice versa. Or try writing in second person, *you*. Alternately, work with a poem in progress by changing the voice.

Objective: To open up possibilities for new work or work in progress by exploring how voice affects the degree of intimacy between poem and reader.

Exercise 2: Lyric Address

Write a poem that addresses itself to a particular *you*—such as the beloved, the reader, or the dead. For example, you could write a love poem, letter poem, instructional poem, or elegy. Notice how this new approach facilitates changes in your style, tone, and diction.

Objective: By crafting a poem that claims a particular *you* as its interlocutor, you'll become more conscious of whom or what you're addressing in your work.

Exercise 3: Persona Poems

For this poem try adopting a new voice and perspective. For example, if most of your poems have been serious, try adopting an ironic or satirical stance. Consider using an invented character, a persona, to speak the lines of your poem. Or consider writing the entire poem as a dramatic monologue: a poem in which the speaker addresses a defined listener in a specific situation.

Objective: By trying out a different speaker, voice, or persona you may free yourself to reveal more emotionally or to simply stretch your range of writing styles.

eight | revision

first thought, best thought?

TIBETAN BUDDHIST MASTER CHÖGYAM Trungpa Rinpoche (1939–87) used the phrase "first thought, best thought" to refer to the vitality of the moment of perception before judgment, and his student, poet Allen Ginsberg, applied this idea to writing, when he spoke of "the first thought you had on your mind, the first thought you thought before you thought you should have a formal thought." Ginsberg's idea of capturing the mind in motion continues to be appealing to many of us, especially when we're just beginning, since it implies that if we jot down the idea quickly enough, we'll be communicating authentically.

Although most guides to creative writing will summarily dismiss this idea, stressing the importance of revision in any serious poet's life, I'd like to suggest that you adopt a *both/and* strategy (as opposed to *either/or*). What exactly do I mean by *both/and*? Apply both "first thought, best thought" *and* revise. As we've touched upon earlier, it's important to give yourself absolute free reign when you're writing in your notebook or recording on your phone: when you're first gathering ideas. This means that every time that inner voice pops up in your head, suggesting that what you're doing is no good, or that it fails to meet expectations, you need to banish this voice immediately. And if you can't entirely banish it at first, at least turn down the volume as much as possible, and just get in there and *play, flow, make a mess.* Write without thinking too much about what you're doing in this first stage. Then, when you've had some time to step away, come back to what you've written to reshape it, get feedback from others, and revise, revise, revise. And always keep every draft as you go. For most of us, this means establishing a new system of saving drafts on the computer (along with the handwritten scraps and phone notes), instead of simply deleting or changing the poem within a single document. Why is it important to save all these first thoughts? Because you may, in fact, lose some of that original vitality as you revise, and you may want to dive back into an earlier draft to discover lines, images, or whole sections that you dismissed too quickly. After all, once you've revised to your heart's content, you'll be the final judge of what version to keep. Your final poem will likely represent a melding of first thoughts with later ones.

Why is it so important to revise and to revise thoroughly, rather than merely tinkering or correcting typos and the like? Although our first thoughts can often contain many of the essential nutrients we need, including energy, emotions, and ideas, crafting powerful poems also involves cultivating these initial thoughts (or seeds) by putting into practice the techniques we've been studying. And like plant cultivation, growing a poem often involves allowing time to process the poem, to let it live in your heart and mind, to see how it looks days, weeks (or sometimes even months or years) later. This remains a somewhat mysterious part of any act of artistic production: most poets, writers, and artists find that solutions to complex problems often arrive after they've stepped away and come back. This element of time can be tricky to manage if you're working under a deadline for an assignment. If this is the case, my suggestion is to simulate breaks by getting a few drafts underway, switching off working on them, and then returning to them. Your professor may also build in a bit of time to revise, if you've been assigned a final portfolio at the end of the unit or semester.

The other reason to try your hand at different versions of the same poem is to stretch: to learn new techniques by trying them on for size. For instance, how can you really know whether short lines suit your subject matter if you've never tried writing in long lines? How can you see if you've found the most vivid images, a rhythm that moves readers, or a powerful way of approaching a topic, if you've never shared your work with readers and pushed yourself to revise based on some of their suggestions? Even if you end up not liking the results of your experiments, you'll develop a kind of muscle memory in the process that will serve you well when you're writing future poems. It may be that *this* poem should be kept in short lines after all, but down the road, your long-line experiment comes in handy. It's helpful to think about what you're learning along the way, instead of becoming too fixated on an individual piece. Keep asking yourself how your thoughts and skills are changing, and you'll see that you're growing in leaps and bounds, by staying loose and trying different ways of crafting poems.

Revision Strategies

At the end of this chapter, you'll be invited to engage with a folio of a student poem in progress and to try out several modes of revision, including collaborative and solo strategies. In general, however, there are three basic categories of revision: **editing out** unnecessary words, phrases, lines, or sections; **adding in**; and **reorganizing** or rewriting. The first category tends to be the easiest for most of us. Here, you're acting as a sculptor, carving away at the poem to render it tighter and more powerful. The other two categories, adding in and reorganizing, tend to be more difficult. Many poets describe the work involved as feeling or thinking their way back into the space of the poem. A typical scenario if you're in a workshop class, for example, is that you've received the feedback that something seems to be missing in a poem, or that classmates would love to read an extra stanza or two of the narrative you've been crafting. If you're game, you'll need to sit with the poem and think of things you can add. There's no right way to do this, but if you can remain relaxed and try writing more than you need, you'll likely be able to find at least a few good new lines to add back in.

In terms of changing or reworking existing material, here are a few questions to ask, as a group or solo:

- Do you have more than one poem idea within a single poem? If so, consider crafting more than one poem out of the material.
- Are there parts of your poem that would be stronger if they were moved—from beginning to end, for example? Try moving things around to see what happens.
- Are existing poems in some way fragmentary? If so, could they be knit together into one longer poem or series?

All of these questions prompt you to consider moving parts of a poem around—within the same poem or into entirely new work. You may need to do some writing back in to make connections once you've done this juggling, which involves reimagining whole poems, but you'll find it's worth the work involved. You may even find that you've crafted entirely new poems (and more of them).

When Enough Is Enough

How can you tell when your poems are complete? When it comes to revision, many poems are in some sense never finished, even once they're published. In fact, often a poem that first appeared in a literary journal is altered once it appears in a book. On the other hand, however, you do need to develop a sense of when you can feel comfortable sending a poem out into the world. So, a better question might be: when is it complete *enough*? When is it good enough for you to stand by it?

After all is said and done, after you've taken in the comments and suggestions from others and tried many different versions, you are the ultimate judge, and judging can be difficult. With practice, however, you'll get a hunch that the poem has fulfilled its own goals. For some of us, this develops more as a feeling or intuition than as an intellectual idea. And for some poems, unfortunately, this feeling never comes, indicating that a poem is still lacking an essential ingredient. Hold on to these unfinished works; you may find a way to complete them when you return weeks, months, or even years later. Remember to consider all of it—the reading you do, your initial inspiration, your notes, drafts, and versions—as part of an ongoing process of artistic development. Being a poet requires patience. But most of all it requires love: of the practice itself, the space it affords, what you can learn from it, and what it allows you to share with others.

Readings

Folio: A Poem in Progress

The following folio consists of an annotated early draft, a final draft, and a process statement by my former student, Kaden Unger. As you read, compare Kaden's approaches to revision with your own.

~~*a cow has four stomachs;*~~

dedicated to alan turing, ~~*who committed suicide by cyanide poisoning after being subjected to chemical castration.*~~

there's a body inside
my body my

heart has eight
chambers to

share with the other body.
haunting the tips of my

fingers sometimes go numb
sometimes waking up

naked, wondering
how my sweater got

on the floor;
we hurl as one.

tell me this body
belongs to me

because i can't peel
flesh from muscle

the heave of a full breath
slices of clementines;

the moral dilemma of
a cracked code.

Final Draft

enigma;

dedicated to alan turing.

there's a body inside
my body my
heart has eight
chambers to
share with the other body.
haunting—the tips of my
fingers sometimes go numb
sometimes waking up
naked, wondering
how my shirt got
on the floor;
we hurl as one.
tell me this body
belongs to me
because i can't peel
flesh from muscle.
the   heave of a full breath
the slices of clementines;
the moral dilemma of
a cracked code.

Process Statement

A lot of my writing process happens without much intention. I tend to write mainly in my Notes app, usually after I think of a particular line that I might like to include in a poem. After I have that line, I can expand and create a poem from there. The way a poem comes to its final form has a lot to do with aesthetics, as well. My poem "enigma" originally was two lines per stanza. However, combined with the way it was read aloud and the visual aspect, I edited it so it was one long stanza. I read all my poems out loud now because of "enigma," as I feel it can dictate how the poem looks and flows.

The stanzas don't always dictate every piece of how my poems should be read. In "enigma," there are many instances of enjambment that also create a certain flow. I also use spaces and lack of capitalization to emphasize the way a line or word is meant to be read. For example, towards the end of "enigma," I write: "the   heave of a full breath / the slices of clementines;" The spaces between "the" and "heave" are meant to be read as sucking in air to emphasize that heave.

Another important part of my process takes place in the titles. Originally, "enigma" was named "a cow has four stomachs." It didn't necessarily have anything to do with the poem, but at that time I was experimenting with the way titles affect poetry. While I do still like that title, after workshopping the poem with peers, we came to the conclusion that the poem would benefit from a title that connected to the poem itself. "Enigma" is a poem dedicated to Alan Turing, a mathematician who created faster techniques to break the German army's ciphers sent using the Enigma machine. Turing was arrested, charged for homosexual acts, and subjected to chemical castration, after which he committed suicide. It was important to me as a queer writer to dedicate some of my work to queer people through history, like Turing. My writing process, aside from aesthetics and flow, is a reaction to the world around me.

Craft Questions

- Besides "flow" or rhythm, how does Kaden's choice to change the form of the poem, from couplets to a single stanza, affect your experience?
- Reflect on Kaden's use of the lowercase and white space. What do these typographical elements add to the poem? Would you consider using similar elements? Why or why not?
- Kaden mentions the importance of finding the right title for poems. Look back over some of the titles in previous readings, and discuss your methods for titling your own poems. Do you generally use titles that offer information on the poem's topic, or is the relationship between your titles and poems looser and more associative? Do you prefer short or long titles?
- Note the dedication to Turing. Are there poems you'd consider dedicating to an important person in your life: someone you know personally or a public figure?

Exercises

Exercise 1: Two Heads Are Better Than One

Try one or more of these with a classmate or friend:

1. Exchange poems. Mark each other's best lines and swap back. Start your poem again, using only the marked lines and writing new ones where it seems necessary.

2. Exchange poems. Rewrite each other's poems according to your own inclinations—consider line breaks, sound, image, and metaphor.

3. Try a collaborative poem. Combine your two poems by alternating lines, one then the other, or by writing a completely new poem together.

Objective: To shake loose your normal way of doing things by joining forces with a voice different from your own.

Exercise 2: Read It Over; Turn It Over

Read your poem aloud several times, and record it on your phone. Listen for the way it sounds, rhythmically, musically. Are there places that sound "off"? Too many words in a line? Revise according to sound, paying special attention to articles (e.g., *a/the*) and prepositions (e.g., *of/over*). Take out any extra words, and add words wherever it feels necessary. Keep reading aloud until you are satisfied with how the poem sounds.

Alternately, after reading over a poem in progress several times, turn it over, so that you cannot read it again. Start over with what you remember.

Objective: To train yourself to revise by sound, so that your poems take on a lyrical power. To hold yourself to the standard of best or most memorable lines.

Exercise 3: Beginnings and Endings

Focus on the beginning and ending of a poem in progress. Where does the real action or energy of the poem start? If you find that you lead up to this moment slowly, maybe by setting the scene, ask yourself if this introduction is necessary. Can you cut it, tighten it up, or change it for a sharper opening? Similarly, ask yourself whether the ending of your poem is as impactful as it can be. Does the poem contain a powerful line, and then keep going? Can you cut, tighten, or change the last few lines?

Objective: To grab your reader's attention at the outset and to help them hold the poem in mind after it has ended.

PART II | STORIES

introduction

the bridge between fact and fiction

WHEN YOU THINK OF various types of prose writing, what forms come to mind? Maybe you're writing essays in some of your courses, or you're used to reading articles online, in the newspaper, or in the library databases. Maybe you've recently read a biography, historical text, or manual of some sort. What distinguishes fictional stories from these other prose pieces?

According to the *Oxford English Dictionary*, the definitions of the word *fiction* include "arbitrary invention"; "that which is fashioned or framed"; "a device, a fabric"; "the action of 'feigning' or inventing imaginary incidents, existences, states of things ... whether for the purpose of deception or otherwise"; and "the species of literature which is concerned with the narration of imaginary events and the portraiture of imaginary characters; fictitious composition ... prose novels and stories collectively." As these various descriptions suggest, ideas of *fabrication*, *imagination*, and even *deception* are central to the definition of fiction.

If we stop to consider these ideas more deeply, we find that the bridge between fact and fiction is actually often blurred in all kinds of stories: from those we tell orally to the various sub-genres of fiction, including

creative nonfiction, or nonfiction anchored in actual experience while drawing on the expressive, imaginative capacities of creative writing. In this text, we'll focus on fictional short stories, but throughout you'll be guided in methods to draw from your actual experiences, emotions, and ideas to help you invent characters, situations, and worlds. This process of transformation—from fact to fiction—will make the stories you write feel more authentic, believable, and resonant.

The fiction we'll focus on will mainly be short stories, which generally run anywhere from about 1,500 words (6 double-spaced pages) to 6,000 words (24 double-spaced pages). Along the way, we'll also read and discuss some **short-short stories**, sometimes referred to as **flash fictions**, which run from 500 (2 double-spaced pages) to 2,000 (8 double-spaced pages) long. Both of these forms are relatively brief, compared to full-length **novellas** (in between a short story and a novel in length) and **novels**. The brevity of the forms we'll be working with necessitates that we engage our reader right from the start, and that we limit the number of characters and plot twists. This doesn't preclude you from creating a complex, moving experience, however. Quite to the contrary. Not only can you accomplish a great deal in the little package of the short story, but by learning to craft stories, you'll be learning many important tools for any writer, regardless of genre, including where to begin and end, where to zoom in and what to leave out, and how to create a world for your reader to inhabit.

Further, by engaging in the practice of crafting stories you are participating in a tradition that spans centuries and continents. Originally orally recited, and first recorded on cave walls, stories are essential to all human cultures as a means of sharing, remembering, and passing down information, experiences, and emotions. Who doesn't like a good story? If you check, almost all of our communications and many of our forms of entertainment involve some aspect of narrative. And whether you're planning to spend your life as a professional fiction writer, trying the craft out for a course, or writing for your own enjoyment, the process of crafting short stories is bound to take you on a challenging and satisfying adventure.

Fiction's Basic Elements

In the following pages, we will mainly be focused on *realistic* short stories, or those that could plausibly take place, as opposed to *speculative fiction*, which incorporates elements that do not exist in our reality. The reason for this is twofold. First, this guide is intended to be portable and accessible—to avoid bloat. Next, when you're first starting off in any creative endeavor, it's helpful to learn some of the conventions before moving on to alternative forms. That being said, as you'll soon discover, there's plenty of adventure, invention, and discovery within the genre of realistic fiction. And, in fact, some of the stories we'll read test the bounds of plausibility in intriguing ways.

Within the genre of realistic short stories, here are the main elements we'll explore:

- Subject Matter
- Details
- Viewpoint
- Characterization
- Plot
- Setting
- Voice and Tone

What are some techniques you can use to get started writing stories and what will you write about? Is there promising **subject matter** within your own experience that you can draw on for your stories? Mining for, identifying, and beginning to use this material is the subject of chapter 9. In this chapter, we'll also be reviewing techniques for active reading to prepare us to read and discuss others' stories as we develop our own. And, of course, we'll be thinking about subject matter all along as we do this reading, discussing, and developing.

Take a moment to think about the best storyteller you know. There's usually one in every group of friends. What methods does this person use (maybe unconsciously) to captivate their audience, hold their attention, or make them laugh? In contrast, are there things that less effective storytellers routinely do, or forget to do? Although oral stories necessarily differ from written ones, they share some basic elements. For one, if you listen closely enough, good storytellers often exaggerate (or even make up) vivid, evocative **details**, while editing out details that would likely bore their audience. We'll discuss methods of generating and selecting just the right details to hold your reader's attention in chapter 10.

Similarly, good storytellers also tend to cut to the chase. Starting **in medias res**, or in the middle of things, they plunge us into the action, and rather than meandering for too long, they quickly build up a sense of **tension** by focusing on some sort of conflict between people or within an individual. Building suspense or interest around this source of tension, confident storytellers craft scenes that lead up to a **climax** or tipping point, ultimately providing a sense of resolution, conclusion, or ending. If you've already tried writing short stories, you may have found that managing these elements of structure and pacing, making sure something both believable and compelling happens, can be more difficult than it first seems. Often this process involves creating more than one line of tension, while simultaneously taking a less-is-more approach when it comes to twists. In addition, focusing on the passage of time within the story, in part by considering the use of **flashback**, or including an earlier scene, can take some practice. To develop these skills, we'll focus on **plot**, or the sequence of events, in chapter 13.

The way in which the story is told, including its **viewpoint**, or person telling the story, be it first person (*I/we*), second person (*you*), or third person (*he/she/they*), is often more finely considered in written stories than in spoken ones, and we'll look at this element in chapter 11. Finding the right viewpoint is central to finding the story's focus, so we'll try out a range of possibilities to determine the strongest vantage point. Along with this, we'll consider the impact of verb tense. It may be that one of your characters will tell your story, that you'll decide to use a third-person narrator, or that you'll choose another viewpoint. Whatever the case, from the beginning to the end of the process of crafting a story, you'll be thinking about your main character or protagonist, as well as the other characters that populate your story. It's not necessary to create many characters for a short story, but the ones you create should feel real to you. Even if you don't include all of the details of their lives, preferences, background, and so on, you should have an idea of these things yourself; after all, you're the expert on your characters. In fact, many fiction writers report that their characters seem to take on a life of their own, occupying a similar space in their mind to that of actual people.

We'll work in chapter 12 on getting to know characters in order to bring them to life. What makes characters believable, unique, and memorable? How can we depict characters in action or through dialogue, as well as through description, to make them seem real? How can we build plot around one or several well-developed characters? These are some of the questions we'll also address in chapter 13. In fact, if we develop a certain mastery over characterization, many of the story's other elements will seem to fall into place, including its **setting**: the story's places, times, and seasons. In chapter 14 we'll work with setting by considering, for example, the choice to base our story in a real or imagined place, the decision to include various degrees of specificity, and the topics of time and historical period. Not only does the setting of a story render it more vivid, it can also be used symbolically to amplify existing themes.

Finally, we'll consider **style** and **tone**. Style generally refers to the way the story is written, whereas tone refers to the story's attitude or mood. Chapter 15 considers various styles and tones, and details the ways in which **diction** (word choice) and **syntax** (sentence structure) all contribute to building a story's style. To complete our study of short fiction, we'll read and practice writing stories that are more experimental in nature—that take risks with style, form, and subject matter. Here we *will* begin to think about ways to deviate from convention, despite our focus on realism. What happens when you write a story in one long paragraph as a series of instructions? Can you craft an effective short story out of a series of texts between characters? The sky's the limit, once we've gained some mastery over our craft.

Ultimately, you'll know that your story is "working" when the seemingly complex and difficult process of building characters, scenes, and plot, starts to feel more seamless, and when the balance between dialogue, action, and **exposition** (background information or description), feels natural and unforced. And you'll know that your stories are coming into focus when they not only resonate with your own experience, with the stories that you've long held in your heart and wanted to tell, but when they resonate with others: your classmates, professor, friends, and writing partners. If we're just beginning to write stories, developing the various elements can feel a bit daunting. But gradually, the question of elements will dissolve into broader questions of experience, subject matter, and areas of concern.

What are the stories you're uniquely able to tell and how can you render them relevant and moving to others? This question of subject matter is one of the larger questions we'll be asking throughout. What is the story you'd write if no one were going to read it or critique it? At the beginning, I encourage you to just get in the sandbox and start playing: take notes, jot down ideas, and exercise your imagination without worry or concern. Look over your playful first thoughts later to discover hidden gems that you may be able to develop. Let those gems of ideas generate other ideas. What's really the most interesting part of the story you have in mind? Here's where our adventure starts.

nine | getting started

the crafting of a story

One of the most common questions of aspiring fiction writers is *What do I have to write about*? You may have some ideas for **subject matter** but not be sure how to develop them, or you may even feel that your lived experience is not interesting enough to spark engaging stories in the first place. This kind of doubt is extremely common. In fact, at some point, writers at all stages experience the feeling that they've run out of ideas, need to live more interesting lives in order to write, or that they're better off just borrowing from common tropes and plots from existing fiction, movies, and television instead of trying to generate unique stories of their own. Depending on the degree, self-doubt can be distracting or even debilitating. Therefore, it's important at the outset to try your best to banish it by beginning to identify as someone with plenty of unique stories to tell. After all, there's only one you. Even if you've grown up in a family of close-knit siblings, each sibling has experienced the family dynamics and household differently. Even if you live in a small, quiet town where nothing much seems to happen, if you learn to observe the characters, setting, and goings-on around you more carefully, you'll see that there's plenty of drama and interest to draw on for stories. After all, the human condition, in itself—being born, growing older, dying—is vastly mysterious terrain, as are the social dynamics between people, their relationships with each other and with themselves: their struggles, triumphs, and disappointments.

In fact, as mentioned in the introduction, low-key questions and situations often spark wonderful short stories whereas elaborate plots and large casts of characters are often more difficult to render realistically within the compression of the form. And depending on your level of experience, it may be easier to start small and build up to longer, more complex stories as you go. All this being said, the question remains: *How to begin?* The short answer is: begin with your actual lived experience.

Begin by noticing and noting the people, places, things, and happenings directly around you or from your past. Keep a notebook or journal, small enough to carry with you, as well as your phone, to jot down or record ideas, lists, and bits of **dialogue** or conversation. You never know when something may strike you. For many of us, the best ideas come when we're sleepy or just about to doze off. And many creative people have particularly active dream lives. As unappealing as it may feel to turn on the light to jot down that last idea before falling asleep or recording your dreams before you've gotten out of the bed in the morning, it's good to catch it when it comes: before you forget it.

Once you've gotten in the habit of taking notes and doing some free writing, you may still struggle with carving out the necessary time to develop your first thoughts into stories. For many, this involves a process of trial and error: writing at a certain time each day, for example, or carving out a larger chunk of time a couple of times each week. Most fiction writers require a good deal of uninterrupted time to develop their ideas, and if you find that time is in short supply, this can pose problems. In this case, you'll have to get creative. Can you cancel appointments and get off of work on a Saturday to complete a story in progress? Can you write for an hour or two first thing in the morning or last thing at night? In any case, expect that your stories will require your time. Rather than this feeling like a burden, however, the time you're able to make for your creative work will feel precious. You may even find yourself craving it, guarding it, and trying to extend it. This is how you'll know you're hooked!

Alternately, if you've got lots of time on your hands, you may encounter another kind of obstacle: that all-too-familiar mode of procrastination. For some reason, we writers tend to have a difficult time getting started, and we can drag our heels when we feel stuck. The important thing here is again to find a schedule that works for you: a schedule that's realistic enough to stick to. Consider the analogy with exercise. If you aren't normally very athletic, but need to get in shape, it's usually better to find some mode of exercise that's fairly easy and enjoyable in order to begin and continue. Once you're comfortable going to the gym for classes, or walking three days per week, you can gradually extend the time you're spending or the degree of difficulty in each exercise session. On the other hand, if you begin by setting an unrealistic goal for yourself of running ten miles per day from the start, you may very well quickly come to dread your own regime and burn out. So, whether you have a lot of time or a little, make the process enjoyable by not only keeping your writing sessions relatively low-key at first, but also by writing in a comfortable spot at a time when you're sharp.

Are you a morning or evening person? When do you get your best ideas? Do you prefer writing at home or in a library, café, or other setting? There's no right place or schedule, only a right one for you personally. And this may change as you and your writing change. So, stay flexible while prioritizing your writing time and space. Once you've made this space, you'll somehow find more and more time and energy for your writing as you become more immersed in the world you're creating. As laborious as writing stories can sometimes feel, there is also much joy to be found in this kind of creative labor. As you hone your craft, you're bringing your imaginative life into focus so that others can benefit.

Sources

As we've discussed, your actual lived experience is often the best place to start when first writing stories. Not only are you the expert on your own life, but also by using the concrete details you've experienced first-hand (the faded pink-and-white check dress you wanted to wear every day as a toddler; the flirtatious exchanges between the bus-driver of your route and her favorite daily passenger), you are more likely to avoid **clichés**, **melodrama**, and **stock characters** or stereotypes. Although it can be tempting to write a fantasy-version of your own life, you're better off sticking with reality at this stage, and gradually transforming it: by melding scenes, people, and stories, and by creating equally believable details.

We'll discuss details in greater depth in the following chapter. But for now, it may be helpful to begin by thinking about your relationships with family, friends, neighbors, older or younger people, and romantic partners, past or present. It's almost impossible to find a relationship that doesn't contain some degree of mixed emotion or **ambivalence**, as well as some sense of mystery, areas that are unresolved, and areas of **conflict**. All of these elements make for powerful stories. As you begin to transform people into characters, start by changing their names and picking and choosing aspects from each. For example, your aunt Rose's height and confidence may be melded with your neighbor's tendency to throw loud parties.

If after mining your own experience for material, you find that you're still coming up short, it may be helpful to review the following list of sources. If you're in a class, you could discuss the ones you find useful and add some of your own to the list.

1. Personal Experiences: Are there experiences that shaped you, changed your perspective, or that simply stand out in your mind? These need not be overtly dramatic to prove valuable as sources. Powerful stories often simply chart some change in the protagonist's understanding. A character may struggle with issues of self-esteem until they meet someone whose sense of humor coaxes them out of their shell; in another story, a character may realize the importance of forgiveness after a conflict with a friend whom they find out is deeply damaged.

2. Memorable Incidents: Are there specific incidents you've witnessed that have stuck with you? Maybe your kitchen once caught on fire, or you saw someone stealing food from a supermarket shelf. What do you know about the incident? What don't you know? Fiction writers often fabricate entire stories around a memorable incident or moment. Again, this need not be a high-speed chase or bank robbery; it might be a relatively ordinary occurrence that sparks a story: your ninety-year old neighbor wears his pajamas to retrieve his mail at the end of his driveway each day until …; a houseguest stays long after they're welcome, sparking a confrontation.

3. Family Relationships: No matter how close or distant, most of us have families, so, unsurprisingly, this is a fertile ground for stories. Consider what you know about your family members, what you don't know and would like to find out, and what you really *wouldn't* want to know if given the chance. Also, spend some time thinking about the complexities of your family relationships. Likely, you'll find personality traits, conflicts, and mysteries that you can use for your stories. As usual, feel free to mix and match traits from different individuals in order to create characters.

4. Romantic Relationships: Most of us have had at least one romantic relationship that has since ended. What did you love about that person you were with? What drove you crazy? In what ways were you compatible or incompatible? What were some of the sources of conflict, ambivalence, or tension? By reflecting back on this relationship with honesty, you'll be able to avoid writing cliché love stories, and instead find material for unique, believable characters and plots.

5. Other Influential Relationships: Many successful stories pair younger and older characters or include a generational mix. Spend some time contemplating people in your own life that have been especially influential, especially those who are much older or younger than you. Were there areas of misunderstanding? What did you learn from them? What may they have learned from you?

6. Observations: Everyday observations, the kind you jot down in your notebook or record on your phone, are rife with possibilities. Don't be too choosy at first. Just jot down your description of the smell in the air, the expression on the face of someone you love, the way a car in front of you screeched to a halt. When you come back to these observations later, you may find a good story-starter or a description you can use in an existing story to build atmosphere and texture.

7. Places: Even those of us who don't have particularly good memories seem to hold certain places in our mind. And creating a vivid setting or sense of place is an essential part of crafting short stories. Think back to the places that are most memorable and evocative for you: your grandmother's attic, the basketball court where you spent most of your free time, a place to which you regularly escaped. Call on your five senses to describe these places in detail. It's very likely that you'll be able to use one of these places or a composite for a short story.

Active Reading

Most writers agree that reading the work of others is the most important thing they can do to grow. Reading carefully, with an eye toward craft, will be especially helpful to you as you begin to draft your own stories. The various reading you do—from assignments to your own discoveries—may at times confirm a direction you're taking and, at others, help you uncover possibilities you hadn't ever considered. As you read, almost all of the observations you make and questions you raise are potentially useful; even if you detest a story you're reading for a class, for instance, reading it may help to confirm ways in which you *don't* want to write. The process of imitation and admiration of some techniques and styles and rejection of others is a vital aspect of developing your own aesthetic. Most of us gradually cobble together ways of doing things until our own inclinations begin to emerge. And even then, growing through the reading we do is a lifelong process.

As you read, it's useful to get in the habit of marking up passages that seem significant, notable, and perplexing. This process will likely make the reading you do more active and engaging, as well as serving as a useful reminder when you return to the story. It's also a good idea to get in the habit of looking up words with which you're unfamiliar or rusty in a reputable online dictionary such as merriam-webster.com. In order to model this process of active reading, the following story by contemporary United States writer, Sandra Cisneros (b. 1954) is annotated.

Barbie-Q

Yours is the one with mean eyes and a ponytail. Striped swimsuit, stilettos, sunglasses, and gold hoop earrings. Mine is the one with bubble hair. Red swimsuit, stilettos, pearl earrings, and a wire stand. But that's all we can afford, besides one extra outfit apiece. Yours, "Red Flair," sophisticated A-line coatdress with a Jackie Kennedy pillbox hat, white gloves, handbag, and heels included. Mine, "Solo in the Spotlight," evening elegance in black glitter strapless gown with a puffy skirt at the bottom like a mermaid tail, formal-length gloves, pink chiffon scarf, and mike included. From so much dressing and undressing, the black glitter wears off where her titties stick out. This and a dress invented from an old sock when we cut holes here and here and here, the cuff rolled over for the glamorous, fancy-free, off-the-shoulder look.

relationship btwn speaker & "you"?

great details

Every time the same story. Your Barbie is roommates with my Barbie, and my Barbie's boyfriend comes over and your Barbie steals him, okay? Kiss kiss kiss. Then the two Barbies fight. You dumbbell! He's mine. Oh no he's not, you stinky! Only Ken's invisible, right? Because we don't have money for a stupid-looking boy doll when we'd both rather ask for a new Barbie outfit next Christmas. We have to make do with your mean-eyed Barbie and my bubblehead Barbie and our one outfit apiece not including the sock dress.

speaker's age?

poverty

Until next Sunday when we are walking through the flea market on Maxwell Street and there! Lying on the street next to some tool bits, and platform shoes with the heels all squashed, and a fluorescent green wicker wastebasket, and aluminum foil, and hubcaps, and a pink shag rug, and windshield wiper blades, and dusty mason jars, and a coffee can full of rusty nails. There! Where? Two Mattel boxes. One with the "Career Gal" ensemble, snappy black-and-white business suit, three-quarter-length sleeve jacket with kick-pleated skirt, red sleeveless shell, gloves, pumps, and matching hat included. The other, "Sweet Dreams," dreamy pink-and-white plaid nightgown and matching robe, lace-trimmed slippers,

setting

women's roles

hair-brush and hand mirror included. How much? Please, please, please, please, please, please, please, until they say okay.

dialogue style

On the outside you and me skipping and humming but inside we are doing loopity-loops and pirouetting. Until at the next vendor's stand, next to boxed pies, and bright orange toilet brushes, and rubber gloves, and wrench sets, and bouquets of feather flowers, and glass towel racks, and steel wool, and Alvin and the Chipmunks records, there! And there! And there! And there! and there! and there! and there! Bendable Legs Barbie with her new page-boy hairdo, Midge, Barbie's best friend. Ken, Barbie's boyfriend. Skipper, Barbie's little sister. Tutti and Todd, Barbie and Skipper's tiny twin sister and brother. Skipper's friends, Scooter and Ricky. Alan, Ken's buddy. And Francie, Barbie's MOD'ern cousin.

Everybody today selling toys, all of them damaged with water smelling of smoke. Because a big toy warehouse on Halsted Street burned down yesterday—see there?—the smoke still rising and drifting across the Dan Ryan expressway. And now there is a big fire sale at Maxwell Street, today only.

So what if we didn't get our new Bendable Legs Barbie and Midge and Ken and Skipper and Tutti and Todd and Scooter and Ricky and Alan and Francie in nice clean boxes and had to buy them on Maxwell Street, all water-soaked and sooty. So what if our Barbies smell like smoke when you hold them up to your nose even after you wash and wash and wash them. And if the prettiest doll, Barbie's MOD'ern cousin Francie with real eyelashes, eyelash brush included, has a left foot that's melted a little—so? If you dress her in her new "Prom Pinks" outfit, satin splendor with matching coat, gold belt, clutch, and hair bow included, so long as you don't lift her dress, right?—who's to know.

why don't they care that their toys are damaged?

Craft Questions

- Describe the voice of the speaker. What do we know about her through how she speaks? Who is the "you" in the story?
- What details does Cisneros use to bring the story to life?
- Why do you think Cisneros runs in dialogue without using quotes?
- Note places where the speaker directly addresses the reader. How does this form of address affect the story's tone?
- What gender roles do the Barbies model for the girls? In what ways do the girls seem to accept or reject these roles?

- Identify sources of conflict in the story. Who or what seems to prevail?
- In what ways does Cisneros's story deal with issues of class and race?

Technically a short-short story, "Barbie Q" is a highly compressed, focused piece of fiction. Like a snapshot, Cisneros's piece presents us with an instant in time that nonetheless suggests a story. What do we know about the background, motivations, and relationship between the two characters? What do we know about the world they inhabit? Although you may not be able to agree on a single focus in discussion, it's clear that Cisneros has mapped out a certain territory of thought, feeling, and experience. Her story transports us into its world, letting us make the final determination on what impression we take away with us, rather than leading us to draw a specific moral or conclusion.

Remember, the process of writing is almost always messy. If this is not the case, you may run into problems later. In other words, no matter how attached you may be to a certain idea for a story, it's important to let it live and breathe a life of its own. For example, you may begin by wanting to write about a falling-out between siblings but find that one of your siblings seems rather lifeless in comparison to the other. If you've tried working on both characters, and hit a wall, it might be time to consider that the story would be stronger if you focused on a single protagonist or if you changed the viewpoint entirely. Most often, you'll only discover the real focus of the story as you write, or even after the story is done. As you take up the various suggestions in this chapter, stay open.

To begin writing your own short stories, try a few of the following jump-starts. Have fun. Feel free to alter them as you see fit. And see if you can generate a jump-start or two of your own to share with others. For now, your only goal should be to start generating material; we'll take up ways to shape and craft your material in the chapters that follow.

Exercises

Jump-Starts: Use any of these jump-starts to generate material. Once you've completed an exercise, set it aside for at least a day, come back to it later, and try gradually turning your notes into a story.

1. Write a list of the most fascinating or mysterious people you've encountered. They could be unusual in some way, or maybe you've always wondered about their stories. What are their physical characteristics? What do you know about their lives? What do you want to know? Use one or two of these people as the foundation for characters. Whatever you don't know, make it up.

2. Begin by reading some of the first sentences of the stories collected in this text. Notice what you learn right away and what you want to know more about. Similarly aiming to place your reader **in medias res**, or in the middle of things, write at least five first sentences for five different stories. Choose the one that seems most promising as the beginning of a story.

3. Speak a story, or part of a story, into your phone.

4. Tell two secrets and one lie about yourself. Apply these three ideas to a character.

5. Close your eyes. Imagine a basement you've been in. It could be your current basement, one you grew up with, or one you've visited. You walk down the stairs. When you open your eyes, what is the first object that you see? Describe it.

6. Close your eyes. Imagine that you're taking a long car trip somewhere. When you open your eyes, what do you see? Describe the scene.

7. Find an object in your home to write about. What's the object's backstory? Begin a story by describing the object.

ten | details

creating a world

As you read this book, pause for a minute to take in the scene around you. Are you sitting or lying down? Is it daytime or night? Is your space brightly or dimly lit? What objects do you see? Are there any detectable scents in the air? What about sounds? What temperature is it? How does your body feel? What clothes are you wearing? Is your head rested in one of your hands? Is your phone by your side? Is the light of it visible?

Just as the details of our actual lived experience make the world we inhabit real to us, the details of a story bring it alive for a reader, creating a world for them to inhabit. Without these details, a story can easily feel flat, contrived, and unreal. Although there are some writers who are maximalist in their descriptions and others who intentionally take a minimalist approach, carefully selecting fewer details, our inclination as readers is to grab onto whatever details have been provided. If we simply wanted to be taken from point A to point B in a plot or storyline, or to read a piece written about a certain topic, we'd probably opt for a synopsis, news article, or opinion piece. Instead, stories allow us the opportunity to lose (and ultimately find) ourselves, to reach beyond our own pod, to experience what life might be like for others. In this regard, fiction is enduringly and maybe increasingly meaningful. Not to mention, it's fun.

Before you begin to become more aware of the details in others' stories and to work with them in your own, let's review a few basic definitions. For starters, the *Oxford English Dictionary*'s definition of *detail* includes "attention to particulars" and "to deal with or treat a thing in its individual particulars." As the word *particulars* implies, we're dealing with parts of a thing, with specific, precise aspects: not just a bird, but a small bird with gray and red wings. When we look over the types of details we've discussed in stories so far, we'll find that many are **sensory** in nature, or arising from the five senses. Whereas we tend to focus our attention on crafting visual images, we can expand our repertoire to also include sounds, tastes, smells, and tactile sensations. This is not to suggest that we should force ourselves to use all five senses in every passage we write, especially if this style of description seems foreign to our sensibilities. However, as we become more aware of the importance of details, it's worthwhile to experiment beyond the visual. Eventually, including just the right amount and kind of detail will become practically second nature.

In order to think more about the ways in which carefully selected sensory details can transport us, let's take a look at a short-short story by contemporary United States writer, Jayne Anne Phillips (b. 1952):

✤ Blind Girls

She knew it was only boys in the field, come to watch them drunk on first wine. A radio in the little shack poured out promises of black love and lips. Jesse watched Sally paint her hair with grenadine, dotting the sticky syrup on her arms. The party was in a shack down the hill from her house, beside a field of tall grass where black snakes lay like flat belts. The Ripple bottles were empty and Jesse told pornographic stories about various adults while everyone laughed; about Miss Hicks the home-ec teacher whose hands were dimpled and moist and always touching them. It got darker and the stories got scarier. Finally she told her favorite, the one about the girl and her boyfriend parked on a country road on a night like this, with the wind blowing and then rain, the whole sky sobbing potato juice. Please let's leave, pleads girlie, It sounds like something scratching at the car. For God's sake, grumbles boyfriend, and takes off squealing. At home they find the hook of a crazed amputee caught in the door. Jesse described his yellow face, putrid, and his blotchy stump. She described him panting in the grass, crying and looking for something. She could feel him smelling of raw vegetables, a rejected bleeding cowboy with wheat hair, and she was unfocused. Moaning in the dark and falsetto voices. Don't don't please don't. Nervous laughter. Sally looked out the window of the shack. The grass is moving, she said, Something's crawling in it. No, it's nothing. Yes, there's something coming, and her voice went up at the end. It's just boys trying to scare us. But Sally whined and flailed her arms. On her knees she hugged Jesse's legs and mumbled into her thighs. It's all right, I'll take you up to the house. Sally was stiff, her nails digging the skin. She wouldn't move. Jesse tied a scarf around her eyes and led her like a horse through fire up the hill to the house, one poison light soft in a window. Boys ran out of the field squawling.

Craft Questions

- Which sensory details stand out for you?
- Do any of them repeat or echo each other?
- Notice their order. Do they seem to build to a crescendo?
- Discuss the story's focus. What is it about?
- Do the images tell the story? Are there other elements that move the story along?

Avoiding Abstraction

You've already begun to jot down observations in your notebook or on your phone. You've started to come up with possibilities for stories by mining the material of your actual life, including your relationships, conflicts, and past experiences. So, naturally, you've developed some ideas for stories: a story about divorce, a breakup, the loss of a loved one. There's nothing wrong with these ideas; however, in order to find the ticking time bomb, the story within the story that's aching to come out, you'll need to first get inside this big idea or abstraction: to break it down into its particulars. (And be ready for it to explode or transform.)

Here are some examples of sensory detail used effectively. As you read, try the following exercise alone or with a group. The first one is done for you to model a possible response.

Details vs. Abstractions

1) Underline sensory details that stand out.
2) Note abstract or general ideas the passage brings to life.

> She flew home at Christmas, her mother and her mother's new husband met her at the airport. Her mother hugged her hard and told her she looked pretty, and her mother's new husband shook hands with her and told her, Yes she sure did look pretty, and welcome home.
>
> (Joyce Carol Oates, "Happy")

Seems like a second marriage. The daughter is uncomfortable about meeting the new husband.

> A week had passed since they had made acquaintance. It was a holiday. It was sultry indoors, while on the street the wind whirled the dust round and round, and blew people's hats off. It was a thirsty day, and Gurov often went into the pavilion, and pressed Anna Sergeyevna to have syrup and water or an ice. One did not know what to do with oneself.
>
> (Anton Chekhov, "The Lady with the Dog")

> Why did I think she would come there and act right? Slacks. No hat like the grandmothers and viewers, and groaning all the while. When we stood for hymns she kept her mouth shut. Wouldn't even look at the words on the page. She actually reached in her purse for a mirror to check her lipstick.
>
> (Toni Morrison, "Recitatif")

In each of these examples, the writer deftly *shows* us what to see, feel, and understand. Rather than needing to *tell* us that there was a divorce, that the mother remarried, and that the daughter is reluctantly meeting the mother's new husband for the first time, Joyce Carol Oates sets a scene at the airport, and uses physical action and run-in dialogue to communicate the situation and the daughter's discomfort directly. It's not Divorce with a capital *D* that Oates is writing about; it's this particular family dynamic, this particular situation, these specific characters, which give us, as readers, the chance to feel like we're in the scene, discovering things for ourselves, piecing clues together, drawing our own conclusions. All the while, Oates is leading us where she wants us to go, seamlessly. Powerful stories involve this kind of magical sleight of hand.

Simile and Metaphor

The most common figures of speech are **simile**, a comparison that uses *like* or *as*, and **metaphor**, which implies a comparison. If you take a look at the excerpt below from T.C. Boyle's "Are We Not Men," you may notice a comparison using the word *like*. Here, Boyle uses **figurative language**: language that compares one thing to another, creating a new "figure" or meaning for the reader. Boyle uses simile when he writes that his character "dealt with [each situation] like a five-star general driving the enemy into the sea." Through this comparison, the writer turns up the emotional heat on an already visceral, vivid passage. More often considered when studying poetry, simile and metaphor are nonetheless powerful tools for fiction writers as well. When used effectively, figurative language can heighten sensation and multiply meaning through association, thereby creating a richer, multi-layered experience.

Here are some additional examples of these common **figures of speech**:

Simile

- I didn't ask her how her day had gone—all her days were the same, pedal to the metal, one *situation* after another, all of which she dealt with like a five-star general driving the enemy into the sea.
  (T.C. Boyle, "Are We Not Men?")

- The old woman watched him with her arms folded across her chest *as if* she were the owner of the sun, and the daughter watched, her head thrust forward and her fat helpless hands hanging at the wrists.
  (Flannery O'Connor, "The Life You Save May Be Your Own")

- My stomach twists *like* an earthworm after the rain.
  (Meg Pokrass, "Like a Family")

- The child-you believed this and locked it inside your brain, and your adult mind grew up around that idea *like* a tree that grows next to a barbed wire fence, its trunk expanding year by year, ring by ring, burying the barbed wire deeper in its bark.
  (Chad B. Anderson, "Maidencane")

- Time slipped away that way lately, *as if* behind a curtain then out again as something else, here as an internet hole, there as a walk on your street you insisted on calling a hike with your wife and son, here as a book your eyes look at, that you don't comprehend, there as crippling depression, here as observing circling turkey vultures, there as your ever-imminent anxiety, here as a failed Zoom call, there as a home-schooling shift with your son, here as April, May already gone, there as the obsession over the body count, the nameless numbers rising on endless graphics of animated maps.
  (Tommy Orange, "The Team")

Metaphor

- When the storm of grief had spent itself she went away to her room alone.
  (Kate Chopin, "Story of an Hour")

- ... until you are a mad dog just biting yourself for sympathy, because there is no relenting, and there is no hand that falls, and there is no woman to come home and take you in her arms.
  (Louise Erdrich, "I'm a Mad Dog Biting Myself for Sympathy")

- In the midst of Camel smoke hanging lower and thicker than a September monsoon, No-Horse rode high, his PIMC-issued wheelchair transfigured—a magical chariot drawn by two blond, beer-clumsy palominos perfumed with coconut sunscreen and dollar-fifty Budweisers.

  (Natalie Díaz, "The Gospel of Guy No-Horse")

- Time passes in pages and in dried-up pens.

  (Kendra Fortmeyer, "Things I Know to Be True")

Clearly, each simile and metaphor works a little differently; there isn't a one-size-fits-all approach. But it's best if your figures of speech provide an associative leap, a moment of surprise. And *like* an actual leap, we need to find that sweet spot; if it's too big a leap, we might fumble, and if it's too small, we might not really move much (or be moved).

Ultimately, rather than artificially force yourself to use metaphor or simile in your stories, simply remain open to the idea as you write. Let these phrases emerge naturally, since they work best when they amplify other elements already at play. And how much you use figurative language will depend upon your overall aesthetic; some writers are decidedly more poetic than others. That being said, if you're struggling to revise a particularly flat passage in a story, you may find that a comparison helps to bring it alive.

Symbolism

Wherever your writing falls on the spectrum from literal to metaphorical, it's useful to consider the fact that no image appears without a reason. After all, you've had to select it from innumerable possibilities. Why have you decided to describe a character's bike in detail (maybe the character lives in a city, is athletic, or is environmentally conscious)? Why is the changing foliage of the tree outside a character's window described in detail (maybe to give a sense of the story's setting, including the season)? Images not only bring the story to life, generally; they can also be used to help develop character, setting, situation, and theme. As we'll see in Mary Robison's "Yours" in chapter 14, the changing foliage and jack-o-lanterns of late October foreshadow the story's climax, and are closely tied-in with its theme.

In Robison's case, the jack-o-lanterns become a **symbol**, or an image that stands for more than it literally connotes, creating additional layers of meaning. We're all familiar with symbols that carry agreed upon meanings: the dove normally connotes peace; the cross normally connotes Christ's crucifixion and Christianity. Similarly, stories often use images to refer to familiar symbolic meanings. Rather than refer to a single definition, however, symbols in stories call to mind a range of possible associations.

Unlike figures of speech, symbols begin not by comparison, but by simply using images. Once we read the story over several times, and consider context and interconnections, we begin to suspect that something deeper is at work. When you use the same or similar image multiple times or spend a comparatively long time describing it, you clue your reader into the possibility of symbolic meaning.

Again, it's best not to force symbolism; simply remain open to the possibility of it emerging organically. For example, if you read over a draft of a story, and find that you've mentioned lamplight and other forms of light multiple times, you might ask yourself if these images are needlessly repetitive or whether they tie-in with a possible theme, such as insight. If you answer the latter, you may want to revise them with that objective in mind. This process often takes some practice; it's easy to use symbolic suggestion too consciously or heavy-handedly, but with some practice, you'll learn to use it subtly to evoke layers of meaning, allowing your reader to make the final conclusions.

Notes on Cliché

Given the abundance of formulaic plots and characters in contemporary movies and television shows, it's no wonder that many writers will, at some point, use hackneyed or clichéd storylines without even realizing it. To be more alert to this pitfall, it's important to keep reading (as well as watching innovative movies and TV). In addition, there are certain basic premises bound to lead you in the direction of cliché. Here are some of the most common:

- *It was all a dream.* Whereas your dreams themselves can serve as a source for some interesting images and material, the common practice of framing a fantastical story as a dream (*but this was just a dream*) can make for a tired and somewhat lazy set-up. Instead of trusting your own writing to do the work of creating a believable world for your reader, you're using the premise of the dream to do that work for you. Paradoxically, the story most often ends up feeling even more artificial and contrived.

- *Vampires and goblins, oh my.* It's possible to write an inventive, satirical, new take on the overused plotlines of spooky thrillers, but when you're just starting out, it's best to steer clear of this formula. For even if your story is well written, it will probably end up being a one-off:

readers may follow the plotline to the end, but they'll be unlikely to want to return to your story.

- *Stranger than fiction.* Sometimes things that have actually happened to you are too strange to be believed in fiction. You may have been involved in a car chase. Or a friendly, nondescript neighbor may have been involved in a tragedy that ended up on the news. At first these events may seem like the perfect material for a short story. After all, they involve a dramatic, riveting plot. But, before you use them, consider whether they will feel fresh, new, and believable to a reader. Are there elements of the actual experience that made it unique or different from the stories we've seen again and again on television?

- *Sugary sweet.* We've all enjoyed a good Hallmark movie when we're feeling low: a young woman moves from her small town to the big city to take a position at a top law firm only to fall in love with her high school sweetheart on a visit home one Christmas. (You know the rest.) There's nothing wrong with a love story, but, again, think about what makes it believable, complex, and unique. By unconsciously borrowing a stock plot, you'll risk losing your reader to boredom.

- *Is this my story to tell*? Want to write about someone or a group of people very different from yourself? That's an honest enough impulse for a fiction writer. But be aware that, if you do, you could be crossing some lines. Are you really set up to write your story from the point of view of a homeless veteran if you've never had either experience? Unless you know an individual in this position well enough to really get a sense of their history, thoughts, motivations, and daily life, you may end up painting in broad strokes, falling prey to sentimentality, and even stereotyping.

Keep in mind that these are not rules. They're simply a set of signposts to help you avoid common dead-ends as you begin to draft short stories. Ultimately, by mining your own unique experience, and by including fresh sensory details throughout, you'll be well on your way to writing powerful, moving stories that others will want to read again and again.

Reading

Andre Dubus II (1936–99)
The Intruder

Because Kenneth Girard loved his parents and his sister and because he could not tell them why he went to the woods, his first moments there were always uncomfortable ones, as if he had left the house to commit a sin. But he was thirteen and he could not say that he was going to sit on a hill and wait for the silence and trees and sky to close in on him, wait until they all became a part of him, and thought and memory ceased and the voices began. He could only say that he was going for a walk and, since there was so much more to say, he felt cowardly and deceitful and more lonely than before.

He could not say that on the hill he became great, that he had saved a beautiful girl from a river (the voice then had been gentle and serious and she had loved him), or that he had ridden into town, his clothes dusty, his black hat pulled low over his sunburned face, and an hour later had ridden away with four fresh notches on the butt of his six-gun, or that with the count three-and-two and the bases loaded, he had driven the ball so far and high that the outfielders did not even move, or that he had waded through surf and sprinted over sand, firing his Tommy gun and shouting to his soldiers behind him.

Now he was capturing a farmhouse. In the late movie the night before, the farmhouse had been very important, though no one ever said why, and sitting there in the summer dusk, he watched the backs of his soldiers as they advanced through the woods below him and crossed the clear, shallow creek and climbed the hill that he faced. Occasionally, he lifted his twenty-two-caliber rifle and fired at a rusty tin-can across the creek, the can becoming a Nazi face in a window as he squeezed the trigger and the voices filled him: *You got him, Captain. You got him.* For half an hour he sat and fired at the can, and anyone who might have seen him could never know that he was doing anything else, that he had been wounded in the shoulder and lost half his men, but had captured the farmhouse.

Kenneth looked up through the trees, which were darker green now. While he had been watching his battle, the earth, too, had become darker, shadowed, with patches of late sun on the grass and brown fallen pine needles. He stood up, then looked down at the creek, and across it, at the hill on the other side. His soldiers were gone. He was hungry, and he turned and walked back through the woods.

Then he remembered that his mother and father were going to a party in town that night and he would be alone with Connie. He liked being alone, but, even more, he liked being alone with his sister. She was nearly seventeen; her skin was fair, her cheeks colored, and she had long black hair that came down to her shoulders; on the right side of her face, a wave of it reached the corner of her eye. She was the most beautiful girl he knew. She was also the only person with whom, for his entire life, he had been nearly perfectly at ease. He could be silent with her or he could say whatever occurred to him and he never had to think about it first to assure himself that it was not foolish or, worse, uninteresting.

Leaving the woods, he climbed the last gentle slope and entered the house. He leaned his rifle in a corner of his room, which faced the quiet, blacktop road, and went to the bathroom and washed his hands. Standing at the lavatory, he looked into the mirror. He suddenly felt as if he had told a lie. He was looking at his face and, as he did several times each day, telling himself, without words, that it was a handsome face. His skin was fair, as Connie's was, and he had color in his cheeks; but his hair, carefully parted and combed, was more brown than black. He believed that Connie thought he was exactly like her, that he was talkative and well-liked. But she never saw him with his classmates. He felt that he was deceiving her.

He left the house and went into the outdoor kitchen and sat on a bench at the long, uncovered table and folded his arms on it.

"Did you kill anything?" Connie said.

"Tin cans."

His father turned from the stove with a skillet of white perch in his hand.

"They're good ones," he said.

"Mine are the best," Kenneth said.

"You didn't catch but two."

"They're the best."

His mother put a plate in front of him, then opened a can of beer and sat beside him. He sat quietly, watching his father at the stove. Then he looked at his mother's hand, holding the beer can. There were veins and several freckles on the back of it. Farther up her forearm was a small yellow bruise; the flesh at her elbow was wrinkled. He looked at her face. People said that he and Connie looked like her, so he supposed it was true, but he could not see the resemblance.

"Daddy and I are going to the Gossetts' tonight," she said.

"I know."

"I wrote the phone number down," his father said. "It's under the phone."

"Okay."

His father was not tall either, but his shoulders were broad. Kenneth wondered if his would be like that when he grew older. His father was the only one in the family who tanned in the sun.

"And *please*, Connie," his mother said, "will you go to sleep at a reasonable hour? It's hard enough to get you up for Mass when you've had a good night's sleep."

"Why don't we go into town for the evening Mass?"

"No. I don't like it hanging over my head all day."

"All right. When will y'all be home?"

"About two. And that doesn't mean read in bed till then. You need your sleep."

"We'll go to bed early," Connie said.

His father served fried perch and hush puppies onto their plates and they had French bread and catsup and Tabasco sauce and iced tea. After supper, his father read the newspaper and his mother read a Reader's Digest condensation, then they showered and dressed and at seven-thirty, they left. He and Connie followed them to the door. Connie kissed them, then he did. His mother and father looked happy and he felt good about that.

"We'll be back about two," his mother said. "Keep the doors locked."

"Definitely," Connie said. "And we'll bar the windows."

"Well, you never know. Y'all be good. G'night."

"Hold down the fort, son," his father said.

"I will."

Then they were gone, the screen door slamming behind them, and Connie left the sunporch, but he stood at the door, listening to the car starting and watching its headlights as it backed down the trail through the yard, then turned into the road and drove away. Still he did not move. He loved the nights at the camp when they were left alone. At home, there was a disturbing climate about their evenings alone, for distant voices of boys in the neighborhood reminded him that he was not alone entirely by choice. Here, there were no sounds.

He latched the screen and went into the living room. Connie was sitting in the rocking chair near the fireplace, smoking a cigarette. She looked at him, then flicked ashes into an ashtray on her lap.

"Now don't you tell on me."

"I didn't know you did that."

"Please don't tell. Daddy would skin me alive."

"I won't."

He could not watch her. He looked around the room for a book.

"Douglas is coming tonight," she said.

"Oh." He picked up the Reader's Digest book and pretended to look at it. "Y'all going to watch TV?" he said.

"Not if you want to."

"It doesn't matter."

"You watch it. You like Saturday nights."

She looked as if she had been smoking for a long time, all during the summer and possibly the school year, too, for months or even a year without his knowing it. He was hurt. He laid down the book.

"Think I'll go outside for a while," he said.

He went onto the sunporch and out the door and walked down the sloping car trail that led to the road. He stopped at the gate, which was open, and leaned on it. Forgetting Connie, he looked over his shoulder at the camp, thinking that he would never tire of it. They had been there for six weeks, since early June, his father coming on Friday evenings and leaving early Monday mornings, driving sixty miles to their home in southern Louisiana. Kenneth fished during the day, swam with Connie in the creeks, read novels about baseball, and watched the major league games on television. He thought winter at the camp was better, though. They came on week-ends and hunted squirrels and there was a fireplace.

He looked down the road. The closest camp was half a mile away, on the opposite side of the road, and he could see its yellow lighted windows through the trees. *That's the house. Quiet now. We'll sneak through the woods and get the guard, then charge the house. Come on.* Leaning against the gate, he stared into the trees across the road and saw himself leading his soldiers through the woods. They reached the guard. His back was turned and Kenneth crawled close to him, then stood up and slapped a hand over the guard's mouth and stabbed him in the back. They rushed the house and Kenneth reached the door first and kicked it open. The general looked up from his desk, then tried to get his pistol from his holster. Kenneth shot him with his Tommy gun. *Grab those papers, men. Let's get out of here.* They got the papers and ran outside and Kenneth stopped to throw a hand grenade through the door. He reached the woods before it exploded.

He turned from the gate and walked toward the house, looking around him at the dark pines. He entered the sunporch and latched the screen, then he smelled chocolate, and he went to the kitchen. Connie was stirring a pot of fudge on the stove. She had changed to a fresh pale blue shirt, the tails of it hanging almost to the bottom of her white shorts.

"It'll be a while," she said.

He nodded, watching her hand and the spoon. He thought of Douglas coming and began to feel nervous.

"What time's Douglas coming?"

"Any minute now. Let me know if you hear his car."

"All right."

He went to his room and picked up his rifle, then he saw the magazine on the chest of drawers and he leaned the rifle in the corner again. Suddenly his mouth was dry. He got the magazine and quickly turned the pages until he found her: she was stepping out of the surf on the French Riviera, laughing, as if the man with her had just said something funny.

She was blonde and very tan and she wore a bikini. The photograph was in color. For several moments he looked at it, then he got the rifle and cleaning kit and sat in the rocking chair in the living room, with the rifle across his lap. He put a patch on the cleaning rod and dipped it in bore cleaner and pushed it down the barrel, the handle of the rod clanging against the muzzle. He worked slowly, pausing often to listen for Douglas's car, because he wanted to be cleaning the rifle when Douglas came. Because Douglas was a tackle on the high school football team in the town, and Kenneth had never been on a football team, and never would be.

The football players made him more uncomfortable than the others. They walked into the living room and firmly shook his father's hand, then his hand, beginning to talk as soon as they entered, and they sat and waited for Connie, their talking never ceasing, their big chests and shoulders leaned forward, their faces slowly turning as they looked at each picture on the wall, at the designs on the rug, at the furniture, passing over Kenneth as if he were another chair, filling the room with a feeling of strength and self-confidence that defeated him, paralyzing his tongue and even his mind, so that he merely sat in thoughtless anxiety, hoping they would not speak to him, hoping especially that they would not ask: *You play football*? Two of them had and he never forgot it. He had answered with a mute, affirming nod.

He had always been shy and, because of it, he had stayed on the periphery of sports for as long as he could remember. When his teachers forced him to play, he spent an anxious hour trying not to become involved, praying in right field that no balls would come his way, lingering on the outside of the huddle so that no one would look up and see his face and decide to throw him a pass on the next play.

But he found that there was one thing he could do and he did it alone, or with his father: he could shoot and he could hunt. He felt that shooting was the only thing that had ever been easy for him. Schoolwork was, too, but he considered that a curse.

He was not disturbed by the boys who were not athletes, unless, for some reason, they were confident anyway. While they sat and waited for Connie, he was cheerful and teasing and they seemed to like him. The girls were best. He walked into the living room and they stopped their talking and laughing and all of them greeted him and sometimes they said: "Connie, he's so cute," or "I wish you were three years older," and he said: "Me, too," and tried to be witty and usually was.

He heard a car outside.

"Douglas is here," he called.

Connie came through the living room, one hand arranging the wave of hair near her right eye, and went into the sunporch. Slowly, Kenneth wiped the rifle with an oily rag. He heard Douglas's loud voice and laughter and heavy footsteps on the sunporch, then they came into the living room. Kenneth raised his face.

"Hi," he said.

"How's it going?"

"All right."

Douglas Bakewell was not tall. He had blond hair, cut so short on top that you could see his scalp, and a reddish face, and sunburned arms, covered with bleached hair. A polo shirt fit tightly over his chest and shoulders and biceps.

"Whatcha got there?" Douglas said.

"Twenty-two."

"Let's see."

"Better dry it."

He briskly wiped it with a dry cloth and handed it to Douglas. Quickly, Douglas worked the bolt, aimed at the ceiling, and pulled the trigger.

"Nice trigger," he said.

He held it in front of his waist and looked at it, then gave it to Kenneth. "Well, girl," he said, turning to Connie, "where's the beer?"

"Sit down and I'll get you one."

She went to the kitchen. Douglas sat on the couch and Kenneth picked up his cleaning kit and, not looking at Douglas, walked into his bedroom. He stayed there until Connie returned from the kitchen, then he went into the living room. They were sitting on the couch. Connie was smoking again. Kenneth kept walking toward the sunporch.

"I'll let you know when the fudge is ready," Connie said.

"All right."

On the sunporch, he turned on the television and sat in front of it. He watched ten minutes of a Western before he was relaxed again, before he settled in his chair, oblivious to the quiet talking in the living room, his mind beginning to wander happily, as a gunfighter in dark clothes moved across the screen.

By the time the fudge was ready, he was watching a detective story, and when Connie called him, he said: "Okay, in a minute," but did not move, and finally she came to the sunporch with a saucer of fudge and set it on a small table beside his chair.

"When that's over, you better go to bed," she said.

"I'm not sleepy."

"You know what Mother said."

"*You're* staying up."

"Course I am. I'm also a little older than you."

"I want to see the late show."

"No!"

"Yes, I am."

"I'll tell Daddy."

"He doesn't care."

"I'll tell him you wouldn't listen to me."

"I'll tell him you smoke."

"Oh, I could *wring* your neck!"

She went to the living room. He tried to concentrate on the Western, but it was ruined. The late show came on and he had seen it several months before and did not want to see it again, but he would not go to bed. He watched absently. Then he had to urinate. He got up and went into the living room, walking quickly, only glancing at them once, but when he did, Connie smiled and, with her voice friendly again, said: "What is it?"

He stopped and looked at her. "*Red River.*"

He smiled.

"I already saw it," he said.

"You watching it again?"

"Maybe so."

"Okay."

He went to the bathroom and when he came back, they were gone. He went to the sunporch. Connie and Douglas were standing near the back door. The television was turned off. Kenneth wondered if Connie had seen *Red River.* If she had not, he could tell her what had happened during the part she missed. Douglas was whispering to Connie, his face close to hers. Then he looked at Kenneth.

"Night," he said.

"G'night," Kenneth said.

He was gone. Kenneth picked up the saucer his fudge had been on and took it to the kitchen and put it in the sink. He heard Douglas's car backing down the trail, and he went to the sunporch, but Connie was not there, so he went to the bathroom door and said: "You seen *Red River*?"

"Yes."

"You taking a bath?"

"Just washing my face. I'm going to bed."

He stood quietly for a moment. Then he went into the living room and got a magazine and sat in the rocking chair, looking at the people in the advertisements. Connie came in, wearing a robe. She leaned over his chair and he looked up and she kissed him.

"Goodnight," she said.

"G'night."

"You going to bed soon?"

"In a minute."

She got her cigarettes and an ashtray from the coffee table and went to her room and closed the door. After a while, he heard her getting into bed.

He looked at half the magazine, then laid it on the floor. Being awake in a house where everyone else was sleeping made him lonely. He went to the sunporch and latched the screen, then closed the door and locked it. He left the light on, but turned out the one in the living room. Then he went to his room and took off everything but his shorts. He was about to turn out the light when he looked at the chest of drawers and saw the magazine. He hesitated. Then he picked it up and found the girl and looked at the exposed tops of her breasts and at her navel and below it. Suddenly he closed the magazine and raised his eyes to the ceiling, then closed them and said three Hail Mary's. Without looking at it, he picked up the magazine and took it to the living room, and went back to his bedroom and lay on his belly on the floor and started doing push-ups. He had no trouble with the first eight, then they became harder, and by the fifteenth he was breathing fast and his whole body was trembling as he pushed himself up from the floor. He did one more, then stood up and turned out the light and got into bed.

His room extended forward of the rest of the house so that, from his bed, he could look through the window to his left and see the living room and Connie's bedroom. He rolled on his back and pulled the sheet up to his chest. He could hear crickets outside his window.

He flexed his right arm and felt the bicep. It seemed firmer than it had in June, when he started doing push-ups every night. He closed his eyes and began the Lord's Prayer and got as far as *Thy kingdom come* before he heard it.

Now it was not the crickets that he heard. He heard his own breathing and the bedsprings as his body tensed, then he heard it again, somewhere in front of the house: a cracking twig, a rustle of dried leaves, a foot on hard earth. Slowly, he rolled on his left side and looked out the window. He waited to be sure, but he did not have to, then he waited to decide what he would do and he did not have to wait for that either, because he already knew, and he looked at the far corner of the room where his rifle was, though he could not see it, and he looked out the window again, staring at the windows of the living room and Connie's room, forcing himself to keep his eyes there, as if it would be all right if the prowler did not come into his vision, did not come close to the house; but listening to the slow footsteps, Kenneth knew that he would.

Get up. Get up and get the rifle. If you don't do it now, he might come to this window and look in and then it'll be too late.

For a moment, he did not breathe. Then, slowly, stopping at each sound of the bedsprings, he rolled out of bed and crouched on the floor beneath the window. He did not move. He listened to his breathing, for there was no other sound, not even crickets, and he began to tremble, thinking the prowler might be standing above him, looking through his window at the empty bed. He held his breath. Then he heard the footsteps again, in front of the house, closer now, and he thought: *He's by the pines in front of Connie's room.* He crawled away from the window, thinking of a large bearded man standing in the pine trees thirty yards from Connie's room, studying the house and deciding which window to use, then he stood up and walked on tiptoes to the chest of drawers and moved his hand over the top of it until he touched the handful of bullets, his fingers quickly closing on them, and he picked up the rifle and took out the magazine and loaded it, then inserted it again and laid the extra bullets on the chest of drawers. Now he had to work the bolt. He pulled it up and back and eased it forward again.

Staying close to the wall, he tiptoed back to the window, stopping at the edge of it, afraid to look out and see a face looking in. He heard nothing. He looked through the windows in the opposite wall, thinking that if the prowler had heard him getting the rifle, he could have run back to the road, back to wherever he had come from, or he could still be hiding in the pines, or he could have circled to the rear of the house to hide again and listen, but there was no way of knowing and he would have to stand in the room, listening, until his father came home. He thought of going to wake Connie, but he was afraid to move. Then he heard him again, near the pines, coming toward the house. He kneeled and pressed his shoulder against the wall, moving his face slightly, just enough to look out the screen and see the prowler walking toward Connie's window, stopping there and looking over his shoulder at the front yard and the road, then reaching out and touching the screen.

Kenneth rose and moved away from the wall, standing close to his bed now; he aimed through the screen, found the side of the man's head, then fired. A scream filled the house, the yard, his mind, and he thought at first it was the prowler, who was lying on the ground now, but it was a high, shrieking scream, it was Connie, and he ran into the living room, but she was already on the sunporch, unlocking the back door, not screaming now, but crying, pulling open the wooden door and hitting the screen with both hands, then stopping to unlatch it, and he yelled: "Connie!"

She turned, her hair swinging around her cheek.

"Get away from me!"

Then she ran outside, the screen door slamming, the shriek starting again, a long high wail, ending in front of the house with: "*Douglas, Douglas, Douglas*!" Then he knew.

Afterward, it seemed that the events of a year had occurred in an hour and, to Kenneth, even that hour seemed to have a quality of neither speed nor slowness, but a kind of suspension, as if time were not passing at all. He remembered somehow calling his father and crying into the phone: "I shot Douglas Bakewell," and because of the crying, his father kept saying: "What's that, son? What did you say?" and then he lay face down on his bed and cried, thinking of Connie outside with Douglas, hearing her sometimes when his own sounds lulled, and sometimes thinking of Connie inside with Douglas, if he had not shot him. He remembered the siren when it was far away and their voices as they brought Connie into the house. The doctor had come first, then his mother and father, then the sheriff; but, remembering, it was as if they all came at once, for there was always a soothing or questioning face over his bed. He remembered the footsteps and hushed voices as they carried the body past his window, while his mother sat on the bed and stroked his forehead and cheek. He would never forget that.

Now the doctor and sheriff were gone and it seemed terribly late, almost sunrise. His father came into the room, carrying a glass of water, and sat on the bed.

"Take this," he said. "It'll make you sleep."

Kenneth sat up and took the pill from his father's palm and placed it on his tongue, then drank the water. He lay on his back and looked at his father's face. Then he began to cry.

"I thought it was a prowler," he said.

"It was, son. A prowler. We've told you that."

"But Connie went out there and she stayed all that time and she kept saying '*Douglas*' over and over, I heard her—"

"She wasn't out there with *him*. She was just out in the yard. She was in shock. She meant she wanted Douglas to be there with her. To help."

"No, *no*. It was *him*."

"It was a prowler. You did right. There's no telling what he might have done."

Kenneth looked away.

"He was going in her room," he said. "That's why she went to bed early. So I'd go to bed."

"It was a prowler," his father said.

Now Kenneth was sleepy. He closed his eyes and the night ran together in his mind and he remembered the rifle in the corner and thought: *I'll throw it in the creek tomorrow. I never want to see it again.* He would be asleep soon. He saw himself standing on the hill and throwing his rifle into the creek, then the creek became an ocean, and he stood on a high cliff and for a moment he was a mighty angel, throwing all guns and cruelty and sex and tears into the sea.

Craft Questions

- How are physical details used to describe the characters and their relationships with each other?
- In what ways does Kenneth's imaginary life and real life become blurred?
- What details foreshadow the climax of the story?
- Does Kenneth's gun function as a symbol? If so, what does it symbolize?

Exercises

Exercise 1: Personal Transformation

Start by writing a very brief synopsis of your life in one paragraph. Include information about your parents, where you grew up, your physical attributes, and any other details you find important. Next, read over your synopsis, and take out some of the facts, substituting them with made-up information. The more specific the details you include, the better. Try using this transformed synopsis as the basis for a character in one of your short stories.

Objective: To transform details from your actual lived experience into fiction.

Exercise 2: There's No Place Like Home

Close your eyes. Spend some time visualizing your childhood room. When you open your eyes, jot down as many details as you can. Read over your list, and circle the most evocative, interesting details. Try using some of this description in a story.

Objective: To draw sensory detail from a place you know well in order to begin a story or to develop a story in progress.

Exercise 3: Object Lesson

Choose an object in your home to describe in detail, using all five senses in your description. Are there details that naturally suggest symbolic meaning? If not, try describing another object. Using Dubus's descriptions of Kenneth's gun as a guide, write a paragraph in which your object gradually takes on symbolic meaning.

Objective: To practice hinting at symbolic meaning without making it overbearing or cliché.

eleven viewpoint

whose story is it?

As you begin working on a short story, you'll want to spend some time considering who's telling it. Finding the right **viewpoint** is central to finding the story's focus, so even if you've already started writing from a viewpoint that feels right, it's worth considering, and even trying out, a range of possibilities to determine the strongest vantage point, before you get too far along. It may be that one of your characters will tell the story, that you'll decide to use a **third-person** narrator (*he/she/they*), or that you'll choose to use multiple viewpoints. Whatever the case, not only will your viewpoint help to determine the voice and tone of your story, it will also determine what we learn and what's left up to the imagination.

For example, if you're working on a story of a mugging, consider telling it from some of the most commonly used perspectives: **first person**: *I*; **second person**: *you*; **third person omniscient** (all-knowing): *he/she/they*; **third person limited** (seen through one of the character's eyes or limited in some other way). In this instance, you could use the first person to narrate the story from the victim's point of view, the mugger's, a bystander's, a police person's; the possibilities continue. Or, instead, you could use the second person, often a tricky viewpoint to pull off, but worth a try here if you want to involve the reader directly. Or, you could use a third person omniscient narrator or a limited one (focusing mostly on the victim's experience, for example). In other words, there are many ways to tell the story, and your choice will determine the story's **focus**: who or what it's about on a deeper level. Is it a story about the victim's fear and survival? About a mugger's motivation or desperation? About the ways in which such crimes are impacting a community?

As complex a decision as this is, if you take a little time to try out different possibilities, you'll likely be able to intuit which viewpoint seems to generate the most interesting, believable story, and which viewpoints create dead-ends or render the story flat. That being said, let's begin by exploring some of the advantages and blind spots of various viewpoints, so that you'll know what you're getting into.

First or Third Person

For many beginning writers, it feels most natural to use the first person to narrate. After all, first person seems immediate and personal; an individual is telling us their own story, using their own unique voice. Keep in mind, however, that if you choose this viewpoint it's important to consider a few possibilities and potential pitfalls.

First, even when you're using the first person, your reader will assume that the narrator is, in fact, a fictional character. This assumption presupposes that you've achieved enough distance from your own experience that you're willing and able to transform it for the sake of crafting believable, moving fiction. If this isn't the case, if you find yourself clinging to characters and events because *they are real*, or because *they actually happened*, the material may still be too raw to use *as is* for a story. In this case, you may want to begin by switching to third person to achieve some distance.

Next, if you're using first person, keep in mind that the character who is telling the story can either be the **protagonist** (the main character) or another character, and they can either be closely involved with the story or more detached from it. The following opening passage illustrates these distinctions.

> My father was a fox farmer. That is, he raised silver foxes, in pens; and in the fall and early winter, when their fur was prime, he killed them and skinned them and sold their pelts to the Hudson's Bay Company or the Montreal Fur Traders. These companies supplied us with heroic calendars to hang, one on each side of the kitchen door. Against a background of cold blue sky and black pine forests and treacherous northern rivers, plumed adventurers planted the flags of England or of France; magnificent savages bent their backs to the portage.

> For several weeks before Christmas, my father worked after supper in the cellar of our house. The cellar was white-washed, and lit by a hundred-watt bulb over the worktable. My brother Laird and I sat on the top step and watched.
>
> (Alice Munro, "Boys and Girls")

Craft Questions

- How involved or detached does the narrator seem to be?
- Do you think that the narrator of "Boys and Girls" is the protagonist or another character?

In some cases, a first-person narrator addresses an **auditor** or listener. "Snow," a short-short story by contemporary United States writer, Ann Beattie (b. 1947), uses this technique in dramatic ways.

> I remember the cold night you brought in a pile of logs and a chipmunk jumped off as you lowered your arms. "What do you think *you're* doing in here?" you said, as it ran through the living room. It went through the library and stopped at the front door as though it knew the house well. This would be difficult for anyone to believe, except perhaps as the subject of a poem. Our first week in the house was spent scraping, finding some of the house's secrets, like wallpaper underneath wallpaper. In the kitchen, a pattern of white-gold trellises supported purple grapes as big and round as Ping-Pong balls. When we painted the walls yellow, I thought of the bits of grape that remained underneath and imagined the vine popping through, the way some plants can tenaciously push through anything. The day of the big snow, when you had to shovel the walk and couldn't find your cap and asked me how to wind a towel so that it would stay on your head—you, in the white towel turban, like a crazy king of snow. People liked the idea of our being together, leaving the city for the country. So many people visited, and the fireplace made all of them want to tell amazing stories; the child who happened to be standing on the right corner when the door of the ice cream truck came open and hundreds of Popsicles crashed out; the man standing on the beach, sand sparkling in the sun, one bit glinting more than the rest, stooping to find a diamond ring. Did they talk about amazing things because they thought we'd turn into one of them? Now I think they probably guessed it wouldn't work. It was as hopeless as giving a child a matched cup and saucer. Remember the night out on the lawn, knee-deep in snow, chins

pointed at the sky as the wind whirled down all that whiteness? It seemed that the world had been turned upside down, and we were looking into an enormous field of Queen Anne's lace. Later, headlights off, our car was the first to ride through the newly fallen snow. The world outside the car looked solarized.

You remember it differently. You remember that the cold settled in stages, that a small curve of light was shaved from the moon night after night, until you were no longer surprised the sky was black, that the chipmunk ran to hide in the dark, not simply to a door that led to its escape. Our visitors told the same stories people always tell. One night, giving me a lesson in storytelling, you said, "Any life will seem dramatic if you omit mention of most of it."

This, then, for drama: I drove back to that house not long ago. It was April, and Allen had died. In spite of all the visitors, Allen, next door, had been the good friend in bad times. I sat with his wife in their living room, looking out the glass doors to the backyard, and there was Allen's pool, still covered with black plastic that had been stretched across it for winter. It had rained, and as the rain fell, the cover collected more and more water until it finally spilled onto the concrete. When I left that day, I drove past what had been our house. Three or four crocuses were blooming in the front—just a few dots of white, no field of snow. I felt embarrassed for them. They couldn't compete.

This is a story, told the way you say stories should be told: Somebody grew up, fell in love, and spent a winter with her lover in the country. This, of course, is the barest outline, and futile to discuss. It's as pointless as throwing birdseed on the ground while snow still falls fast. Who expects small things to survive when even the largest get lost? People forget years and remember moments. Seconds and symbols are left to sum things up: the black shroud over the pool. Love, in its shortest form, becomes a word. What I remember about all that time is one winter. The snow. Even now, saying "snow," my lips move so that they kiss the air.

No mention has been made of the snowplow that seemed always to be there, scraping snow off our narrow road—an artery cleared, though neither of us could have said where the heart was.

Craft Questions

- Who is the you the narrator addresses?
- How would you describe the difference between the two characters' memories?
- Although a first-person narrative is implied throughout, the viewpoint of the story shifts in individual paragraphs. Describe each shift.
- In what way does Beattie's story comment on the nature of storytelling itself?

Just as we often underestimate the complexity of first-person narrators, we often underestimate the flexibility of stories written in the third person. For starters, here are a few questions to ask yourself if you decide to write your story in third person:

- Is my narrator omniscient (all-knowing)?
- If they're not omniscient, which characters' minds can they access?

If you've decided that you don't want to use an omniscient narrator, the story's viewpoint is usually considered **limited third person**. In limited third person, your narrator may see more through the perceptions of one of the characters than the others (sometimes called **close third person**), or they may be limited in some other way: by how much they can or cannot see into the minds of characters, by their knowledge of past and present events, and so on. So, although it may be tempting simply to view the first person as the more immediate, intimate option, and the third person as inherently more distant or formal, this is not always the case.

Alternatives: Second Person and Multiple Viewpoints

Although the second person is used far less often than first or third person, it too offers interesting possibilities. It can refer to a listener, character, or the reader directly. And in stories such as Beattie's, a first-person narrator will occasionally switch to the second person. For another example of a narrative that switches to the second person, take this passage from "What You Pawn I Will Redeem," by contemporary United States writer Sherman Alexie (b. 1966):

> Probably none of this interests you. Homeless Indians are everywhere in Seattle. We're common and boring, and you walk right on by us, with maybe a look of anger or disgust or even sadness at the terrible fate of the noble savage. But we have dreams and families. I'm friends with a homeless Plains Indian man whose son is the editor of a bigtime newspaper back east.

We'll read and discuss the entirety of Alexie's story in the next chapter, but for now, notice the bold way in which the second person engages and implicates us, as readers, in the stereotyping and racism Alexie's narrator calls out.

It's worth noting that although Beattie's and Alexie's stories are unmistakably contemporary, using **multiple viewpoints** and speaking directly to the reader are not brand new inventions. Modern writers such as William Faulkner (1897–1962) are known for using multiple viewpoints in their novels to stunning effect. And eighteenth- and nineteenth-century British writers such as Jane Austen (1775–1817) and Charlotte Brontë (1816–55) addressed their readers directly through so-called **authorial intrusion** (in sentences beginning with "*Dear reader*," for instance). In general, multiple viewpoints are more common in novels than they are in short stories, maybe because the novel form affords more time and space to distinguish and develop various points of view. This is not to say that you can't try using multiple viewpoints, though, as Beattie, Alexie, and others have done with powerful results.

Reliability

Whatever the viewpoint of your story, the question of reliability or believability is bound to come up in your reader's mind, just as it does in life. To what extent do we trust the narrator as an authority? What do they know? What don't they know? What are they hiding? Are there things of which they're temporarily unaware? After all, no one, except for maybe an omniscient being (or narrator) can be in multiple places at the same time, perceiving everything that's happening.

The good news is that instead of these limitations in place, time, and perspective creating a limitation for your story, they can work to your advantage, if you're aware of how to use them. For instance, maybe your narrator is piecing together a series of seemingly disparate perceptions, and memory itself becomes a theme, as in Beattie's "Snow."

Although Beattie's narrator is in some way limited or initially unaware, the narrator's overall credibility is not in question, as it is when you create an **unreliable narrator**. There are times, however, that you may want to purposely create an unreliable narrator in order to make the style of the narration or the relationship between the reader and the story more complex and interesting. For, as we know in life, when people lie or stretch the truth, they often paradoxically reveal truths about themselves or the world around them.

Here are a few general things to keep in mind if you're considering using an unreliable narrator:

- Keep it consistent. Even if you've purposely made your narrator a teller of tall-tales, you'll want to keep the basics of action, dialogue, and plot believable. This will keep your readers from being confused, as well as helping them to quickly see that you've *purposely* distorted the narrator's perception and the way in which the story is told.

- Different Types. Types of unreliable narrators include naïve narrators, such as children or those who are mentally ill; braggarts or those who exaggerate; liars; and those who intentionally play with conventions of truth telling. You need not closely adhere to one of these formulas; in fact, you'll want to be sure to avoid cliché. However, thinking about *why* and *how* your narrator is unreliable is helpful.

- Third person. If you're using a third-person narrator, your reader will probably assume that the story is true because it's narrated by an outside observer. So, if you want to use an unreliable third-person narrator, consider creating a world in which you've suspended normal rules of reality. For an example, see Steven Schutzman's "The Bank Robbery" in chapter 15.

To begin to explore unreliable narrators, take a look at this opening passage from the widely popular novel *Catcher in the Rye* by twentieth-century United States writer J.D. Salinger (1919–2010):

> If you really want to hear about it, the first thing you'll probably want to know is where I was born, and what my lousy childhood was like, and how my parents were occupied and all before they had me, and all that David Copperfield kind of crap, but I don't feel like going into it, if you want to know the truth. In the first place, that stuff bores me, and in the second place, my parents would have two hemorrhages apiece if I told anything pretty personal about them. They're quite touchy about anything like that, especially my father. They're nice and all—I'm not saying that—but they're also touchy as hell. Besides, I'm not going to tell you my whole goddam autobiography or anything. I'll just tell you about this madman stuff that happened to me last Christmas just before I got pretty run-down and had to come out and take it easy. I mean that's all I told D.B. about, and he's my brother and all. He's in Hollywood. That isn't too far from this crumby place, and he comes over and visits me practically every week end. He's going to drive me home when I go home next month maybe. He just got a Jaguar. One of those little English jobs that can do around two hundred miles an hour. It cost him damn near four thousand bucks. He's got a lot of dough, now. He didn't use to. He used to be just a regular writer, when he

was home. He wrote this terrific book of short stories, *The Secret Goldfish*, in case you never heard of him. The best one in it was "The Secret Goldfish." It was about this little kid that wouldn't let anybody look at his goldfish because he'd bought it with his own money. It killed me. Now he's out in Hollywood, D.B., being a prostitute. If there's one thing I hate, it's the movies. Don't even mention them to me.

Craft Questions

- What aspects does narrator Holden Caulfield seem to exaggerate, distort, or make up?
- Which aspects of this opening do you believe or take for granted as reality?
- Which phrases clue you in to the biases, limitations, or unreliability of this narrator?

Identifying Your Story's Focus

As you may know, Holden Caulfield is the protagonist as well as the narrator of *Catcher in the Rye*. So, his mental angst as a troubled teenager, as expressed in this opening and throughout, constitutes a central part of Salinger's novel. As such, we could also call Holden the focus of the story. Again, this is not always the case; in other stories, the narrator is not the focus.

The term *focus* can also be used to refer to what the story is about on a deeper level, which, in turn, is closely related to the idea of **theme**, or the aspect of the story that relates to the human condition generally. As you write, ask yourself how your story would be different if it were written from a different viewpoint. And, again, try various possibilities (in a few paragraphs), before getting too far along. See which feels and sounds best. Use your intuition. Determining your story's focus may take a little longer. Understanding the story underneath the story, the subject matter that you really want to explore, beyond the obvious plot points and scene changes, can feel daunting at first. The important thing is to really *listen* to your own work. In fact, it may be the aspects of your story that feel messiest and least resolved that offer clues to the subject you're exploring. In chapter 16, we'll explore a folio of a student story from its beginning stage of composition, through marked drafts, to completion. This should provide you with a concrete illustration of the work involved in bringing a story to life. As you read the different iterations of this story, pay special attention to the way that its focus gradually shifted and emerged. The seeds of this focus were there all along, but it wasn't until the final draft that the viewpoint, focus, and themes of the story really came together to speak powerfully in unison.

Reading

Ann Pancake (b. 1963)
Me and My Daddy Listen to Bob Marley

In the good Granma smells Mish stands—nighttime powder and church perfume—his fingers tumbling the man in his pocket. His daddy peels the foil from the tiny package he has taken from Gran's dressing table drawer. Daddy, hand tremoring, fishes in the package's dropper of water, snares the lens on a finger and daubs it at his eye as Mish watches. It's not out of curiosity for the contacts—those he has seen his whole life, whenever Daddy can get them, Mish is used to that, looking on from the low single bed at Daddy's house, bedtime, get-up time, Daddy picking plastic in and out of his eyes. Mish watches for the funniness of Daddy at the same dressing table where Granma combs her hair and puts on her make-up, for the strangeness in Gran's mirror of Daddy's raggedy-brimmed Stihl cap, his penny-colored beard. With the effort to keep his eye open, Daddy's top lip is raised, and in the mirror, Mish can see the two big front teeth browning from the middle out. Then the lens pops in, and as though having the thing in his eye grants him the gift of seeing behind, Daddy speaks.

"I told you, wait for me downstairs."

Daddy's right eye streams, and the man somersaults in Mish's pocket.

"Well." Daddy is whispering. "Be very, very quiet. We can't wake Pappy up."

Mish feels around him his coat.

Daddy presses the other contact at the other eye, his hand quivering, the lens falling onto the table top, and he quiet-cusses. They are very tear-able, very expensive. The contact goes in, and Daddy is stepping away from the mirror, blinking hard, then he turns back, sweeps the little packages into the pockets of his coat, and as he passes Mish, he hisses, "You wait right here, Mish. You hear me? I'll be right back."

Mish follows Daddy. Daddy doesn't hear the rustle-roar of his coat, just like he didn't hear it when Mish walked into Gran's room to watch. Arms held away from his body, his feet in slow motion, Daddy wobbles down the hallway like a cartoon wolf, Mish swishing behind, them passing the bathroom, the closet, to the open door of Pappy's room, where Mish stops. The smells of this room are the inside-out of the Gran room smells—unflushed toilet smells, dead thing in the ditch smells, smells of crusted laundry—and Mish does not go in, he never does.

A floorboard shrieks. Daddy's outsplayed elbow hooks Pappy's hat rack, the rack bobs, but Daddy teeters on, balancing on the toes of his boots until he can reach into the clutter on Pappy's high chest of drawers. From the door, Mish can see only the standing-up things on the dresser. He knows there is a picture of old-timey people, of Uncle David as a grown-up, another of Daddy as a little boy, looking exactly like a Mish with blond hair. Daddy is unfolding Pappy's hip-worn wallet, and Mish flicks his eyes to the caterpillar shape under the rusty knit blanket on the bed, Pappy's head on its end. The spooky pink of Pappy's shut eyelids without his glasses over them. Mish looks back to Daddy, one hand replacing the wallet, the other tucking bills into his jeans pocket, then back to Pappy. Mish sucks a quick breath. Pappy's blue eyes are open. They hold Mish's there.

Then Daddy is hurrying through the door, scooping up Mish as he does, and they are down the stairs and into the kitchen where Daddy sets Mish on his feet. "Shhhh." He grabs a block of cheese from the refrigerator, a package of lunchmeat, reaches across to the breadbox and snags one of Gran's mini doughnuts for Mish—Mish crams it in his mouth right there—and Daddy swings Mish up again, Daddy grunting, staggering back a step, the enormous coat, the cheese and lunch meat, Mish's lengthening legs, then he finds his footing and they slam out the back door.

It is late afternoon, the land winter-hard and unsnowed, the air hard also, Christmas three weeks past. Gran's car is gone, her at Walmart in Renfield a long drive away, exchanging one of Daddy's Christmas presents. Daddy is strapping Mish into his carseat in the old car of Pappy's that Daddy has been driving since he had his wreck in Pappy's newer one—Mish was at Mommy's during that—then they are tearing out of Gran's driveway, gravel splattering, and the Cavalier leaps onto the highway.

Daddy leans into the gas. They swallow Route 30, fast, faster, spewing it spent behind, and as Gran's house vanishes and the woods close in, them alone except for the cars passing in the other lane, Mish feels the man who lives in Daddy ease down. The Cavalier insides are sealed, invisible to the other cars, just *whush* and gone, and by the time they swing onto the county back road that goes to Daddy's house, Daddy has loosened enough to scrabble in the mess on the front seat floor. "Listen, Mish," he calls over his shoulder. "Tater made me this for Christmas." He thrusts a cassette into the deck and begins to sing, a high, chokey string. It is not Bob. Mish reaches into his coat pockets and pulls out the Silver Surfer in one hand, a red Power Ranger in the other.

He'd waited until lunch on the couch at Mommy's in his new coat, a Dallas Cowboys coat given him for Christmas by Gran, the coat reaching almost to his knees on one end and almost to his ears on the other, *Now I got it a couple sizes too big so you can grow into it*, a Ninja Turtle shell, Ranger armor, the Dallas Cowboys coat *is* football pads. The Dallas Cowboys are his daddy's favorite team, and the noise of its nylon, the "I'm here!" crash, the blue star on its back with a white border around it, and sometimes Mish can feel the star there behind him, lit up and hot. Him on the couch and Mommy on the phone, her face bearing down as she made the fourth call to Daddy, then fifth. She sucked a breath and blew it out. "Take off that coat, Mish. You're gonna burn up."

Carlin sat cross-legged in front of the TV, thumbing the iPod his own daddy got him for Christmas, while Kenzie, whose daddy got her nothing, perched at the kitchen bar where Mommy'd put her because she couldn't keep her hands to herself. Kenzie pitched at Mish pizza coupons folded tight and hard when Mommy couldn't see—"You look like you're a hole with your head sticking out!"—but Mish heard her voice only at a distance, didn't hear her words at all. He was watching Carlin. "Wet me wissen," Mish said it again, low, conspiratorial, his tone simultaneously pleading and leaden with respect. "Wet *me* wissen, Cawwin," because Carlin, thirteen, sometimes gave up a kindness if it cost him nothing (Kenzie, nine, a deer fly, poison ivy, never gave anything at all). But Carlin, bent in concentration, his mouth slightly open, two juicy scabs under his lip, the thumb scrolling, pretended not to hear even though the buds weren't in his ears. "Pwease, Cawwin, wet me wissen," Mish tried again. "Wet we wissen. Wet we wissen," Kenzie simpered, and Mommy yelled, "Lay off, Kenzie! Mish, Steve's pulling in." Kenzie threw a refrigerator magnet at Mish. "Just three hours late. I guess that's not bad, a busy man like he is. Mish, let's get that coat zipped up—"

Now they are looping down Bonehaul Ridge, the last hill before the last curve before Daddy's house. Daddy's singing trickles to a hush. He brakes, and as they creep up on the curve, Mish slips his men back into his pockets. The car comes to a stop, the man who lives in Daddy back on his feet, finger to his lips, and Mish watches, too. Late afternoon, just this side of dark, Mish holds his breath. But the road in front of Daddy's house is vacant. No taillights of waiting cars. No figure slumped on the crumbly steps. They lurch forward, turn into the dirt tracks by the side porch, and pull around back where they park right up against the chimney. The yard brown waves of high winter weeds, dogless doghouse coughing bright garbage. Mish strokes with his thumb the Power Ranger's chest.

Their breaths steam around them while Daddy quivers the key in the side door padlock. Mish encases himself deeper in the coat, higher in it, his hands in his pockets to his forearms, his shoulders hackled to his ears. The man in Daddy is full raised now, Mish can see him, behind Daddy's bones. The man is flat and black, out of heavy construction paper snipped, a shape only, and only recently has Mish learned, from a Marvel Comics coloring book, the man's name: Quickshiver. The lock unslots, and Mish trails Daddy through the dim, stale kitchen, into the window-blanketed front room, dark as a groundhog burrow, and Mish, coat whispering, feels right away with his feet for the men he left on the floor last Sunday. Daddy squats to prime the kerosene heater, a stubborn cast-off of Gran and Pappy's, and all around Mish, as ever-present and familiar as the house's sour smell, presses the house's black burring, a static not ear-heard in the way Quickshiver is not eye-seen. Mish finds a man, then two, with his toes, and then he stands still, careful not to smash. With the men safe, he can let down a little, take his hands from the coat. He can feel Bob Marley behind him on the wall, tracing warm the rim of the star on his coat. The heater finally flares, Daddy scrambles upright, and in the pink-orange glow, Mish does his quick accounting: the Blue Power Ranger, Spiderman, the Hulk, Dash Incredible, Luke Skywalker, and a swarm of tiny knights. Mish's shoulders ease.

Then he turns around, and out of the dark Bob soars. Bob a beam through the static, radiant and still, and although the heater lights only Bob's chest, chin, and mouth, Mish sees the rest clear. Bob has made his face the colors he likes, red, yellow, and green, something Mish'd like to do, something even Jesus cannot, and under the toboggan hat-thing, Mish knows, three little birds nest in Bob's blacksnake hair. Bob does not worry, you see it in his smile, smoke curling it like Santa Claus's in Gran's *Night Before Christmas* book, only Bob is real. When Mish turns away, he feels the heat again on his back, and he starts to kneel to his men, to reach, when a hand closes over his shoulder.

"C'mon, buddy. Let's eat."

Mish sits cross-legged on the kitchen table with a bowl between his legs, gulping Froot Loops as fast as he can. Daddy is watching the window, dipping into a mustard jar pickle loaf slices he's rolled into tubes, a Budweiser humming in his other hand. Quickshiver crouches. Between bites, Daddy rubs his eyes, pulls now and again on their lids. Mish blinks. Daddy's opened the oven door for heat. They eat in the red U of its element and in a disk of light from a small, goose-necked desk lamp. The room is off the road, but from the side window where Daddy sits, you can see a car's headlights glint off the aluminum "No Hunting" sign tacked to the fence before the car pulls up by the house. Mish hits the bottom of his bowl and slides off the table.

"Keep that overhead off," Daddy says. He watches the window.

Mish stands in the dark doorway. From the floor, the men pull, invisible. To see them at all, he'll have to sit very near the hot cylinder of heater, but right after he thinks that, it doesn't matter anymore. Kneeling, he draws the Silver Surfer and the Power Ranger from his pockets and sets them among the others in their scattered circle. The air over the men is static-less, Mish can feel, and glassy. The black burring pushed up and away. For the first time since this morning, he wriggles out of his coat and lets it drop behind him. Bob has his back. He picks up The Hulk.

The calm almost instantly comes, like a vein from The Hulk into Mish's palm, then up his arm to his heart. The other men begin pulling, showing Mish, and Mish knows what to do. He divides them into the sides they ask for, setting them up for their fight, and as he does, the glassy dome settles, Mish barely notices it with his mind, but the rest of him knows. The dome cupping over, embracing, and inside, only Mish and the men. And soon, Mish hears the murmur, the quiet telling, it comes from his mouth and at the same time from outside of him—

"Mish! C'mere!"

Mish stops.

"Mish!" An amplified hiss. "C'mere!"

Mish leans back. He looks at his men. Then, pulling on his coat, he climbs to his feet and rustles to the kitchen.

Daddy's face is squashed against the window glass. "Look out here." Daddy reaches behind him and snaps off the lamp. Mish rests his chin on the sill and circles his face with his hands like Daddy is doing.

"Look hard. Let your eyes adjust."

Mish stretches big his eyes.

"Do you see something? There by the sycamore?"

Mish strains.

"Somebody moving?"

"I jush see a buncha weedj."

"You're sure?"

Mish looks a little longer, for the sake of Quickshiver. "Nuh-uh. Nuttin dere, Daddy."

Daddy angles his hands around his face, desperate to confirm it. When Mish turns back to his men, Daddy gives up and follows to his own front room spot, the straight chair with the stained pillow drawn up to a crack between blanket-drape and window-frame. He lights his nerve medicine. Mish strips off his coat and studies his men. Half of them sleep in the roofless Lincoln Log house, the other half in the Hot Wheels garage. It is Spiderman wants to be picked up first. Mish does.

Again, the immediate grounding, the vein from man to heart. Whoever Mish holds in his hand, he enters, the man pulling, a speaking way under words, Mish simultaneously following the man and directing him. The men strap on their weapons, pump their muscles, toss back their heads—The Hulk, Luke, Spidey, Knight—Mish both Mish and men and more, the dome settling good now, the block of the black burr. The further he sinks, the calmer he deeps, the good real weight of the men's real world, anchor weight, ballast weight, so different from the daddy weight. Mish speaking not only the men's parts, but the story in-between, and always, every word of the murmur understood. Now the men are shouting challenges to each other, girding for the fight, Mish and the men completely endomed, Bob unworrying overhead like a tricolor moon. The first man dies, the second one, the first man resurrects, the dome holding away—

"Mish! Do you have to pee?"

Mish's mouth crackles, two knights crashing.

"Mish, I said, do you have to pee?"

Mish blows out a breath and sits back on his thighs. While one hand has been moving the men, the other has been holding his crotch. "Uh-uh," he mutters, almost to himself.

"Yeah, you do. Do you want me to come up with you?"

He's let go of his pants and picked up Spiderman, trying to follow him back.

"Mish, do you want me to come?" The voice sharpens. "I'm not cleaning up another mess, I'll tell you that."

"Nooo," Mish groans.

"Well, watch that hole. Hear me?"

Up the dark narrow steps, Mish climbs. The hole in the bathroom floor finally opened all the way through a month ago. The hole's right in front of the toilet, so to pee, you have to straddle it, which Daddy can do, or you have to sidle around and pee from the side, which Mish has to do. Many a time, in daylight, Mish has squatted over the hole and peered down to the stove. Its black coils, its scaley, unwashed pans, the streaked dishtowels borrowed from Gran. Once he dropped a man through to see what would happen, one of the faceless olive army men—he wouldn't have done it to most of the others. When it hit the stovetop, Daddy jumped and cussed. Sometimes, looking through, Mish imagines the what if? of falling himself and frying on a burner. Sometimes, in the night, the bathroom lit, the downstairs dark, like now, Mish sees the hole as not dropping into Daddy's kitchen at all. Mish sees it leading right out of the house to someplace else.

⋆

The day after Christmas Mish stood on the footstool in the bathroom off Gran's kitchen, his men battling in the sink. Through the dome arched over them, the shut bathroom door, Mish heard Gran and Uncle David walk into the kitchen and their chairs scrape. Then the grown-up talk, of no more import than the toilet running, as Rescue Hatchet dove off the faucet to save Dash from Darth—when, suddenly, Mish heard his real name. He stopped.

It was Uncle David, of course, who said it. Uncle David, who only came twice a year, *at most*, twice a year, *if that*. And now he was saying it again, in a string of words Mish couldn't reverse and unscramble.

"Steve is thirty-eight years old, Mom. Thirty-eight years old. And has never held a job longer than, what? Three months?"

"Well, he looks better than he has in years. And just happier than he's ever been—"

"Looks better than he has in years with his two front teeth rotted out."

Through Mish, a coldness was unrolling. Starting in his chest, uncurling even into his arms and his legs.

"You know what I mean. Good color in his face. And not all skinny like he has been."

Mish hunched back over the sink, his mouth moving. Rescue Hatchet hacked at Spiderman now.

"… don't understand why nothing's come of what happened last summer."

"Well, I'll tell you, David, the court system in this county, it's unbelievable how busy they are. At the magistrate's, I heard they're backed up for six months…."

Mish made his murmur louder.

"Did you and Dad really press those charges? Or did you just say you did?"

"He's doing better than he has in so, so long. Why, he walked in here yesterday morning with a wrapped present in his hand—"

"Mom, did you press those charges?" Uncle David asked.

Mish threw open the bathroom door and leapt into the kitchen, "Boo!" He landed with a smack on both feet. Uncle David's and Gran's faces snapped toward him like they were fixed on the same pivot. "Ba-ha-ha-ha-ha-ha!" Mish bellowed his best villain laugh. After a couple seconds, Uncle David laughed, too.

"C'mere, Matthew. C'mon. Give me a hug. I'm leaving this afternoon."

"Don't pay any attention to Uncle David," Daddy tells him every time. "He thinks he's better than us."

Mish grinned, shook his head, and ran.

*

Downstairs, the phone rings. Mish freezes. The insides of his ears stand up like a dog's. He lowers himself closer to the floor hole, head tilted. Hears only a wordless rumble spiked here and there by a snicker. He tiptoes to the top of the stairs, but he can tell nothing from there either. He waits.

"Hey, Mish," Daddy calls. "Get down here get your coat on. We gotta take a quick ride."

Mish's chest clenches. He backs up a few steps and leans into the dark wall, the plaster cold against his cheek.

"It's not a big deal. You can sleep while we're there. And Tater should be around."

Mish breathes deep and blows it loud enough for Daddy to hear, his lips flapping like a horse's.

"C'mon, Mish, it's not a big deal. I'm not gonna stay long."

"Can I sleep in da car?"

"No, it's too cold for you to sleep in the car."

"Daaa-deee."

"Listen, it'll be a nice ride. We'll listen to Bob. And afterwards, we'll stop at Burger King to get you that new toy."

"Wha new toy?"

"I can't remember, I saw it on TV at Gran's. Some kind of man. Now come on down."

"I din see it on teebee at Mommysh."

"Well, I saw it. Get your coat on."

Mish stops on each step, brings his feet together, sighs. When he shuffles into the front room, he sees that Daddy has already swapped the threadbare Stihl cap for the newer one with the Nike swoosh. He's pulling on the canvas coat he got when the Salvation Army came in for the flood victims over in Maddox last year. His usual coat, the one with the tape over the holes to hold in the stuffing, lies on the floor, worryingly close to the men. When Daddy tugs Mish to him, Mish droops, his arms limp, head sagging, and while Daddy threads him into the Dallas Cowboys sleeves, Mish wrinkles his nose against the reek of spilled kerosene in Daddy's coat. Then Daddy is duelling with the zipper, hands buzzing, the cussing a steady grit, but over his shoulder, Mish notices Bob, heaterlit on the wall. Daddy glares at his hands, stiffens and shakes them. Tries the zipper again. Mish watches Bob, tall and easy on his wall, the smoke from his smile, Mish knows—happiness. Bob can make the feeling seen. The star on Mish's back starts to heat, then to ray, and finally the anticipation of Bob in the car overrides what waits at the end. "Your zipper's broke," Daddy says. Mish stoops quick, snatches the two nearest men, and stuffs one in each pocket.

They hurtle past the "No Hunting" sign. They hairpin back up Bonehaul Ridge. With each yard of asphalt collapsing behind, Quickshiver inside Daddy lies a little more down, the safety of being between place and place, Mish knows this without knowing whose knowing it is. They chute through trees, the house static receding, then burst out into a star-gray field, closer, closer, closer drawing to Bob, and when Mish pulls out the men and sees they are Luke Skywalker and Dash Incredible, he smiles. The Cavalier cuts loose on the first of the road's few straights, and Mish can't help but bounce in his seat, this is where Daddy always asks. And then Daddy does, he calls over his shoulder, Quickshiver nothing but a black puddle at his bottom, "What do you want to listen to, Mish?"

And Mish says, "Bob!"

And Daddy says, "Me, too!"

And Daddy steers with his thigh while he respools the cassette on his pinky, the men warming up in acrobatic leaps, until, finally, Daddy jabs the tape in the deck. And instantly, they are swallowed—Mish, men, Daddy—in the belly of Bob.

Rhythm of reggae, happy heartbeat and a half, Mish reeling it into the cave of his ribs, his pulse recalibrated, the soothe, the joy. The throb patterning, echoing, the loops of the curves, the hills' nods and lifts, Mish swaying, the men flying, the car, Mish knows, if seen from outside, red green and yellow glow, colors of Bob. The Cavalier dances the bends, the banks, and Daddy stringy-sings, *This is my message to you - ou -ou.* And Mish's happiness rides on a pillar of memory, sedimented, three years old. Last week, last month, yes, but down, back, further than that, to when Mish stayed at Daddy's half the week, further back still to when Daddy lived at Mommy's house. So much in those layers dark, dangly, shivery, loud, but all that vanishes in the happiness of Bob. The Bob memory constant, soaking up through the sediment and richening each level—memory, memory, memory—whenever Mish was fussy or inconsolable or too tired to sleep, Daddy strapping him in the car, punching the cassette, and they ride in the cradle car to Rockabye Bob.

And three weeks ago, on Christmas night, Carlin stretched out on the bottom bunk with his iPod in his ears, his eyes as blank as if he lay in his coffin, Mish standing behind him, Mish straining with marvel, straining with want, all that glorybig music held in a wafer no thicker than ten Pokemon cards. "Wet me wissen," Mish outright begged, too desperate even to calculate, manipulate, "Wet me wissen," while Carlin paid him no more mind than he did the fluffs of crud under the bed. "Pweeeese, Caw-win, wet me wissen," Mish peering now directly into his face, poking him gently on the shoulder. Until Carlin, his eyes still dead, reached out, planted a hand on Mish's chest, and pushed. Once.

Mish staggered backwards, the tears geysering behind his face. He grabbed the nearest object, a Transformers sticker book, and swung at Carlin. As he did, he yelled, "Me and *my* daddy wissen to Bob Mawwee." And the tears weren't anymore.

Daddy turns the volume halfway down. "Now, Mish."

"Yeah?"

"Don't say anything to anybody about us taking this ride, okay?"

"Okay."

"It'll just be between you and me."

"Okay."

"Don't say anything to Mommy. Or Gran. Even if they ask."

"Yeah."

Daddy cranks the music back up, even louder than before. It is the Bob beat that propels Mish's blood through his veins. Bob is heart. The car tremors, Mish feels the speaker thrumming against his legs, his hips—beat; beat; beat, beat-beat—and he settles back in his seat, the men catching their breaths in his lap, *everything's gonna be*, music carrying rhythm carry, the car a rocker. Lullabye Bob.

The loss of motion wakes him. He flexes his fingers. One man is still there. One he has dropped. Daddy's unstrapping him—Mish tucks the man in his pocket—lifting him out, and Mish buries his face for a second in Daddy's jacket against the cold, which has shocked him full awake, immediate and blunt. The cold has blacked the night darker, crisped the stars whiter, but over Daddy's shoulder, Mish can see clouds like a dirty blanket pulling over distant sky. They are parked just off the hardtop in the mouth of a dirt road leading into a broad field, and Daddy sets him on his feet on the hood of the car. Mish can feel its heat through his tennis shoes. "See the house, Mish?"

Mish looks past the winter grass, bowed and brittle-humped in the three-quarter moon. The house is the only thing rising off the flat of the field until the mountains start again. Mish nods.

"Can you see cars around it?"

Mish nods. Quickshiver is taut on his toes, his hands splayed, head cocked. Mish pulls his coat sleeve against his side, a muted crackle. Daddy is standing on the ground right next to Mish on the hood, one arm around his waist, and Mish thinks of the apples. "Can you start this for me, buddy?" Mish, bearing down with his small front teeth, breaking the peel and gnawing around in the white to give Daddy a good opening.

Daddy takes a finger and stretches the corner of his eye, his lip lifting. "Do you see Tater's truck?"

Mish squints. "Yeah." Tater's truck is easy. A big white Ford extended cab.

"Okay, good." Daddy pulls the corner of his eye again. "Now this is important. This is important, Mish. Look at all of them."

Mish is looking.

"Do you see a blue Toyota Four-Runner?"

Mish wiggles out of the arm around his waist and lifts onto his toes. A heaviness has come into him. One that makes him bigger and tireder. He knew his cars before he knew his colors, that's what Daddy always says, and Mish squints again, drawing on the stingy moon, to untangle the snarl of vehicles around the house. He can't tell blue in the dark, but the shape of a Four-Runner he can.

"Nuh-uh," he says.

"You're sure?"

Mish nods sharp, twice. "Only Toyoda's a Tacoma."

Daddy slaps the star on his back. "Okay. Good. Good job, Mish."

They roll through the field, the house swelling in the windshield. Bob is gone. Daddy drives to the right to straddle the road ruts, the wash of grass against metal, the car cold now because Daddy left the door open while they were looking for the Four Runner. As the house grows larger, clearer, the heaviness drains out of Mish, leaving something worse. When it's summer, Daddy lets him sleep in the carseat, he leaves the door open for air, and sometimes Mish doesn't even wake up. But in the winter, he has to go inside. The car pitches into a deep hole and Mish is thrown forward, and he thinks to reach behind him, to the star, but the carseat straps bind him. Then Daddy's carrying him, crunching through frozen mud to planks across cinderblocks that climb to the front door, and when the planks wobble, Daddy stumbles to the side, Mish scissors his legs around Daddy's waist, Daddy finds his balance, and the door opens.

The party explodes in Mish's face. Laughter without fun, heat without warmth, smoke without smile, every party he's ever entered, and the grownup bodies packed upright and reeling, an October cornfield, rattle and wind. "Hey, Steve!" somebody yells, then somebody else calls it, too, and Daddy grins and yells back. The top half of Tater swims out of the crowd, him brandishing a quart-sized Sheetz cup. "Mish! How you doing?" He strips Mish from Daddy and squashes him to his soft chest, Tater in a T-shirt odored of cigarettes and mildew, and the cup's straw pokes Mish's head and whatever is in it splashes a little on Mish. "Ricky's got it," Tater says, and Daddy says, "Where's he at?" and Tater says, "He'll be here." Past Tater, Mish sees a silver Christmas tree on a table, listing to one side, drooped with brassy, teardrop ornaments, each exactly the same.

He is set on his feet into the cornfield of legs. No, not corn. Brush, thicket, thorn, briar, the legs pressing, posting, buckling, shifting, and Mish clings to Daddy's jeans pocket to avoid being swept down. "Who's this?" The lady stoops to Mish, and her face reminds Mish of the file Daddy uses to sharpen the chainsaw.

"This is my son, Mish."

"Mish?" This is what they always say.

"That's what I call him. He's named after me, my initials smashed together."

"Oh, isn't he handsome?" They always say that, too, unless they say "cute."

"Yeah, looks just like me when I was little."

"What did Santa Claus bring you, Mish?"

"He can't talk very good, I'm the only one who understands him."

Daddy ruffles Mish's hair. Mish ducks. "You got some place he can sleep?"

Then Daddy is steering him by his shoulders through more legs. There's not even room enough for Daddy to pick him back up. Mish stumbles around mud-splattered workboots, plasticky high heels, tennis shoes with mismatched shoestrings, Christmas gift clogs. He watches the feet, his head lowered, to save him from belts and butts, zippers and belly fat. Hands reach down to pet him—"Ahhh, cute!"—Mish fighting the urge to bite Daddy's fingers, until they're in a skinny hall, passing a vibrating washing machine, and finally entering a back room where Daddy swings Mish onto a coat-heaped bed. He pulls Mish out of the Dallas Cowboys coat and wraps the coat around him like a blanket. Then he sheds his own coat and spreads that over Mish, too.

"Will he fall off?" the file lady asks.

"Nah, nah. He's three years old."

Daddy leans in as if to kiss Mish goodnight. Mish snakes an arm out of the coats, snatches Daddy's Nike cap, and flings it as hard as he can. One of Daddy's hands flies to his head, the other tomahawks out to intercept the cap. It misses. And there is Daddy's head, naked. The smashed wads of his balding hair like damp caterpillars crawling his scalp, the patchy bare places in between. The file lady giggles at Mish, and Daddy sweeps his cap off the floor, jams it on his head, and shoots Mish a scarlet look. Mish shoots the look right back.

"Sleep tight, cutie." The file lady's voice.

The door shuts, ugly music damps by a third. Mish slings Daddy's reeking coat off himself. He rolls out of the Dallas Cowboys one. Then, his brow hard, his teeth steeled, him holding tight to the Cowboys coat, he windmills his arms and his legs to make a clearing for himself. Furious snow-angel, the foreign coats rolling and bunching away, some of them tumbling onto the floor. Mish's breath comes hard and coarse, and he picks up Daddy's coat and heaves it over the bed edge, too. Then he seizes the Cowboys coat in both hands and clashes it together, nylon on nylon, drowning the horrible music, the coat louder, louder, the coat hollering, screaming. And then Mish stops. His breath comes more quietly. He turns on his side and hugs the coat towards him. He opens his eyes and there's the label where Granma inked his name. M-I-S-H. Matthew Steven Halliday, Junior.

It wasn't long after he began Head Start the fall before that Kenzie started the game. "Let's play school!" She'd grab Mish and push him onto the couch. "I'm the speech therapist! You're the kid!" Her hands pinning his shoulders, one knee on his thigh, Mish squirming, while Kenzie swooped in and out of his face. "Repeat!" in-swoop, "After!" out-swoop, "Me!" in. Then she would hover, inches from his nose, her breath odored of cold, boiled potatoes. "Ma!" she'd bleat. Then, her tongue tipping out and sucking back, thick. "Thew! Ma-Thew!" Mish wiggling, grunting, shoving her away. "Ma! Thew!" Twisting his head to the side, clamping tight his eyes. "Thew! Thew! Repeat!"

Mish reaches into his Dallas Cowboys pocket and touches the man there. It is Dash Incredible. Luke he dropped in the car. He holds Dash quietly in the pocket. He doesn't bring him out into the room.

Suddenly, Mish is being arranged in the carseat again. He recognizes this from deep in a hole of sleep, and after the recognition, he sinks back, but then a knowing pricks him. He blinks, half-opens his eyes, closes them, reopens. And begins clambering up to awake. As he does, he reaches for the man in his pocket. But the man is not there. Daddy is blundering his seat straps, his hands revved to their highest, bumblebees, propellers, the buckles clacking, missing. His face so close to Mish's Mish can feel the heat off it, smell the salt of sweat. Then Mish feels that it's not just the man who's not there, the pocket isn't there, either, and then Mish understands: the Dallas Cowboys coat is not there.

"Wheresh? Wheresh?"

He is swaddled in Daddy's stinky jacket again. He sees Daddy's flannel is gone too, him in only his long-john shirt, the yellowed armpits ripped, the sleeves pushed up, and Mish hears himself say, "Wheresh my Dawash Cowboysh coat?"

Daddy is slamming Mish's door and reeling around the front of the Cavalier, one hand scratching vicious the back of his neck, then he drops in the driver's seat. Mish shakes his way out of Daddy's coat and throws his head around, sweeps his arms, hunting the dark car insides for his own coat, and he asks again, panic sparking his voice, "Wheresh my Dawash Cowboysh coat?"

Daddy taps a close-parked car, then another, cusses, pulls forward, tries again. Now he's gaping over his shoulder so he can see behind him better, showing his face to Mish, but Daddy doesn't look at him. "Calm down, Mish. I had to loan it to Ricky for a few days. Then you'll get it right back."

"Wicky? Who Wicky?"

Daddy escapes the mess of cars and throws it into Drive. "Ricky needed it for a few days. Then you'll get it back." They are bouncing down the dirt road, and Mish twists in his seat, the house, little, littler, littler behind them, and then, Mish remembers. Dash is in the coat pocket.

"Go ba ge i! Go ba ge i!"

He is shrieking, his words unravelled to how he talked a year ago, two years ago, Mish hears it but cannot help it. The dirt road levels and they plunge even faster, and Mish smacks the seat beside him, searching for the fallen Luke Skywalker, but hits only Dorito crumbs. Then Mish feels the pressing in his chest. The cave begins to creak. The black to leak. Mish grabs hard, pushes back, and when he shouts next, it is a command, no whine in it. "Take me back to Mommysh!"

At the hard top, Daddy jets left without braking.

"Take me back to Mommysh!"

"Mish," Daddy says. "Are you a baby or a man?"

"Take me!"

"I can't, Mish." One front tire drifts onto the shoulder, snags on the pavement lip, the ripping sound of asphalt against rubber, and Daddy jerks it back up, the car swerving into the left lane, then sailing back right. "This is how the judge did it. I've told you a thousand times." He talks the after-party talk, each word deliberate, an egg laid. "It's not my decision. You're with me from Saturday morning to Sunday evening. We have to do what the judge says."

"I doan care wha da judge saysh!"

"Well, I do. It's the law." Now Daddy does look at Mish, his I'm-a-grown-up-and-you're-not look. He turns back to the windshield, his forefinger massaging the corner of his eye. "C'mon, Mish." Now he's lightened his tone, a phony breeze in it. "We'll go in to Burger King tomorrow and get you that man."

Mish's lips are sucked tight in his mouth. His fists are clenched, his arms, too, his stomach, all of him seizing against it, pushing back. But the cave—gradually, excruciatingly—opens. Mish's chest slow-cleaving, the stones cracking, the walls unsealing, until, like always, the first part can't help but spill out. The first part not even plain pain, but the warm wave of pity, and not even for himself, pity for the coat and for Dash, left behind. But once the pity's free, nothing can stop what it's blocked. The grief batter-rams Mish's chest and leaps torrenting out.

The G.I. Joe left at Ponderosa, the Superman shoes outgrown, Kingy run away and the monstrous stench from the ditch, Mommy breaking up with Aaron who liked to play Spiderman, Daddy gone a long time away so the doctors could help him. Daddy gone a long time away. The loss is a tidal wave and Mish strains against it, shoulder to boulder, leaning, gasping, his fingertips shredding from the rough of the rock (*Crybaby. Stop that right now* (*no woman, no cry. No woman, no cry*)). Until, finally, Mish feels it. The breach swings back. The cave, heavily, slowly, closing its walls. The rift shrinking from yawn, to gap, to slit to, finally, nothing at all. Mish breathes. As his heart shuts, all that black loss is anvilled, smelted. Into a tower of flame-colored mad. And the right words come.

"I'm gonna tell," Mish says. His voice is even. Only he can feel the buzz underneath.

Daddy hesitates. It's less than a second, but Mish hears it.

"You're gonna tell what?"

"Dat you sto dat money fom Pappy." On "you stole," Mish feels a spurt of fear, exhilarating. Not of Daddy, but himself.

Daddy watches the road. Mish watches Daddy. "Pappy owed me that money, Mish. For that wood I cut. I just didn't want to interrupt his nap."

"Dat you sto Gransh contacsh." The cave is sealed completely now, and Mish feels himself growing bigger, even without the coat.

Daddy is quiet. Then, "I'm not going to argue with you, Mish."

"Dat you sto my Dawash Cowboysh coat."

Daddy whips his head around, and the bare anger in his face pumps Mish even bigger. Mish almost smiles, and Daddy sputters, in the tone of the wrongly accused that works so well on Gran. "Mish, I did not steal the coat. I loaned it to Ricky. I'll get it back when I get paid at the end of the week."

"You doan eben hab a job!"

Daddy is watching the road again, each hand clamped on its side of the wheel, his shoulders squared. The model of the safe driver. Trees along the road scroll up gray then disappear. When Daddy speaks this time, his voice is flat again.

"This is between you and me, Mish. It's between men. Babies tell Mommy and Granma." Daddy glances over his shoulder. "You keep our secret … I'll get you an iPod." He nods. "Yeah, how about that, buddy? Like Carlin's."

Mish sits motionless in his carseat. It has begun to snow, the flakes driving against the windshield haphazard, bewildered. Then Mish feels, there in the front seat, Quickshiver inside Daddy ease down. Quickshiver drops his shoulders, unkinks his neck, loosens his knees, and lies down. And with each step Quickshiver unwinds, Mish flares a notch tighter. Breath to Mish's ember, gas to his blaze. Now both Quickshiver and Daddy think it is over, Mish bought off by a lie, and the cave again bulges, Mish squeezing with all his power back. Daddy is ejecting the Bob tape, jabbing in his new one, and right when he is lifting his finger to PLAY, Mish says, "I'm gonna tell Uncle Dabid."

Daddy's hand freezes, finger extended. For one cold moment, everything hangs in air.

Then Daddy is slamming on the brakes, Mish shot through with gratification and fear, a hah! and *uh-oh,* all at once, the car yanked onto the shoulder. With a thud-crunch Daddy throws the gear into Park and twists all the way around, his knee against the back of the front seat, in his eyes a full white circle around each iris, Mish sees them clear. Daddy squeezes the front seat back.

"Mish, listen." He speaks from between the rotted teeth, the others gritted. "You listen." He moistens his lips. "Even if you tell Uncle David, let's say you sit right down and tell him." Daddy's eyes grip Mish's. "Do you think he'd understand anything you said?"

Daddy's eyes hold Mish's. The dry screek of the windshield wipers on too fast, the snow too thin. Behind Daddy, the snow spins, scattershot, eddying, like it's not even down it's falling, not even sky it comes from. Finally Daddy turns. Inside Mish, a hundred things scutter away into dark. Daddy drives.

★

Daddy carries Mish, wound in the canvas coat, through the black kitchen and into the blacker front room, tripping over Mish's men. He totes him up the stairs. He sets Mish down in the cold bedroom, switches on the bedside lamp, and clatters over a stack of CD's. Mish lets the coat spill off him and onto the floor, then, like every Saturday night, he follows Daddy to the bathroom. Both of them wary around the floor hole, Mish pees first, as he always does, Daddy waiting, then Mish waits for Daddy. Back in the bedroom, Daddy shakes out the old Gran covers on the unmade bed, tugs off Mish's shoes, and scoots him under. He drops his cap on the floor and strips off his jeans, his heel catching in the folds and almost bringing him down. Then he crawls under and pulls Mish to him.

"I love you, Mish," he mumbles. He kisses Mish, hard, on his forehead. He reaches over and snaps off the lamp.

Mish lies still, not touching Daddy. He tries to turn himself into a stick on the very edge of the bed. But it is cold in the bedroom, the bed a twin, the blankets thin, Daddy warm. Mish draws a little closer, still careful not to touch him.

"Shit," Daddy says.

He flops over, clicks the lamp, and swings his bare legs over the side of the bed. Rummaging in the junk on the bedside stand, he comes up with a grubby contact case. He pinches the contacts from his eyes and slides them into the case. Then he worms back under the covers and after a single blast of outbreath, begins to snore. The lamp blares on.

Mish squeezes his eyes shut. The light bleeds through. He opens them. The lamp's plastic body is shaped like a lamb. It was Daddy and Uncle David's when they were little boys. Mish watches it. Then he widens his gaze to the photos curling on their tacks on the wall. Various Mishes from baby on up. Daddy snores louder.

Mish slips out of bed. He pads into the hall, the floor numbing his feet. He stops at the top of the steps, where the bedroom lamp throws light before the staircase diminishes into dark. "Ma," he whispers. Then he concentrates, his brow hard. "Yew."

Mish sighs. He licks the roof of his mouth. "Ma," he says again, full-voiced. Then he lifts his tongue, positions it between his teeth like Kenzie does, and sucks it back. "Foo," it says.

Mish drops down one step. He tries again. "Ma. Foo." One more step, and he tries it quick, all run together, a little spit flying, "Ma-foo."

He blows out his breath, knocks his head gently against the wall, and descends another step. And this time he doesn't even try. He just opens his mouth. *Matthew.*

He stops. Not quite believing, he tries again. *Matthew.* Although his ear still doubts, his mind hears it clear. *Matthew*, he practices in his head. *Matthew. Matthew*, once for each cold stair, until he steps into the room where all his men wait.

Craft Questions

- How does Pancake's use of the close third person impact the story?
- What do we learn about Mish through his speech and actions? About his father? What remains mysterious?
- How would the story be different if it were told from the father's point of view?

Exercises

Exercise 1: Whose Story Is It?

Expand upon one of your notebook free writing exercises or look back over a piece of writing on which you are currently working, and try switching the point-of-view from first person to third person omniscient or vice versa. Get far enough along in each version to see which one you prefer.

Objective: To try out more than one viewpoint to get an intuitive sense of which one works better for a particular story, before getting too far along.

Exercise 2: Working with the Second Person

Write about a situation in which you were badly stressed, and address a specific you.

Or:

Write about the situation in the second person, keeping in mind that you're trying to make your reader identify with and become you.

Objective: To experiment with two different uses of second-person point-of-view to see how this viewpoint can impact narrative voice.

Exercise 3: Whom Can We Believe?

Imagine this situation: You are walking down a dark street at night and you are mugged—a person demands your money, then knocks you to the ground before running away.

Tell the account from the perspective of two of the following characters, using a first-person narrator each time. One of the narrators is reliable, and the other one is not.

The victim (you)
The mugger
A police officer
Your therapist

Objective: To experience the impact of the narrator, in general, and to try your hand at writing from the perspective of an unreliable narrator, in particular.

twelve characterization

getting to know you

We humans are inherently social creatures. Even the most reclusive of us spend a great deal of our time with others: interacting with family, forming friendships, falling in love, admiring, desiring, and critiquing those around us, and so on. Not surprisingly, as readers we're instantly drawn to the characters that populate stories: what they're up to, what makes them tick, their motivations, conflicts, frustrations, goals, and actions. So, as you consider ways to bring your stories to life, it's essential that you develop your characters in as much detail as possible. Getting to know your characters, so that they become real to *you*, will help to ensure that they become real to *us*, your readers, even if every detail you conjure doesn't ultimately end up in your story.

In addition, by using your life experience and imagination to fully develop your characters, you can often determine some of your story's plot. For example, if two characters with very different personalities meet and fall in love, you can be sure that there will be some lines of tension, some twists and turns, along the way, not to mention the internal tension these differences may bring up for each character. Will they stay together, break up, or find some way of resolving, or even thriving, on their differences?

What will they learn about each other and themselves in the process? Are they really more alike, in the end, than their superficial differences at first suggest? Depending on your answers to these questions, you have the makings of several different story arcs or plotlines.

Round and Flat Characters

To develop truly **round** characters with many different aspects for your reader to experience, it's helpful to begin by thinking of people you know. In the end, however, there is a sleight of hand involved in giving your reader the sense that they are actually getting to know your characters in real time, as real people. If you simply record all you know of a person in paragraphs of description, your story will drag and fall flat. On the other hand, consider how we get to know people in real life. For example, imagine that you're at a party and you walk up to an interesting stranger. How do you first get to know them? Probably by how they look, talk, and act, and by asking questions to elicit more information. Similarly, *physical traits*, *action*, and *dialogue* are our first clues to character. So, although you, as writer, may already know everything there is to know about your characters, assume that your reader is just getting to know them, clue by clue.

Sometimes you'll purposely end up also using **flat** characters, or those that simply adhere to readers' expectations: for instance, the bartender who makes small-talk with your protagonist each week when he visits his neighborhood spot, or the annoying neighbors who are constantly using their leaf blower. These characters serve some purpose in the story, but are not fully developed, nor do they necessarily need to be. However, if you find that your main characters are falling into stereotypes—the troubled teen, the bitchy ex-girlfriend—you may want to rethink them, remembering to make them not only consistent, but complex and unique, so that they truly have a life of their own beyond familiar tropes.

Creating Consistent, Complex, Unique Characters

The most basic aspect of characterization involves *consistency*. Although it might be interesting to read a story where a normally honest, law-abiding character steals something from a convenience store, we're bound to feel confused if this inconsistency isn't in some way developed or explained. For example, maybe we later find out that the character was deprived as a child and maintained a sense of deprivation long after she was able to pay for the things she desired. So, while fiction writers are often engaged in creating an element of surprise, their characters need to adhere to some semblance of consistency for that surprise to take on meaning.

In addition, as we've discussed, the round characters you create need to possess some degree of *complexity* in order to hold your reader's interest. For example, if a character is difficult—plotting, selfish, demanding—we probably want to know what made them this way and what other qualities might offset this dominant trait. After all, people are very rarely all one thing or the other, and our contradictions are often what make us most interesting.

Again, jotting down character traits of the various people you know or whom you have encountered will help you avoid falling into the trap of using stock or cliché characters. As you write, work on revealing more than one trait or motivation, while keeping an eye on ways to bring those traits together into a coherent whole. One way of thinking about this process is through **lines of tension** or conflict, a topic we'll explore in greater depth in the following chapter. By developing both *internal* and *external* lines of tension, you'll create more complex, believable, compelling characters.

Dialogue

How do you and your closest friends speak to each other? Is there one of your friends who's usually the funniest? One who poses probing questions and really listens for answers? Is there a great storyteller in your crew? Do you and your friends often use slang in conversation? Do you curse? There's no reason to jettison whatever idiosyncrasies you notice in the speech of people around you when it comes to writing stories. In fact, it's a really good idea to get in the habit of recording (on paper or on your phone) the way that people talk (with their permission, of course). Your efforts in observation are bound to help you as you create **dialogue** or speech that sounds real. Even though **dialect**, which uses regional speech, can sometimes overwhelm a story, especially if you've altered spelling, working with diction and word order to incorporate elements of characters' identities is a wonderful way of bringing them to life.

Although there are always exceptions and experiments, the convention for most dialogue is to place it in quotation marks. And most writers indent each time a new speaker speaks. When the speech of a single character continues for more than one paragraph, use opening quotation marks at the beginning of each new paragraph, but no closing marks until the end of that character's speech. And although it may be tempting to vary your **dialogue tags** ("he said," "she said," or "they said"), it is less cumbersome for a reader if you keep them simple, instead of peppering your story with verbs such as "exclaim" and "retort." Similarly, you won't need to use many adverbs (e.g., "she said angrily") if your dialogue effectively communicates characters' emotions. In fact, if the speech of your characters is truly clear and distinct, you may be able to strategically dispense with dialogue tags altogether.

As you read the following short-short story by twentieth-century United States writer Ernest Hemingway (1899–1961), you'll see these methods in action. The voices of "Hills Like White Elephants" are so distinct that not only has Hemingway frequently dispensed with dialogue tags, but he's also managed to reveal most of the story's background, plot, and theme through the dialogue while hardly using any paragraphs of **exposition** (paragraphs that offer direct information). This is another thing that dialogue can do for your stories, even if they end up being less dialogue-heavy than Hemingway's: dialogue can move your stories along.

Hills Like White Elephants

The hills across the valley of the Ebro[1] were long and white. On this side there was no shade and no trees and the station was between two lines of rails in the sun. Close against the side of the station there was the warm shadow of the building and a curtain, made of strings of bamboo beads, hung across the open door into the bar, to keep out flies. The American and the girl with him sat at a table in the shade, outside the building. It was very hot and the express from Barcelona would come in forty minutes. It stopped at this junction for two minutes and went on to Madrid.

"What should we drink?" the girl asked. She had taken off her hat and put it on the table.

"It's pretty hot," the man said.

"Let's drink beer."

"Dos cervezas," the man said into the curtain.

"Big ones?" a woman asked from the doorway.

"Yes. Two big ones."

The woman brought two glasses of beer and two felt pads. She put the felt pads and the beer glasses on the table and looked at the man and the girl. The girl was looking off at the line of hills. They were white in the sun and the country was brown and dry.

"They look like white elephants," she said.

"I've never seen one," the man drank his beer.

"No, you wouldn't have."

"I might have," the man said. "Just because you say I wouldn't have doesn't prove anything."

The girl looked at the bead curtain. "They've painted something on it," she said. "What does it say?"

"Anis del Toro. It's a drink."

---

1 A river in Northern Spain.

"Could we try it?"

The man called "Listen" through the curtain. The woman came out from the bar.

"Four reales."[1]

"We want two Anis del Toro."

"With water?"

"Do you want it with water?"

"I don't know," the girl said. "Is it good with water?"

"It's all right."

"You want them with water?" asked the woman.

"Yes, with water."

"It tastes like licorice," the girl said and put the glass down.

"That's the way with everything."

"Yes," said the girl. "Everything tastes of licorice. Especially all the things you've waited so long for, like absinthe."

"Oh, cut it out."

"You started it," the girl said. "I was being amused. I was having a fine time."

"Well, let's try and have a fine time."

"All right. I was trying. I said the mountains looked like white elephants. Wasn't that bright?"

"That was bright."

"I wanted to try this new drink. That's all we do, isn't it—look at things and try new drinks?"

"I guess so."

The girl looked across at the hills.

"They're lovely hills," she said. "They don't really look like white elephants. I just meant the coloring of their skin through the trees."

"Should we have another drink?"

"All right."

The warm wind blew the bead curtain against the table.

"The beer's nice and cool," the man said.

"It's lovely," the girl said.

"It's really an awfully simple operation, Jig," the man said. "It's not really an operation at all."

The girl looked at the ground the table legs rested on.

"I know you wouldn't mind it, Jig. It's really not anything. It's just to let the air in." The girl did not say anything.

"I'll go with you and I'll stay with you all the time. They just let the air in and then it's all perfectly natural."

"Then what will we do afterward?"

---

1 Spanish coins.

"We'll be fine afterward. Just like we were before."

"What makes you think so?"

"That's the only thing that bothers us. It's the only thing that's made us unhappy."

The girl looked at the bead curtain, put her hand out and took hold of two of the strings of beads.

"And you think then we'll be all right and be happy."

"I know we will. You don't have to be afraid. I've known lots of people that have done it."

"So have I," said the girl. "And afterward they were all so happy."

"Well," the man said, "if you don't want to you don't have to. I wouldn't have you do it if you didn't want to. But I know it's perfectly simple."

"And you really want to?"

"I think it's the best thing to do. But I don't want you to do it if you don't really want to."

"And if I do it you'll be happy and things will be like they were and you'll love me?"

"I love you now. You know I love you."

"I know. But if I do it, then it will be nice again if I say things are like white elephants, and you'll like it?"

"I'll love it. I love it now but I just can't think about it. You know how I get when I worry."

"If I do it you won't ever worry?"

"I won't worry about that because it's perfectly simple."

"Then I'll do it. Because I don't care about me."

"What do you mean?"

"I don't care about me."

"Well, I care about you."

"Oh, yes. But I don't care about me. And I'll do it and then everything will be fine."

"I don't want you to do it if you feel that way."

The girl stood up and walked to the end of the station. Across, on the other side, were fields of grain and trees along the banks of the Ebro. Faraway, beyond the river, were mountains. The shadow of a cloud moved across the field of grain and she saw the river through the trees.

"And we could have all this," she said. "And we could have everything and every day we make it more impossible."

"What did you say?"

"I said we could have everything."

"We can have everything."

"No, we can't."

"We can have the whole world."

"No, we can't."

"We can go everywhere."

"No, we can't. It isn't ours any more."

"It's ours."

"No, it isn't. And once they take it away, you never get it back."

"But they haven't taken it away."

"We'll wait and see."

"Come on back in the shade," he said. "You mustn't feel that way."

"I don't feel any way," the girl said. "I just know things."

"I don't want you to do anything that you don't want to do—"

"Nor that isn't good for me," she said. "I know. Could we have another beer?"

"All right. But you've got to realize—"

"I realize," the girl said. "Can't we maybe stop talking?"

They sat down at the table and the girl looked across at the hills on the dry side of the valley and the man looked at her and at the table.

"You've got to realize," he said, "that I don't want you to do it if you don't want to. I'm perfectly willing to go through with it if it means anything to you."

"Doesn't it mean anything to you? We could get along."

"Of course it does. But I don't want anybody but you. I don't want anyone else. And I know it's perfectly simple."

"Yes, you know it's perfectly simple."

"It's all right for you to say that, but I do know it."

"Would you do something for me now?"

"I'd do anything for you."

"Would you please please please please please please please stop talking?"

He did not say anything but looked at the bags against the wall of the station. There were labels on them from all the hotels where they had spent nights.

"But I don't want you to," he said, "I don't care anything about it."

"I'll scream," the girl said.

The woman came out through the curtains with two glasses of beer and put them down on the damp felt pads. "The train comes in five minutes," she said.

"What did she say?" asked the girl.

"That the train is coming in five minutes."

The girl smiled brightly at the woman, to thank her.

"I'd better take the bags over to the other side of the station," the man said. She smiled at him.

"All right. Then come back and we'll finish the beer."

He picked up the two heavy bags and carried them around the station to the other tracks. He looked up the tracks but could not see the train. Coming back, he walked through the barroom, where people waiting for the train were drinking. He drank an Anis at the bar and looked at the people. They were all waiting reasonably for the train. He went out through the bead curtain. She was sitting at the table and smiled at him.

"Do you feel better?" he asked.

"I feel fine," she said. "There's nothing wrong with me. I feel fine."

Craft Questions

- What do we learn about the two characters through how they speak?
- What are they arguing about?
- How is tension built up?
- Is there a climax? A resolution?
- Critics have disagreed on whether or not the story can be considered feminist? What's your opinion?

To round out our discussion of dialogue, be aware of situations in which dialogue should *not* be used. If it's not helping to advance your characterization, but merely summarizing minor plot points, you may be best off transforming it into paraphrase. For example, take the following passage of dialogue:

> "Joe, let's go to the party."
> "Ok."
> "I'll drive. I have a new convertible."
> "Great."

And try this instead:

> With an air of excitement, Emily suggested to Joe that they leave for the party in her new convertible.

In addition, detailed information and lengthy but uninteresting conversations are often best paraphrased. For instance, a character might mention how hot it is one afternoon, but be less likely to say it's 97 degrees at 2:15. Or two characters might be discussing what they should do to make ends meet, but you could just as well describe the conversation: "they sat at the kitchen table for hours, discussing whether they could get new jobs or sell one of their cars." In general, keep your dialogue lively and engaging. And Hemingway aside, when you're first starting to write stories, try for a balance between dialogue, thoughts, and actions.

Thoughts

So much of our life is spent in thought. So, if you want your stories to be realistic and multi-layered, you'll surely want to include some of what your characters are thinking. There are several effective ways to do this. But before we get into the nitty gritty, spend some time considering your own thought processes and doing some stream-of-consciousness writing. A simple way of doing this is to set a timer for five to seven minutes and start writing whatever thoughts come to mind without stopping, reading over, or critiquing what you've written. Most likely, you'll find that your natural thoughts are pretty unstructured. And it's unlikely that you've spent time thinking about basic facts such as, "I'm a twenty-year-old college student taking a creative writing class." Why is this important to observe? Just as recording how people actually speak prepares you to write realistic dialogue, considering how you (and others) actually think prepares you for including realistic thoughts in your stories.

Most of the time, thoughts included in stories are not placed in quotation marks or in italics. In some cases, there is a signal phrase, such as "she thought" or "he felt" to indicate what's happening, and in other cases, the fact that the passage is thought is merely implied. For instance, compare these two passages from Andre Dubus's, "The Intruder," included in chapter 10:

> He suddenly felt as if he had told a lie. He was looking at his face and, as he did several times each day, telling himself, without words, that it was a handsome face.

> Afterward, it seemed that the events of a year had occurred in an hour and, to Kenneth, even that hour seemed to have a quality of neither speed nor slowness, but a kind of suspension, as if time were not passing at all.

In both cases, we're in Kenneth's mind. However, whereas the verb *felt* and the phrase *telling himself* indicate this fact in the first passage, the third person limited narration is enough of an indicator in the second. In fact, throughout his story, Dubus immerses us in various levels of Kenneth's thought: from thoughts and memories to the voices he hears within the imaginary world he's created. By re-reading "The Intruder" and the other stories collected in this text, you'll gain a better understanding of the multiple possibilities for including characters' thoughts in your own work.

Actions

How characters act, individually and in relation to one another, is another major factor involved in characterization. Not only do the little gestures—the nervous ticks, facial expressions and postures—show us how a character feels, the actions in which they engage clue us into characters' habits, psychology, and motives. For examples, think back on some of the stories we've explored so far. First, again consider Dubus's characterization of Kenneth in "The Intruder." In particular, take a look back on this scene:

> He went to his room and picked up his rifle, then he saw the magazine on the chest of drawers and he leaned the rifle in the corner again. Suddenly his mouth was dry. He got the magazine and quickly turned the pages until he found her: she was stepping out of the surf on the French Riviera, laughing, as if the man with her had just said something funny. She was blonde and very tan and she wore a bikini. The photograph was in color. For several moments he looked at it, then he got the rifle and cleaning kit and sat in the rocking chair in the living room, with the rifle across his lap. He put a patch on the cleaning rod and dipped it in bore cleaner and pushed it down the barrel, the handle of the rod clanging against the muzzle. He worked slowly, pausing often to listen for Douglas's car, because he wanted to be cleaning the rifle when Douglas came. Because Douglas was a tackle on the high school football team in the town, and Kenneth had never been on a football team, and never would be.

Craft Questions

- What do Kenneth's actions in this scene suggest about his psychological state of mind: his desires, obsessions, and anxieties?
- How might this scene, in particular, foreshadow what's to come?

On a different note, consider two brief passages from Hemingway's "Hills Like White Elephants." First, Hemingway *shows* us that the two characters have been traveling for some time together:

> He did not say anything but looked at the bags against the wall of the station. There were labels on them from all the hotels where they had spent nights.

Several paragraphs later, Hemingway writes:

> He picked up the two heavy bags and carried them around the station to the other tracks.

Craft Question

- From "looked at" to "picked up," Hemingway spends a comparatively long time describing the seemingly mundane action of tending to travel bags. What might the bags symbolically imply?

Regardless of the level of detail and thematic depth, both Dubus and Hemingway deliver information about the characters' personalities and relationships with each other through action. Rather than *telling* us about internal and external conflicts, both writers bring those conflicts to life through the characters' actions in the world around them.

Ultimately, it's the combination of dialogue, thoughts, and action that creates unique, realistic characters. And although we've looked at each of these aspects separately, as you write, you're likely to forget about these guidelines if you're truly engaged in the world you're creating. In revision, however, you may want to play around with altering the balance between these various modes to see what happens. For example, if you've created a story with very little dialogue, ask yourself if this lack is an important aspect of the story, or whether the story may actually benefit from the addition of characters' voices. As always, there's no real rule; you have to play around with different options to determine what works, and getting feedback from your professor and peers is often very helpful as you ask yourself these questions. Most importantly, have fun! If you become obsessed with developing your characters, you're likely on the right track.

Reading

Sherman Alexie (b. 1966)
What You Pawn I Will Redeem

Noon

One day you have a home and the next you don't, but I'm not going to tell you my particular reasons for being homeless, because it's my secret story, and Indians have to work hard to keep secrets from hungry white folks.

I'm a Spokane Indian boy, an Interior Salish, and my people have lived within a hundred-mile radius of Spokane, Washington, for at least ten thousand years. I grew up in Spokane, moved to Seattle twenty-three years ago for college, flunked out after two semesters, worked various blue- and bluer-collar jobs, married two or three times, fathered two or three kids, and then went crazy. Of course, crazy is not the official definition of my mental problem, but I don't think asocial disorder fits it, either, because that makes me sound like I'm a serial killer or something. I've never hurt another human being, or, at least, not physically. I've broken a few hearts in my time, but we've all done that, so I'm nothing special in that regard. I'm a boring heartbreaker, too. I never dated or married more than one woman at a time. I didn't break hearts into pieces overnight. I broke them slowly and carefully. And I didn't set any land-speed records running out the door. Piece by piece, I disappeared. I've been disappearing ever since.

I've been homeless for six years now. If there's such a thing as an effective homeless man, then I suppose I'm effective. Being homeless is probably the only thing I've ever been good at. I know where to get the best free food. I've made friends with restaurant and convenience-store managers who let me use their bathrooms. And I don't mean the public bathrooms, either. I mean the employees' bathrooms, the clean ones hidden behind the kitchen or the pantry or the cooler. I know it sounds strange to be proud of this, but it means a lot to me, being trustworthy enough to piss in somebody else's clean bathroom. Maybe you don't understand the value of a clean bathroom, but I do.

Probably none of this interests you. Homeless Indians are everywhere in Seattle. We're common and boring, and you walk right on by us, with maybe a look of anger or disgust or even sadness at the terrible fate of the noble savage. But we have dreams and families. I'm friends with a homeless Plains Indian man whose son is the editor of a big-time newspaper back East. Of course, that's his story, but we Indians are great storytellers and liars and mythmakers, so maybe that Plains Indian hobo is just a plain old everyday Indian. I'm kind of suspicious of him, because he identifies himself only as Plains Indian, a generic term, and not by a specific tribe. When I asked him why he wouldn't tell me exactly what he is, he said, "Do any of us know exactly what we are?" Yeah, great, a philosophizing Indian. "Hey," I said, "you got to have a home to be that homely." He just laughed and flipped me the eagle and walked away.

I wander the streets with a regular crew—my teammates, my defenders, my posse. It's Rose of Sharon, Junior, and me. We matter to one another if we don't matter to anybody else. Rose of Sharon is a big woman, about seven feet tall if you're measuring over-all effect and about five feet tall if you're only talking about the physical. She's a Yakama Indian of the Wishram variety. Junior is a Colville, but there are about 199 tribes that make up the Colville, so he could be anything. He's good-looking, though, like he just stepped out of some "Don't Litter the Earth" public-service advertisement.

He's got those great big cheekbones that are like planets, you know, with little moons orbiting them. He gets me jealous, jealous, and jealous. If you put Junior and me next to each other, he's the Before Columbus Arrived Indian and I'm the After Columbus Arrived Indian. I am living proof of the horrible damage that colonialism has done to us Skins. But I'm not going to let you know how scared I sometimes get of history and its ways. I'm a strong man, and I know that silence is the best method of dealing with white folks.

This whole story really started at lunchtime, when Rose of Sharon, Junior, and I were panning the handle down at Pike Place Market. After about two hours of negotiating, we earned five dollars—good enough for a bottle of fortified courage from the most beautiful 7-Eleven in the world. So we headed over that way, feeling like warrior drunks, and we walked past this pawnshop I'd never noticed before. And that was strange, because we Indians have built-in pawnshop radar. But the strangest thing of all was the old powwow-dance regalia I saw hanging in the window.

"That's my grandmother's regalia," I said to Rose of Sharon and Junior.

"How you know for sure?" Junior asked.

I didn't know for sure, because I hadn't seen that regalia in person ever. I'd only seen photographs of my grandmother dancing in it. And those were taken before somebody stole it from her, fifty years ago. But it sure looked like my memory of it, and it had all the same color feathers and beads that my family sewed into our powwow regalia.

"There's only one way to know for sure," I said.

So Rose of Sharon, Junior, and I walked into the pawnshop and greeted the old white man working behind the counter.

"How can I help you?" he asked.

"That's my grandmother's powwow regalia in your window," I said. "Somebody stole it from her fifty years ago, and my family has been searching for it ever since."

The pawnbroker looked at me like I was a liar. I understood. Pawnshops are filled with liars.

"I'm not lying," I said. "Ask my friends here. They'll tell you."

"He's the most honest Indian I know," Rose of Sharon said.

"All right, honest Indian," the pawnbroker said. "I'll give you the benefit of the doubt. Can you prove it's your grandmother's regalia?"

Because they don't want to be perfect, because only God is perfect, Indian people sew flaws into their powwow regalia. My family always sewed one yellow bead somewhere on our regalia. But we always hid it so that you had to search really hard to find it.

"If it really is my grandmother's," I said, "there will be one yellow bead hidden somewhere on it."

"All right, then," the pawnbroker said. "Let's take a look."

He pulled the regalia out of the window, laid it down on the glass counter, and we searched for that yellow bead and found it hidden beneath the armpit.

"There it is," the pawnbroker said. He didn't sound surprised. "You were right. This is your grandmother's regalia."

"It's been missing for fifty years," Junior said.

"Hey, Junior," I said. "It's my family's story. Let me tell it."

"All right," he said. "I apologize. You go ahead."

"It's been missing for fifty years," I said.

"That's his family's sad story," Rose of Sharon said. "Are you going to give it back to him?"

"That would be the right thing to do," the pawnbroker said. "But I can't afford to do the right thing. I paid a thousand dollars for this. I can't just give away a thousand dollars."

"We could go to the cops and tell them it was stolen," Rose of Sharon said.

"Hey," I said to her. "Don't go threatening people."

The pawnbroker sighed. He was thinking about the possibilities.

"Well, I suppose you could go to the cops," he said. "But I don't think they'd believe a word you said."

He sounded sad about that. As if he was sorry for taking advantage of our disadvantages.

"What's your name?" the pawnbroker asked me.

"Jackson," I said.

"Is that first or last?"

"Both," I said.

"Are you serious?"

"Yes, it's true. My mother and father named me Jackson Jackson. My family nickname is Jackson Squared. My family is funny."

"All right, Jackson Jackson," the pawnbroker said. "You wouldn't happen to have a thousand dollars, would you?"

"We've got five dollars total," I said.

"That's too bad," he said, and thought hard about the possibilities. "I'd sell it to you for a thousand dollars if you had it. Heck, to make it fair, I'd sell it to you for nine hundred and ninety-nine dollars. I'd lose a dollar. That would be the moral thing to do in this case. To lose a dollar would be the right thing."

"We've got five dollars total," I said again.

"That's too bad," he said once more, and thought harder about the possibilities. "How about this? I'll give you twenty-four hours to come up with nine hundred and ninety-nine dollars. You come back here at lunchtime tomorrow with the money and I'll sell it back to you. How does that sound?"

"It sounds all right," I said.

"All right, then," he said. "We have a deal. And I'll get you started. Here's twenty bucks."

He opened up his wallet and pulled out a crisp twenty-dollar bill and gave it to me. And Rose of Sharon, Junior, and I walked out into the daylight to search for nine hundred and seventy-four more dollars.

1 P.M.

Rose of Sharon, Junior, and I carried our twenty-dollar bill and our five dollars in loose change over to the 7-Eleven and bought three bottles of imagination. We needed to figure out how to raise all that money in only one day. Thinking hard, we huddled in an alley beneath the Alaska Way Viaduct and finished off those bottles—one, two, and three.

2 P.M.

Rose of Sharon was gone when I woke up. I heard later that she had hitchhiked back to Toppenish and was living with her sister on the reservation.

Junior had passed out beside me and was covered in his own vomit, or maybe somebody else's vomit, and my head hurt from thinking, so I left him alone and walked down to the water. I love the smell of ocean water. Salt always smells like memory.

When I got to the wharf, I ran into three Aleut cousins, who sat on a wooden bench and stared out at the bay and cried. Most of the homeless Indians in Seattle come from Alaska. One by one, each of them hopped a big working boat in Anchorage or Barrow or Juneau, fished his way south to Seattle, jumped off the boat with a pocketful of cash to party hard at one of the highly sacred and traditional Indian bars, went broke and broker, and has been trying to find his way back to the boat and the frozen North ever since.

These Aleuts smelled like salmon, I thought, and they told me they were going to sit on that wooden bench until their boat came back.

"How long has your boat been gone?" I asked.

"Eleven years," the elder Aleut said.

I cried with them for a while.

"Hey," I said. "Do you guys have any money I can borrow?"

They didn't.

3 P.M.

I walked back to Junior. He was still out cold. I put my face down near his mouth to make sure he was breathing. He was alive, so I dug around in his bluejeans pockets and found half a cigarette. I smoked it all the way down and thought about my grandmother.

Her name was Agnes, and she died of breast cancer when I was fourteen. My father always thought Agnes caught her tumors from the uranium mine on the reservation. But my mother said the disease started when Agnes was walking back from a powwow one night and got run over by a motorcycle. She broke three ribs, and my mother always said those ribs never healed right, and tumors take over when you don't heal right.

Sitting beside Junior, smelling the smoke and the salt and the vomit, I wondered if my grandmother's cancer started when somebody stole her powwow regalia. Maybe the cancer started in her broken heart and then leaked out into her breasts. I know it's crazy, but I wondered whether I could bring my grandmother back to life if I bought back her regalia.

I needed money, big money, so I left Junior and walked over to the Real Change office.

4 P.M.

Real Change is a multifaceted organization that publishes a newspaper, supports cultural projects that empower the poor and the homeless, and mobilizes the public around poverty issues. Real Change's mission is to organize, educate, and build alliances to create solutions to homelessness and poverty. It exists to provide a voice for poor people in our community.

I memorized Real Change's mission statement because I sometimes sell the newspaper on the streets. But you have to stay sober to sell it, and I'm not always good at staying sober. Anybody can sell the paper. You buy each copy for thirty cents and sell it for a dollar, and you keep the profit.

"I need one thousand four hundred and thirty papers," I said to the Big Boss.

"That's a strange number," he said. "And that's a lot of papers."

"I need them."

The Big Boss pulled out his calculator and did the math.

"It will cost you four hundred and twenty-nine dollars for that many," he said.

"If I had that kind of money, I wouldn't need to sell the papers."

"What's going on, Jackson-to-the-Second-Power?" he asked. He is the only person who calls me that. He's a funny and kind man.

I told him about my grandmother's powwow regalia and how much money I needed in order to buy it back.

"We should call the police," he said.

"I don't want to do that," I said. "It's a quest now. I need to win it back by myself."

"I understand," he said. "And, to be honest, I'd give you the papers to sell if I thought it would work. But the record for the most papers sold in one day by one vender is only three hundred and two."

"That would net me about two hundred bucks," I said.

The Big Boss used his calculator. "Two hundred and eleven dollars and forty cents," he said.

"That's not enough," I said.

"And the most money anybody has made in one day is five hundred and twenty-five. And that's because somebody gave Old Blue five hundred-dollar bills for some dang reason. The average daily net is about thirty dollars."

"This isn't going to work."

"No."

"Can you lend me some money?"

"I can't do that," he said. "If I lend you money, I have to lend money to everybody."

"What can you do?"

"I'll give you fifty papers for free. But don't tell anybody I did it."

"O.K.," I said.

He gathered up the newspapers and handed them to me. I held them to my chest. He hugged me. I carried the newspapers back toward the water.

5 P.M.

Back on the wharf, I stood near the Bainbridge Island Terminal and tried to sell papers to business commuters boarding the ferry.

I sold five in one hour, dumped the other forty-five in a garbage can, and walked into McDonald's, ordered four cheeseburgers for a dollar each, and slowly ate them.

After eating, I walked outside and vomited on the sidewalk. I hated to lose my food so soon after eating it. As an alcoholic Indian with a busted stomach, I always hope I can keep enough food in me to stay alive.

6 P.M.

With one dollar in my pocket, I walked back to Junior. He was still passed out, and I put my ear to his chest and listened for his heartbeat. He was alive, so I took off his shoes and socks and found one dollar in his left sock and fifty cents in his right sock.

With two dollars and fifty cents in my hand, I sat beside Junior and thought about my grandmother and her stories.

When I was thirteen, my grandmother told me a story about the Second World War. She was a nurse at a military hospital in Sydney, Australia. For two years, she healed and comforted American and Australian soldiers.

One day, she tended to a wounded Maori soldier, who had lost his legs to an artillery attack. He was very dark-skinned. His hair was black and curly and his eyes were black and warm. His face was covered with bright tattoos.

"Are you Maori?" he asked my grandmother.

"No," she said. "I'm Spokane Indian. From the United States."

"Ah, yes," he said. "I have heard of your tribes. But you are the first American Indian I have ever met."

"There's a lot of Indian soldiers fighting for the United States," she said. "I have a brother fighting in Germany, and I lost another brother on Okinawa."

"I am sorry," he said. "I was on Okinawa as well. It was terrible."

"I am sorry about your legs," my grandmother said.

"It's funny, isn't it?" he said.

"What's funny?"

"How we brown people are killing other brown people so white people will remain free."

"I hadn't thought of it that way."

"Well, sometimes I think of it that way. And other times I think of it the way they want me to think of it. I get confused."

She fed him morphine.

"Do you believe in Heaven?" he asked.

"Which Heaven?" she asked.

"I'm talking about the Heaven where my legs are waiting for me."

They laughed.

"Of course," he said, "my legs will probably run away from me when I get to Heaven. And how will I ever catch them?"

"You have to get your arms strong," my grandmother said. "So you can run on your hands."

They laughed again.

Sitting beside Junior, I laughed at the memory of my grandmother's story. I put my hand close to Junior's mouth to make sure he was still breathing. Yes, Junior was alive, so I took my two dollars and fifty cents and walked to the Korean grocery store in Pioneer Square.

7 P.M.

At the Korean grocery store, I bought a fifty-cent cigar and two scratch lottery tickets for a dollar each. The maximum cash prize was five hundred dollars a ticket. If I won both, I would have enough money to buy back the regalia.

I loved Mary, the young Korean woman who worked the register. She was the daughter of the owners, and she sang all day.

"I love you," I said when I handed her the money.

"You always say you love me," she said.

"That's because I will always love you."

"You are a sentimental fool."

"I'm a romantic old man."

"Too old for me."

"I know I'm too old for you, but I can dream."

"O.K.," she said. "I agree to be a part of your dreams, but I will only hold your hand in your dreams. No kissing and no sex. Not even in your dreams."

"O.K.," I said. "No sex. Just romance."

"Goodbye, Jackson Jackson, my love. I will see you soon."

I left the store, walked over to Occidental Park, sat on a bench, and smoked my cigar all the way down.

Ten minutes after I finished the cigar, I scratched my first lottery ticket and won nothing. I could win only five hundred dollars now, and that would be only half of what I needed.

Ten minutes after I lost, I scratched the other ticket and won a free ticket—a small consolation and one more chance to win some money.

I walked back to Mary.

"Jackson Jackson," she said. "Have you come back to claim my heart?"

"I won a free ticket," I said.

"Just like a man," she said. "You love money and power more than you love me."

"It's true," I said. "And I'm sorry it's true."

She gave me another scratch ticket, and I took it outside. I like to scratch my tickets in private. Hopeful and sad, I scratched that third ticket and won real money. I carried it back inside to Mary.

"I won a hundred dollars," I said.

She examined the ticket and laughed.

"That's a fortune," she said, and counted out five twenties. Our fingertips touched as she handed me the money. I felt electric and constant.

"Thank you," I said, and gave her one of the bills.

"I can't take that," she said. "It's your money."

"No, it's tribal. It's an Indian thing. When you win, you're supposed to share with your family."

"I'm not your family."

"Yes, you are."

She smiled. She kept the money. With eighty dollars in my pocket, I said goodbye to my dear Mary and walked out into the cold night air.

8 P.M.

I wanted to share the good news with Junior. I walked back to him, but he was gone. I heard later that he had hitchhiked down to Portland, Oregon, and died of exposure in an alley behind the Hilton Hotel.

9 P.M.

Lonesome for Indians, I carried my eighty dollars over to Big Heart's in South Downtown. Big Heart's is an all-Indian bar. Nobody knows how or why Indians migrate to one bar and turn it into an official Indian bar. But Big Heart's has been an Indian bar for twenty-three years. It used to be way up on Aurora Avenue, but a crazy Lummi Indian burned that one down, and the owners moved to the new location, a few blocks south of Safeco Field.

I walked into Big Heart's and counted fifteen Indians—eight men and seven women. I didn't know any of them, but Indians like to belong, so we all pretended to be cousins.

"How much for whiskey shots?" I asked the bartender, a fat white guy.

"You want the bad stuff or the badder stuff?"

"As bad as you got."

"One dollar a shot."

I laid my eighty dollars on the bar top.

"All right," I said. "Me and all my cousins here are going to be drinking eighty shots. How many is that apiece?"

"Counting you," a woman shouted from behind me, "that's five shots for everybody."

I turned to look at her. She was a chubby and pale Indian woman, sitting with a tall and skinny Indian man.

"All right, math genius," I said to her, and then shouted for the whole bar to hear. "Five drinks for everybody!"

All the other Indians rushed the bar, but I sat with the mathematician and her skinny friend. We took our time with our whiskey shots.

"What's your tribe?" I asked.

"I'm Duwamish," she said. "And he's Crow."

"You're a long way from Montana," I said to him.

"I'm Crow," he said. "I flew here."

"What's your name?" I asked them.

"I'm Irene Muse," she said. "And this is Honey Boy."

She shook my hand hard, but he offered his hand as if I was supposed to kiss it. So I did. He giggled and blushed, as much as a dark-skinned Crow can blush.

"You're one of them two-spirits, aren't you?" I asked him.

"I love women," he said. "And I love men."

"Sometimes both at the same time," Irene said.

We laughed.

"Man," I said to Honey Boy. "So you must have about eight or nine spirits going on inside you, enit?"

"Sweetie," he said. "I'll be whatever you want me to be."

"Oh, no," Irene said. "Honey Boy is falling in love."

"It has nothing to do with love," he said.

We laughed.

"Wow," I said. "I'm flattered, Honey Boy, but I don't play on your team."

"Never say never," he said.

"You better be careful," Irene said. "Honey Boy knows all sorts of magic."

"Honey Boy," I said, "you can try to seduce me, but my heart belongs to a woman named Mary."

"Is your Mary a virgin?" Honey Boy asked.

We laughed.

And we drank our whiskey shots until they were gone. But the other Indians bought me more whiskey shots, because I'd been so generous with my money. And Honey Boy pulled out his credit card, and I drank and sailed on that plastic boat.

After a dozen shots, I asked Irene to dance. She refused. But Honey Boy shuffled over to the jukebox, dropped in a quarter, and selected Willie Nelson's "Help Me Make It Through the Night." As Irene and I sat at the table and laughed and drank more whiskey, Honey Boy danced a slow circle around us and sang along with Willie.

"Are you serenading me?" I asked him.

He kept singing and dancing.

"Are you serenading me?" I asked him again.

"He's going to put a spell on you," Irene said.

I leaned over the table, spilling a few drinks, and kissed Irene hard. She kissed me back.

10 P.M.

Irene pushed me into the women's bathroom, into a stall, shut the door behind us, and shoved her hand down my pants. She was short, so I had to lean over to kiss her. I grabbed and squeezed her everywhere I could reach, and she was wonderfully fat, and every part of her body felt like a large, warm, soft breast.

Midnight

Nearly blind with alcohol, I stood alone at the bar and swore I had been standing in the bathroom with Irene only a minute ago.

"One more shot!" I yelled at the bartender.

"You've got no more money!" he yelled back.

"Somebody buy me a drink!" I shouted.

"They've got no more money!"

"Where are Irene and Honey Boy?"

"Long gone!"

2 A.M.

"Closing time!" the bartender shouted at the three or four Indians who were still drinking hard after a long, hard day of drinking. Indian alcoholics are either sprinters or marathoners.

"Where are Irene and Honey Boy?" I asked.

"They've been gone for hours," the bartender said.

"Where'd they go?"

"I told you a hundred times, I don't know."

"What am I supposed to do?"

"It's closing time. I don't care where you go, but you're not staying here."

"You are an ungrateful bastard. I've been good to you."

"You don't leave right now, I'm going to kick your ass."

"Come on, I know how to fight."

He came at me. I don't remember what happened after that.

4 A.M.

I emerged from the blackness and discovered myself walking behind a big warehouse. I didn't know where I was. My face hurt. I felt my nose and decided that it might be broken. Exhausted and cold, I pulled a plastic tarp from a truck bed, wrapped it around me like a faithful lover, and fell asleep in the dirt.

6 A.M.

Somebody kicked me in the ribs. I opened my eyes and looked up at a white cop.

"Jackson," the cop said. "Is that you?"

"Officer Williams," I said. He was a good cop with a sweet tooth. He'd given me hundreds of candy bars over the years. I wonder if he knew I was diabetic.

"What the hell are you doing here?" he asked.

"I was cold and sleepy," I said. "So I lay down."

"You dumb-ass, you passed out on the railroad tracks."

I sat up and looked around. I was lying on the railroad tracks. Dockworkers stared at me. I should have been a railroad-track pizza, a double Indian pepperoni with extra cheese. Sick and scared, I leaned over and puked whiskey.

"What the hell's wrong with you?" Officer Williams asked. "You've never been this stupid."

"It's my grandmother," I said. "She died."

"I'm sorry, man. When did she die?"

"Nineteen seventy-two."

"And you're killing yourself now?"

"I've been killing myself ever since she died."

He shook his head. He was sad for me. Like I said, he was a good cop.

"And somebody beat the hell out of you," he said. "You remember who?"

"Mr. Grief and I went a few rounds."

"It looks like Mr. Grief knocked you out."

"Mr. Grief always wins."

"Come on," he said. "Let's get you out of here."

He helped me up and led me over to his squad car. He put me in the back. "You throw up in there and you're cleaning it up," he said.

"That's fair."

He walked around the car and sat in the driver's seat. "I'm taking you over to detox," he said.

"No, man, that place is awful," I said. "It's full of drunk Indians."

We laughed. He drove away from the docks.

"I don't know how you guys do it," he said.

"What guys?" I asked.

"You Indians. How the hell do you laugh so much? I just picked your ass off the railroad tracks, and you're making jokes. Why the hell do you do that?"

"The two funniest tribes I've ever been around are Indians and Jews, so I guess that says something about the inherent humor of genocide."

We laughed.

"Listen to you, Jackson. You're so smart. Why the hell are you on the street?"

"Give me a thousand dollars and I'll tell you."

"You bet I'd give you a thousand dollars if I knew you'd straighten up your life."

He meant it. He was the second-best cop I'd ever known.

"You're a good cop," I said.

"Come on, Jackson," he said. "Don't blow smoke up my ass."

"No, really, you remind me of my grandfather."

"Yeah, that's what you Indians always tell me."

"No, man, my grandfather was a tribal cop. He was a good cop. He never arrested people. He took care of them. Just like you."

"I've arrested hundreds of scumbags, Jackson. And I've shot a couple in the ass."

"It don't matter. You're not a killer."

"I didn't kill them. I killed their asses. I'm an ass-killer."

We drove through downtown. The missions and shelters had already released their overnighters. Sleepy homeless men and women stood on street corners and stared up at a gray sky. It was the morning after the night of the living dead.

"Do you ever get scared?" I asked Officer Williams.

"What do you mean?"

"I mean, being a cop, is it scary?"

He thought about that for a while. He contemplated it. I liked that about him.

"I guess I try not to think too much about being afraid," he said. "If you think about fear, then you'll be afraid. The job is boring most of the time. Just driving and looking into dark corners, you know, and seeing nothing. But then things get heavy. You're chasing somebody, or fighting them or walking around a dark house, and you just know some crazy guy is hiding around a corner, and hell, yes, it's scary."

"My grandfather was killed in the line of duty," I said.

"I'm sorry. How'd it happen?"

I knew he'd listen closely to my story.

"He worked on the reservation. Everybody knew everybody. It was safe. We aren't like those crazy Sioux or Apache or any of those other warrior tribes. There've only been three murders on my reservation in the last hundred years."

"That is safe."

"Yeah, we Spokane, we're passive, you know. We're mean with words. And we'll cuss out anybody. But we don't shoot people. Or stab them. Not much, anyway."

"So what happened to your grandfather?"

"This man and his girlfriend were fighting down by Little Falls."

"Domestic dispute. Those are the worst."

"Yeah, but this guy was my grandfather's brother. My great-uncle."

"Oh, no."

"Yeah, it was awful. My grandfather just strolled into the house. He'd been there a thousand times. And his brother and his girlfriend were drunk and beating on each other. And my grandfather stepped between them, just as he'd done a hundred times before. And the girlfriend tripped or something. She fell down and hit her head and started crying. And my grandfather kneeled down beside her to make sure she was all right. And for some reason my great-uncle reached down, pulled my grandfather's pistol out of the holster, and shot him in the head."

"That's terrible. I'm sorry."

"Yeah, my great-uncle could never figure out why he did it. He went to prison forever, you know, and he always wrote these long letters. Like fifty pages of tiny little handwriting. And he was always trying to figure out why he did it. He'd write and write and write and try to figure it out. He never did. It's a great big mystery."

"Do you remember your grandfather?"

"A little bit. I remember the funeral. My grandmother wouldn't let them bury him. My father had to drag her away from the grave."

"I don't know what to say."

"I don't, either."

We stopped in front of the detox center.

"We're here," Officer Williams said.

"I can't go in there," I said.

"You have to."

"Please, no. They'll keep me for twenty-four hours. And then it will be too late."

"Too late for what?"

I told him about my grandmother's regalia and the deadline for buying it back.

"If it was stolen, you need to file a report," he said. "I'll investigate it myself. If that thing is really your grandmother's, I'll get it back for you. Legally."

"No," I said. "That's not fair. The pawnbroker didn't know it was stolen. And, besides, I'm on a mission here. I want to be a hero, you know? I want to win it back, like a knight."

"That's romantic crap."

"That may be. But I care about it. It's been a long time since I really cared about something."

Officer Williams turned around in his seat and stared at me. He studied me.

"I'll give you some money," he said. "I don't have much. Only thirty bucks. I'm short until payday. And it's not enough to get back the regalia. But it's something."

"I'll take it," I said.

"I'm giving it to you because I believe in what you believe. I'm hoping, and I don't know why I'm hoping it, but I hope you can turn thirty bucks into a thousand somehow."

"I believe in magic."

"I believe you'll take my money and get drunk on it."

"Then why are you giving it to me?"

"There ain't no such thing as an atheist cop."

"Sure, there is."

"Yeah, well, I'm not an atheist cop."

He let me out of the car, handed me two fivers and a twenty, and shook my hand.

"Take care of yourself, Jackson," he said. "Stay off the railroad tracks."

"I'll try," I said.

He drove away. Carrying my money, I headed back toward the water.

8 A.M.

On the wharf, those three Aleuts still waited on the wooden bench.

"Have you seen your ship?" I asked.

"Seen a lot of ships," the elder Aleut said. "But not our ship."

I sat on the bench with them. We sat in silence for a long time. I wondered if we would fossilize if we sat there long enough.

I thought about my grandmother. I'd never seen her dance in her regalia. And, more than anything, I wished I'd seen her dance at a powwow.

"Do you guys know any songs?" I asked the Aleuts.

"I know all of Hank Williams," the elder Aleut said.

"How about Indian songs?"

"Hank Williams is Indian."

"How about sacred songs?"

"Hank Williams is sacred."

"I'm talking about ceremonial songs. You know, religious ones. The songs you sing back home when you're wishing and hoping."

"What are you wishing and hoping for?"

"I'm wishing my grandmother was still alive."

"Every song I know is about that."

"Well, sing me as many as you can."

The Aleuts sang their strange and beautiful songs. I listened. They sang about my grandmother and about their grandmothers. They were lonesome for the cold and the snow. I was lonesome for everything.

10 A.M.

After the Aleuts finished their last song, we sat in silence for a while. Indians are good at silence.

"Was that the last song?" I asked.

"We sang all the ones we could," the elder Aleut said. "The others are just for our people."

I understood. We Indians have to keep our secrets. And these Aleuts were so secretive they didn't refer to themselves as Indians.

"Are you guys hungry?" I asked.

They looked at one another and communicated without talking.

"We could eat," the elder Aleut said.

11 A.M.

The Aleuts and I walked over to the Big Kitchen, a greasy diner in the International District. I knew they served homeless Indians who'd lucked into money.

"Four for breakfast?" the waitress asked when we stepped inside.

"Yes, we're very hungry," the elder Aleut said.

She took us to a booth near the kitchen. I could smell the food cooking. My stomach growled.

"You guys want separate checks?" the waitress asked.

"No, I'm paying," I said.

"Aren't you the generous one," she said.

"Don't do that," I said.

"Do what?" she asked.

"Don't ask me rhetorical questions. They scare me."

She looked puzzled, and then she laughed.

"O.K., Professor," she said. "I'll only ask you real questions from now on."

"Thank you."

"What do you guys want to eat?"

"That's the best question anybody can ask anybody," I said. "What have you got?"

"How much money you got?" she asked.

"Another good question," I said. "I've got twenty-five dollars I can spend. Bring us all the breakfast you can, plus your tip."

She knew the math.

"All right, that's four specials and four coffees and fifteen per cent for me."

The Aleuts and I waited in silence. Soon enough, the waitress returned and poured us four coffees, and we sipped at them until she returned again, with four plates of food. Eggs, bacon, toast, hash-brown potatoes. It's amazing how much food you can buy for so little money.

Grateful, we feasted.

Noon

I said farewell to the Aleuts and walked toward the pawnshop. I heard later that the Aleuts had waded into the salt water near Dock 47 and disappeared. Some Indians swore they had walked on the water and headed north. Other Indians saw the Aleuts drown. I don't know what happened to them.

I looked for the pawnshop and couldn't find it. I swear it wasn't in the place where it had been before. I walked twenty or thirty blocks looking for the pawnshop, turned corners and bisected intersections, and looked up its name in the phone books and asked people walking past me if they'd ever heard of it. But that pawnshop seemed to have sailed away like a ghost ship. I wanted to cry. And just when I'd given up, when I turned one last corner and thought I might die if I didn't find that pawnshop, there it was, in a space I swear it hadn't occupied a few minutes ago.

I walked inside and greeted the pawnbroker, who looked a little younger than he had before.

"It's you," he said.

"Yes, it's me," I said.

"Jackson Jackson."

"That is my name."

"Where are your friends?"

"They went travelling. But it's O.K. Indians are everywhere."

"Do you have the money?"

"How much do you need again?" I asked, and hoped the price had changed.

"Nine hundred and ninety-nine dollars."

It was still the same price. Of course, it was the same price. Why would it change?

"I don't have that," I said.

"What do you have?"

"Five dollars."

I set the crumpled Lincoln on the countertop. The pawnbroker studied it.

"Is that the same five dollars from yesterday?"

"No, it's different."

He thought about the possibilities.

"Did you work hard for this money?" he asked.

"Yes," I said.

He closed his eyes and thought harder about the possibilities. Then he stepped into the back room and returned with my grandmother's regalia.

"Take it," he said, and held it out to me.

"I don't have the money."

"I don't want your money."

"But I wanted to win it."

"You did win it. Now take it before I change my mind."

Do you know how many good men live in this world? Too many to count!

I took my grandmother's regalia and walked outside. I knew that solitary yellow bead was part of me. I knew I was that yellow bead in part. Outside, I wrapped myself in my grandmother's regalia and breathed her in. I stepped off the sidewalk and into the intersection. Pedestrians stopped. Cars stopped. The city stopped. They all watched me dance with my grandmother. I was my grandmother, dancing.

Craft Questions

- How would you describe the narrator, based on how he talks, thinks, and acts?
- What do other characters reveal about Jackson?
- Three Aleut Indians briefly appear several times and then disappear in the story. Why do you think Alexie included these comparatively undeveloped characters? What do they add to the story?
- How do you make sense of the pawnbroker's surprising act of generosity at the end of the story? How does Alexie "get away with" this apparent inconsistency in characterization?
- Discuss the ways in which Alexie's story challenges (or reinforces) existing stereotypes.

Exercises

Exercise 1: Naming

Write a character sketch for one of the following names: Esther, Buck, or Lily, avoiding standard associations. In your sketch, describe at least the following attributes: body type/size, favorite piece of clothing, one habit (for example, addicted to chocolate), one gesture (for example, twists hair when nervous). After you're done, reconsider the names of the characters in a current short story.

Objective: To work against stereotypes and unexamined associations attached to certain names.

Exercise 2: Developing Character through Place

Write about a landscape you know well (a city, small town, suburb, or rural area) in a way that reveals something about the people who inhabit it.

Objective: To practice depicting characters through the places they inhabit.

Exercise 3: Junk Drawer

Take your current short story, and describe the main character's junk drawer or the trunk of their car. Begin with a list, and be as specific as you can in your description.

Objective: To learn about (and reveal) your character through the objects they possess.

thirteen | plot

time out of mind

WHAT MAKES A STORY accessible, engaging, suspenseful, or humorous? What keeps you listening? If you think of some of your favorite stories, they probably use plenty of vivid detail, and they possess a strong voice and characters. They also consider pace. They seem to know where to speed up and where to linger, as well as when to arrive at the ending. Events, episodes, and revelations are sequenced for clarity and impact, not necessarily according to how things would have actually occurred. As is true in oral storytelling, written short stories necessitate that we are willing and able to rearrange, edit, exaggerate, and stretch the truth in order to create a psychologically complex and satisfying experience.

In fiction, the sequencing of events is referred to as **plot**. You may begin a story with a fairly clear sense of what's going to happen. You may even draft an outline to remind yourself of where you want to take your reader first, next, and last. But for many writers, the process of arriving at an interesting, realistic plot is a bit more involved. In fact, for most writers, the process of plotting a story involves multiple drafts, and this is where workshopping in class or receiving feedback from trusted writers and readers can be particularly helpful. Where does the story seem to drag? Where do you rush through an intriguing scene without taking full advantage of its potential? Is your story too low-energy to hold interest? Too dramatic to be believable? Such questions are bound to arise organically when you're doing the work of revision. That being said, there are some useful ideas we can keep in mind throughout the process of assembling episodes or scenes into a coherent plot.

Beginning in Medias Res

In much of the writing we do, including email, application letters, memos, and essays, we're expected to craft something of an introduction. If we launch right into the middle of what we want to say, it's often considered abrupt, choppy, or disrespectful. However, well-crafted stories often plunge us right **in medias res**, Latin for in the middle of things. Not only does this technique get the action going, it also lets readers piece together elements of the story on their own, without feeling like they're being too firmly led by the artifice of fiction.

In order to see beginnings in action, let's reread the first paragraphs of some of the stories we've encountered so far:

Sandra Cisneros, "Barbie-Q"

> Yours is the one with mean eyes and a ponytail. Striped swimsuit, stilettos, sunglasses, and gold hoop earrings. Mine is the one with bubble hair. Red swimsuit, stilettos, pearl earrings, and a wire stand. But that's all we can afford, besides one extra outfit apiece. Yours, "Red Flair," sophisticated A-line coatdress with a Jackie Kennedy pillbox hat, white gloves, handbag, and heels included. Mine, "Solo in the Spotlight," evening elegance in black glitter strapless gown with a puffy skirt at the bottom like a mermaid tail, formal-length gloves, pink chiffon scarf, and mike included. From so much dressing and undressing, the black glitter wears off where her titties stick out. This and a dress invented from an old sock when we cut holes here and here and here, the cuff rolled over for the glamorous, fancy-free, off-the-shoulder look.

Andre Dubus II, "The Intruder"

> Because Kenneth Girard loved his parents and his sister and because he could not tell them why he went to the woods, his first moments there were always uncomfortable ones, as if he had left the house to commit a sin. But he was thirteen and he could not say that he was going to sit on a hill and wait for the silence and trees and sky

> to close in on him, wait until they all became a part of him, and thought and memory ceased and the voices began. He could only say that he was going for a walk and, since there was so much more to say, he felt cowardly and deceitful and more lonely than before.

Ernest Hemingway, "Hills Like White Elephants"

> The hills across the valley of the Ebro were long and white. On this side there was no shade and no trees and the station was between two lines of rails in the sun. Close against the side of the station there was the warm shadow of the building and a curtain, made of strings of bamboo beads, hung across the open door into the bar, to keep out flies. The American and the girl with him sat at a table in the shade, outside the building. It was very hot and the express from Barcelona would come in forty minutes. It stopped at this junction for two minutes and went on to Madrid.

Sherman Alexie, "What You Pawn I Will Redeem"

> One day you have a home and the next you don't, but I'm not going to tell you my particular reasons for being homeless, because it's my secret story, and Indians have to work hard to keep secrets from hungry white folks.

Craft Questions

- Which is your favorite opening and why?
- Discuss the mood or tone set by the opening of each story.
- What kinds of information do we learn in each? What questions are raised?

Even if you're already deep into the writing of a story, it's not too late to review and revise the opening. In fact, it's often best to go back to the beginning to prune and shape once most or the entire story has been drafted. You may very well find that you can cut the first few paragraphs, leaping right into the mind of your narrator and into the story's action. Similarly, once you've got an initial draft, take a closer look at your ending. Inventive stories often take a final psychological leap at the end without explaining, summing up, or presenting a moral. Maybe you'll decide to end with a single visual detail, central to the story's themes, or with a bit of dialogue or action. For ideas on effective endings, go back and review the stories we've covered thus far. In terms of the plot, your ending need not be dramatic, but it should be resonant. It should make us re-think what we've read and even make us want to read the story again!

Plot Points

You may be familiar with the common triangle often used to illustrate plot progression in stories. Gustav Freytag, the nineteenth-century German playwright and novelist, famously drew a pyramid to represent dramatic structure.

According to Freytag, not only do stories include a beginning, middle, and end (as indicated by the three points of the pyramid), they typically begin with a series of low-key yet dramatic questions and actions (sometimes referred to as **rising action**), lead up to a single climax or tipping point or else a series of climactic moments, progress with a final series of actions (sometimes referred to as **falling action**), and conclude with a **resolution** or ending.

Keep in mind that the shape of your plot may not exactly (or even remotely) follow this formula. In fact, your plot may more closely resemble a triangle with one longer side for rising or falling action, a wave pattern (as the action rises and falls several times), and the list goes on. The basic idea, however, is useful; consider the shape of your story by conceptualizing its beginning, middle, and end, as well as breaking it down into **scenes** or units of action marked by a switch in setting or time.

To practice thinking of scenes as building blocks that can be added together and rearranged to form an effective plot, look back over some of the stories we've read and mark their scene changes. You'll see that in some cases, the writer has used white space to indicate a break in the action; in others, there might be an asterisk or other mark, and often, there is no visual indication. In "What You Pawn I Will Redeem" (chapter 12), for instance, Alexie uses white space along with subtitles (times of day). Why might he have split the story up this way? What aspects of the story does this structure emphasize? Spend some time thinking about and discussing the various options available to you.

So, what actually needs to occur in your story for it to be interesting? Do you need to construct a dramatic climax (a divorce, a personal awakening, a death) at the center or near the end? Not necessarily. In fact, some of the most effective short stories involve rather low-key plotlines, in which, on the surface, not much seems to happen. When building your own story, you may want to consider some area of change felt by your protagonist or by more than one character (especially if your story involves a close relationship). In so doing, there's also the possibility that you'll provoke a change in the reader's view or understanding. In any case, as you revise, ask yourself whether your story currently exists as a series of anecdotes or whether its individual plot points cohere into a satisfying experience. If there's still work to do, don't despair. The process of revising a story can be laborious, but it will pay off. And, overall, the more stories you craft, the easier working with structure will become. You'll still likely puzzle over plot points from time to time, but you'll also develop an intuitive sense of which storylines need tweaking and which might be dead ends altogether. You'll be able to more quickly spot where the kernel of the story really lies and to make the necessary adjustments without overthinking.

Creating Tension

Although we often hear that what drives stories is *conflict*, it may actually be more useful to think in terms of lines of **tension**. Sure, structuring your story around some literal conflict (a fight, change of heart, a breakdown, a loss) will give it a certain focus and help to ensure that something happens. However, there are additional methods of crafting riveting stories: namely, by considering both *internal* (psychological) and *external* (in the character's world) forms of tension. By creating not one but multiple kinds of tension, your story will take on greater depth, subtlety, and believability.

At any stage of crafting your story, ask yourself these questions to explore possible sources of tension:

- What does my character desire that they can't have? Can have?
- What are the difficulties of my character's situation? Will these difficulties be resolved or will they remain unresolved? How and why?
- What does my character like about another character? Dislike?
- In what ways are two of my characters similar? Different?
- What keeps my character up at night?
- What haunts my character psychologically?

Now try adding to this list, individually or as a group. Use promising ideas to develop a story in progress.

Controlling Pace

As you continue to craft and revise your story, you'll likely be tightening it up by cutting or reshaping plot points and passages. You may also be adding more detail, description, and action at this stage. These decisions are largely a matter of regulating the **pace** of your story: the rate at which it unfolds.

One way of conceptualizing pace is to think about how often you reveal key aspects of your characters, significant plot points, and so on. As we've discussed, most stories begin by both raising questions and by quickly revealing important facets of the plot. They then proceed to plant questions, clues, and answers as the story progresses, building up to a climax or series of climactic moments, followed by a sense of resolution in the ending. If you include too many plot twists, your story may feel forced or clichéd. On the other hand, most readers *do* seem to want to experience a sense of unfolding or revelation as they read. For shorter short stories, thinking carefully about the number and frequency of key plot points (as well as characters!) is particularly important, in order to give your reader time to enter, believe, digest, and experience the world you've created. If you're working with a longer short story, your canvas has increased, offering you more room to move.

In general, dialogue tends to speed up a story (think "Hills Like White Elephants"), as does action, whereas description tends to slow things down. When you're first beginning to write stories, it's helpful to try to strike a balance between these modes throughout. This will keep your story from moving either too quickly or too slowly. However, as you become confident as a writer and begin to carve out your own unique style, you may naturally end up relying more heavily on one (or more) of these modes more than the others. Since **style** in fiction is largely a matter of **diction** (word choice) and **syntax** (the structure of sentences), it's also helpful to be conscious of when your sentences are short or long, fast-paced or slow moving, to become more adept at regulating pace and rhythm for maximum impact.

Plot Patterns: Flashback and Flash-Forward

Just as it's important to consider pace, you'll also want to consider the time frame in which your story occurs. Is it set in the present tense, past tense, or does it switch back and forth in time? Does it occur over the time of one day or over a period of years?

Even if your story is mainly structured in chronological order, you may want to include a scene or two from a period of time before the main action occurred: a **flashback**. Not only can flashbacks lend your story texture, they can offer insight into characters' actions, personalities, and relationships, just as meeting a friend's family members or hearing stories about our parents' lives before we were born can help us to understand our friends and family in greater depth.

So, how do you go about including a flashback if you've never before used one? First, think of a trigger. Maybe your character is engaged in a memory that you'd like to render vividly by writing it as a flashback. Next, try using a signal phrase such as "he remembered when...." It's not always necessary to use such a phrase, especially if there's a clear switch in action or setting, but if you're unsure whether your reader will be able to follow the timeline, you may want to use a signal for clarity. By looking over the stories in this text, you'll be able to observe ways that experienced writers blend flashbacks into their stories clearly and seamlessly, with and without signal devices.

Another way to clue your reader in to flashback is to switch verb tense. For instance, if your story is mainly written in present tense, you can simply switch to past tense for the flashback. And if your story is written in past tense, you can use a switch to past perfect ("she *had* followed") as your clue. Remember to include some action and dialogue in your flashback to bring it to life. Then, when you're ready to wrap it up, consider using a second signal phrase such as "but that was years ago," or else simply switch back to a scene written in the story's standard verb tense.

As important as it is to carefully consider verb tense when you're using flashback, it's equally important to consider throughout. Try to keep your verb tense consistent, except when there's a significant reason to change it (as in the case of flashback). If this is a stumbling block for you, try reading your story aloud or having someone read it aloud to you to catch inconsistencies in verb tense.

So, what about **flash-forward**? It's not often used, but it can occasionally come in handy when you want to offer your reader a bird's-eye-view to undercut undue suspense or possible melodrama. In these cases, the reader comes to know more than the characters. In "The Sparks Fly Upward" by contemporary United States writer, Tim Erwin, a man unsuccessfully attempts to reconcile with his wife by involving himself in a money-making scheme: illegally charging people to park in a downtown parking lot. As you read the following passage, notice how Erwin uses flash-forward without falling into the trap of creating too great a distance between the reader and the story.

> All of a sudden, I felt so tired I could hardly stand up straight. I realized I was stranded out here in the sticks, with no way to get back to Gloucester. So I stretched out on the porch swing, put my feet up and closed my eyes. I shucked off my boots. It felt good to

lie down. I didn't know it yet, but across town, police were still getting the last of the cars out of the jammed lot. Finding themselves trapped, the attendants nowhere to be found, there had been arguments, fights, horns overlapping in the night. And one anonymous grievant, in a fit of anger, had thrown a piece of cinder block against the glass window of Lloyd's shop, forming a crack that would spread out in all directions from the solid white center, as fine and complicated as a web. Soon, a call would be placed to my brother in Delray Beach, and he would learn about all this from the local authorities. And pretty soon after that, the morning would come, and my phone would start to ring.

That was ahead of me. But for now, I was getting ready to lower myself into a long, heavy sleep.

Craft Questions

- Where does the flash-forward start and end?
- What purpose does it seem to serve?
- What techniques does Erwin use to keep us involved in the story?

Avoiding Cliché

In the end, the plot of your story will and should be uniquely your own. As freeing as this idea may seem, when you're first starting off, it may also be a bit daunting. And you may be tempted to fall back on tried and true formulas from television, movies, and even some best sellers. Examples include plots based on rags to riches, love triangles, car chases, or a couple driving off into the sunset at the end. This is not to say that you couldn't turn any one of these overused plots into an interesting story if, say, they're given an ironic or self-conscious spin. However, if you find yourself modeling what you've seen elsewhere multiple times, your story may end up suffering from these overused ideas.

So, instead try approaching the structure of your story as a blank canvas for infinite possibilities, including plenty of seemingly ordinary, low-key plotlines that come from things you've experienced or observed. Maybe two sisters grow closer after they experience family difficulties. Or a lonely man takes a walk in his own neighborhood where he meets a neighbor he didn't know lived right down the street, and they get to be friends. Or a college-student struggles to come up with tuition money but finds a way to help an elderly relative who compensates them for their time. Look for the story in everyday life, and then take it from there. You'll be surprised where your story takes you—and your readers!

Reading

Edwidge Danticat (b. 1969)
"A Wall of Fire Rising"

"Listen to what happened today," Guy said as he barged through the rattling door of his tiny shack.

His wife, Lili, was squatting in the middle of their one-room home, spreading cornmeal mush on banana leaves for their supper.

"Listen to what happened *to me* today!" Guy's seven-year-old son—Little Guy—dashed from a corner and grabbed his father's hand. The boy dropped his composition notebook as he leaped to his father, nearly stepping into the corn mush and herring that his mother had set out in a trio of half gourds on the clay floor.

"Our boy is in a play." Lili quickly robbed Little Guy of the honor of telling his father the news.

"A play?" Guy affectionately stroked the boy's hair.

The boy had such tiny corkscrew curls that no amount of brushing could ever make them all look like a single entity. The other boys at the Lycée Jean-Jacques called him "pepper head" because each separate kinky strand was coiled into a tight tiny ball that looked like small peppercorns.

"When is this play?" Guy asked both the boy and his wife. "Are we going to have to buy new clothes for this?"

Lili got up from the floor and inclined her face towards her husband's in order to receive her nightly peck on the cheek.

"What role do you have in the play?" Guy asked, slowly rubbing the tip of his nails across the boy's scalp. His fingers made a soft grating noise with each invisible circle drawn around the perimeters of the boy's head. Guy's fingers finally landed inside the boy's ears, forcing the boy to giggle until he almost gave himself the hiccups.

"Tell me, what is your part in the play?" Guy asked again, pulling his fingers away from his son's ear.

"I am Boukman," the boy huffed out, as though there was some laughter caught in his throat.

"Show Papy your lines," Lili told the boy as she arranged the three open gourds on a piece of plywood raised like a table on two bricks, in the middle of the room. "My love, Boukman is the hero of the play."

The boy went back to the corner where he had been studying and pulled out a thick book carefully covered in brown paper.

"You're going to spend a lifetime learning those." Guy took the book from the boy's hand and flipped through the pages quickly. He had to strain his eyes to see the words by the light of an old kerosene lamp, which that night—like all others—flickered as though it was burning its very last wick.

"All these words seem so long and heavy," Guy said. "You think you can do this, son?"

"He has one very good speech," Lili said. "Page forty, remember, son?"

The boy took back the book from his father. His face was crimped in an of-course-I-remember look as he searched for page forty.

"Bouk-man," Guy struggled with the letters of the slave revolutionary's name as he looked over his son's shoulders. "I see some very hard words here, son."

"He already knows his speech," Lili told her husband.

"Does he now?" asked Guy.

"We've been at it all afternoon," Lili said. "Why don't you go on and recite that speech for your father?"

The boy tipped his head towards the rusting tin on the roof as he prepared to recite his lines.

Lili wiped her hands on an old apron tied around her waist and stopped to listen.

"Remember what you are," Lili said, "a great rebel leader. Remember, it is the revolution."

"Do we want him to be all of that?" Guy asked.

"He is Boukman," Lili said. "What is the only thing on your mind now, Boukman?"

"Supper," Guy whispered, enviously eyeing the food cooling off in the middle of the room. He and the boy looked at each other and began to snicker.

"Tell us the other thing that is on your mind," Lili said, joining in their laughter.

"Freedom!" shouted the boy, as he quickly slipped into his role.

"Louder!" urged Lili.

"Freedom is on my mind!" yelled the boy.

"Why don't you start, son?" said Guy. "If you don't, we'll never get to that other thing that we have on our minds."

The boy closed his eyes and took a deep breath. At first, his lips parted but nothing came out. Lili pushed her head forward as though she were holding her breath. Then like the last burst of lightning out of clearing sky, the boy began.

"A wall of fire is rising and in the ashes, I see the bones of my people. Not only those people whose dark hollow faces I see daily in the fields, but all those souls who have gone ahead to haunt my dreams. At night I relive once more the last caresses from the hand of a loving father, a valiant love, a beloved friend."

It was obvious that this was a speech written by a European man, who gave to the slave revolutionary Boukman the kind of European phrasing that might have sent the real Boukman turning in his grave. However, the speech made Lili and Guy stand on the tips of their toes from great pride. As their applause thundered in the small space of their shack that night, they felt as though for a moment they had been given the rare pleasure of hearing the voice of one of the forefathers of Haitian independence in the forced baritone of their only child. The experience left them both with a strange feeling that they could not explain. It left the hair on the back of their necks standing on end. It left them feeling much more love than they ever knew that they could add to their feeling for their son.

"Bravo," Lili cheered, pressing her son into the folds of her apron. "Long live Boukman and long live my boy."

"Long live our supper," Guy said, quickly batting his eyelashes to keep tears from rolling down his face.

•

The boy kept his eyes on his book as they ate their supper that night. Usually Guy and Lili would not have allowed that, but this was a special occasion. They watched proudly as the boy muttered his lines between swallows of cornmeal.

The boy was still mumbling the same words as the three of them used the last of the rainwater trapped in old gasoline containers and sugarcane pulp from the nearby sugarcane mill to scrub the gourds that they had eaten from.

When things were really bad for the family, they boiled clean sugarcane pulp to make what Lili called her special sweet water tea. It was supposed to suppress gas and kill the vermin in the stomach that made poor children hungry. That and a pinch of salt under the tongue could usually quench hunger until Guy found a day's work or Lili could manage to buy spices on credit and then peddle them for a profit at the marketplace.

That night, anyway, things were good. Everyone had eaten enough to put all their hunger vermin to sleep.

The boy was sitting in front of the shack on an old plastic bucket turned upside down, straining his eyes to find the words on the page. Sometimes when there was no kerosene for the lamp, the boy would have to go sit by the side of the road and study under the street lamps with the rest of the neighborhood children. Tonight, at least, they had a bit of their own light.

Guy bent down by a small clump of old mushrooms near the boy's feet, trying to get a better look at the plant. He emptied the last drops of rainwater from a gasoline container on the mushroom, wetting the bulging toes sticking out of his son's sandals, which were already coming apart around his endlessly growing feet.

Guy tried to pluck some of the mushrooms, which were being pushed into the dust as though they wanted to grow beneath the ground as roots. He took one of the mushrooms in his hand, running his smallest finger over the round bulb. He clipped the stem and buried the top in a thick strand of his wife's hair.

The mushroom looked like a dried insect in Lili's hair.

"It sure makes you look special," Guy said, teasing her.

"Thank you so much," Lili said, tapping her husband's arm. "It's nice to know that I deserve these much more than roses."

Taking his wife's hand, Guy said, "Let's go to the sugar mill."

"Can I study my lines there?" the boy asked.

"You know them well enough already," Guy said.

"I need many repetitions," the boy said.

•

Their feet sounded as though they were playing a wet wind instrument as they slipped in and out of the puddles between the shacks in the shantytown. Near the sugar mill was a large television screen in a iron grill cage that the government had installed so that the shantytown dwellers could watch the state-sponsored news at eight o'clock every night. After the news, a gendarme would come and turn off the television set, taking home the key. On most nights, the people stayed at the site long after this gendarme had gone and told stories to one another beneath the big blank screen. They made bonfires with dried sticks, corn husks, and paper, cursing the authorities under their breath.

There was a crowd already gathering for the nightly news event. The sugar mill workers sat in the front row in chairs or on old buckets.

Lili and Guy passed the group, clinging to their son so that in his childhood naïveté he wouldn't accidentally glance at the wrong person and be called an insolent child. They didn't like the ambiance of the nightly news watch. They spared themselves trouble by going instead to the sugar mill, where in the past year they had discovered their own wonder.

Everyone knew that the family who owned the sugar mill were eccentric "Arabs," Haitians of Lebanese or Palestinian descent whose family had been in the country for generations. The Assad family had a son who, it seems, was into all manner of odd things, the most recent of which was a hot-air balloon, which he had brought to Haiti from America and occasionally flew over the shantytown skies.

As they approached the fence surrounding the field where the large wicker basket and deflated balloon rested on the ground, Guy let go of the hands of both his wife and the boy.

Lili walked on slowly with her son. For the last few weeks, she had been feeling as though Guy was lost to her each time he reached this point, twelve feet away from the balloon. As Guy pushed his hand through the barbed wire, she could tell from the look on his face that he was thinking of sitting inside the square basket while the smooth rainbow surface of the balloon itself floated above his head. During the day, when the field was open, Guy would walk up to the basket, staring at it with the same kind of longing that most men display when they admire very pretty girls.

Lili and the boy stood watching from a distance as Guy tried to push his hand deeper, beyond the chain link fence that separated him from the balloon. He reached into his pants pocket and pulled out a small pocket-knife, sharpening the edges on the metal surface of the fence. When his wife and child moved closer, he put the knife back in his pocket, letting his fingers slide across his son's tightly coiled curls.

"I wager you I can make this thing fly," Guy said.

"Why do you think you can do that?" Lili asked.

"I know it," Guy replied.

He followed her as she circled the sugar mill, leading to their favorite spot under a watch light. Little Guy lagged faithfully behind them. From this distance, the hot-air balloon looked like an odd spaceship.

Lili stretched her body out in the knee-high grass in the field. Guy reached over and tried to touch her between her legs.

"You're not one to worry, Lili," he said. "You're not afraid of the frogs, lizards, or snakes that could be hiding in this grass?"

"I am here with my husband," she said. "You are here to protect me if anything happens."

Guy reached into his shirt pocket and pulled out a lighter and a crumpled piece of paper. He lit the paper until it burned to an ashy film. The burning paper floated in the night breeze for a while, landing in fragments on the grass.

"Did you see that, Lili?" Guy asked with a flame in his eyes brighter than the lighter's. "Did you see how the paper floated when it was burned? This is how that balloon flies."

"What did you mean by saying that you could make it fly?" Lili asked.

"You already know all my secrets," Guy said as the boy came charging towards them.

"Papa, could you play *Lago* with me?" the boy asked.

Lili lay peacefully on the grass as her son and husband played hide-and-seek. Guy kept hiding and his son kept finding him as each time Guy made it easier for the boy.

"We rest now." Guy was becoming breathless.

The stars were circling the peaks of the mountains, dipping into the cane fields belonging to the sugar mill. As Guy caught his breath, the boy raced around the fence, running as fast as he could to purposely make himself dizzy.

"Listen to what happened today," Guy whispered softly in Lili's ear.

"I heard you say that when you walked in the house tonight," Lili said. "With the boy's play, I forgot to ask you."

The boy sneaked up behind them, his face lit up, though his brain was spinning. He wrapped his arms around both their necks.

"We will go back home soon," Lili said.

"Can I recite my lines?" asked the boy.

"We have heard them," Guy said. "Don't tire your lips."

The boy mumbled something under his breath. Guy grabbed his ear and twirled it until it was a tiny ball in his hand. The boy's face contorted with agony as Guy made him kneel in the deep grass in punishment.

Lili looked tortured as she watched the boy squirming in the grass, obviously terrified of the crickets, lizards, and small snakes that might be there.

"Perhaps we should take him home to bed," she said.

"He will never learn," Guy said, "if I say one thing and you say another."

Guy got up and angrily started walking home. Lili walked over, took her son's hand, and raised him from his knees.

"You know you must not mumble," she said.

"I was saying my lines," the boy said.

"Next time say them loud," Lili said, "so he knows what is coming out of your mouth."

That night Lili could hear her son muttering his lines as he tucked himself in his corner of the room and drifted off to sleep. The boy still had the book with his monologue in it clasped under his arm as he slept.

•

Guy stayed outside in front of the shack as Lili undressed for bed. She loosened the ribbon that held the old light blue cotton skirt around her waist and let it drop past her knees. She grabbed half a lemon that she kept in the corner by the folded mat that she and Guy unrolled to sleep on every night. Lili let her blouse drop to the floor as she smoothed the lemon over her ashen legs.

Guy came in just at that moment and saw her bare chest by the light of the smaller castor oil lamp that they used for the later hours of the night. Her skin had coarsened a bit over the years, he thought. Her breasts now drooped from having nursed their son for two years after he was born. It was now easier for him to imagine their son's lips around those breasts than to imagine his anywhere near them.

He turned his face away as she fumbled for her nightgown. He helped her open the mat, tucking the blanket edges underneath.

Fully clothed, Guy dropped onto the mat next to her. He laid his head on her chest, rubbing the spiky edges of his hair against her nipples.

"What was it that happened today?" Lili asked, running her fingers along Guy's hairline, an angular hairline, almost like a triangle, in the middle of his forehead. She nearly didn't marry him because it was said that people with angular hairlines often have very troubled lives.

"I got a few hours' work for tomorrow at the sugar mill," Guy said. "That's what happened today."

"It was such a long time coming," Lili said.

It was almost six months since the last time Guy had gotten work there. The jobs at the sugar mill were few and far between. The people who had them never left, or when they did they would pass the job on to another family member who was already waiting on line.

Guy did not seem overjoyed about the one day's work.

"I wish I had paid more attention when you came in with the news," Lili said. "I was just so happy about the boy."

"I was born in the shadow of that sugar mill," Guy said. "Probably the first thing my mother gave me to drink as a baby was some sweet water tea from the pulp of the sugarcane. If anyone deserves to work there, I should."

"What will you be doing for your day's work?"

"Would you really like to know?"

"There is never any shame in honest work," she said.

"They want me to scrub the latrines."

"It's honest work," Lili said, trying to console him.

"I am still number seventy-eight on the permanent hire list," he said. "I was thinking of putting the boy on the list now, so maybe by the time he becomes a man he can be up for a job."

Lili's body jerked forward, rising straight up in the air. Guy's head dropped with a loud thump onto the mat.

"I don't want him on that list," she said. "For a young boy to be on any list like that might influence his destiny. I don't want him on the list."

"Look at me," Guy said. "If my father had worked there, if he had me on the list, don't you think I would be working?"

"If you have any regard for me," she said, "you will not put him on the list."

She groped for her husband's chest in the dark and laid her head on it. She could hear his heart beating loudly as though it were pumping double, triple its normal rate.

"You won't put the boy on any lists, will you?" she implored.

"Please, Lili, no more about the boy. He will not go on the list."

"Thank you."

"Tonight I was looking at that balloon in the yard behind the sugar mill," he said. "I have been watching it real close."

"I know."

"I have seen the man who owns it," he said. "I've seen him get in it and put it in the sky and go up there like it was some kind of kite and he was the kite master. I see the men who run after it trying to figure out where it will land. Once I was there and I was one of those men who were running and I actually guessed correctly. I picked a spot in the sugarcane fields. I picked the spot from a distance and it actually landed there."

"Let me say something to you, Guy—"

"Pretend that this is the time of miracles and we believed in them. I watched the owner for a long time, and I think I can fly that balloon. The first time I saw him do it, it looked like a miracle, but the more and more I saw it, the more ordinary it became."

"You're probably intelligent enough to do it," she said.

"I am intelligent enough to do it. You're right to say that I can."

"Don't you think about hurting yourself?"

"Think like this. Can't you see yourself up there? Up in the clouds somewhere like some kind of bird?"

"If God wanted people to fly, he would have given us wings on our backs."

"You're right, Lili, you're right. But look what he gave us instead. He gave us reasons to want to fly. He gave us the air, the birds, our son."

"I don't understand you," she said.

"Our son, your son, you do not want him cleaning latrines."

"He can do other things."

"Me too. I can do other things too."

A loud scream came from the corner where the boy was sleeping. Lili and Guy rushed to him and tried to wake him. The boy was trembling when he opened his eyes.

"What is the matter?" Guy asked.

"I cannot remember my lines," the boy said.

Lili tried to string together what she could remember of her son's lines. The words slowly came back to the boy. By the time he fell back to sleep, it was almost dawn.

•

The light was slowly coming up behind the trees. Lili could hear the whispers of the market women, their hisses and swearing as their sandals dug into the sharp-edged rocks on the road.

She turned her back to her husband as she slipped out of her nightgown, quickly putting on her day clothes.

"Imagine this," Guy said from the mat on the floor. "I have never really seen your entire body in broad daylight."

Lili shut the door behind her, making her way out to the yard. The empty gasoline containers rested easily on her head as she walked a few miles to the public water fountains. It was harder to keep them steady when the containers were full. The water splashed all over her blouse and rippled down her back.

The sky was blue as it was most mornings, a dark indigo-shaded turquoise that would get lighter when the sun was fully risen.

Guy and the boy were standing in the yard waiting for her when she got back.

"You did not get much sleep, my handsome boy," she said, running her wet fingers over the boy's face.

"He'll be late for school if we do not go right now," Guy said. "I want to drop him off before I start work."

"Do we remember our lines this morning?" Lili asked, tucking the boy's shirt down deep into his short pants.

"We just recited them," Guy said. "Even I know them now."

Lili watched them walk down the footpath, her eyes following them until they disappeared.

As soon as they were out of sight, she poured the water she had fetched into a large calabash, letting it stand beside the house.

She went back into the room and slipped into a dry blouse. It was never too early to start looking around, to scrape together that night's meal.

•

"Listen to what happened again today," Lili said when Guy walked through the door that afternoon.

Guy blotted his face with a dust rag as he prepared to hear the news. After the day he'd had at the factory, he wanted to sit under a tree and have a leisurely smoke, but he did not want to set a bad example for his son by indulging his very small pleasures.

"You tell him, son," Lili urged the boy, who was quietly sitting in a corner, reading.

"I've got more lines," the boy announced, springing up to his feet. "Papy, do you want to hear them?"

"They are giving him more things to say in the play," Lili explained, "because he did such a good job memorizing so fast."

"My compliments, son. Do you have your new lines memorized too?" Guy asked.

"Why don't you recite your new lines for your father?" Lili said.

The boy walked to the middle of the room and prepared to recite. He cleared his throat, raising his eyes towards the ceiling.

"There is so much sadness in the faces of my people. I have called on their gods, now I call on our gods. I call on our young. I call on our old. I call on our mighty and the weak. I call on everyone and anyone so that we shall all let out one piercing cry that we may either live freely or we should die."

"I see your new lines have as much drama as the old ones," Guy said. He wiped a tear away, walked over to the chair, and took the boy in his arms. He pressed the boy's body against his chest before lowering him to the ground.

"Your new lines are wonderful, son. They're every bit as affecting as the old." He tapped the boy's shoulder and walked out of the house.

"What's the matter with Papy?" the boy asked as the door slammed shut behind Guy.

"His heart hurts," Lili said.

•

After supper, Lili took her son to the field where she knew her husband would be. While the boy ran around, she found her husband sitting in his favorite spot behind the sugar mill.

"Nothing, Lili," he said. "Ask me nothing about this day that I have had."

She sat down on the grass next to him, for once feeling the sharp edges of the grass blades against her ankles.

"You're really good with that boy," he said, drawing circles with his smallest finger on her elbow. "You will make a performer of him. I know you will. You can see the best in that whole situation. It's because you have those stars in your eyes. That's the first thing I noticed about you when I met you. It was your eyes, Lili, so dark and deep. They drew me like danger draws a fool."

He turned over on the grass so that he was staring directly at the moon up in the sky. She could tell that he was also watching the hot-air balloon behind the sugar mill fence out of the corner of his eye.

"Sometimes I know you want to believe in me," he said. "I know you're wishing things for me. You want me to work at the mill. You want me to get a pretty house for us. I know you want these things too, but mostly you want me to feel like a man. That's why you're not one to worry about, Lili. I know you can take things as they come."

"I don't like it when you talk this way," she said.

"Listen to this, Lili. I want to tell you a secret. Sometimes, I just want to take that big balloon and ride it up in the air. I'd like to sail off somewhere and keep floating until I got to a really nice place with a nice plot of land where I could be something new. I'd build my own house, keep my own garden. Just be something new."

"I want you to stay away from there."

"I know you don't think I should take it. That can't keep me from wanting."

"You could be injured. Do you ever think about that?"

"Don't you ever want to be something new?"

"I don't like it," she said.

"Please don't get angry with me," he said, his voice straining almost like the boy's.

"If you were to take that balloon and fly away, would you take me and the boy?"

"First you don't want me to take it and now you want to go?"

"I just want to know that when you dream, me and the boy, we're always in your dreams."

He leaned his head on her shoulders and drifted off to sleep. Her back ached as she sat there with his face pressed against her collar bone. He drooled and the saliva dripped down to her breasts, soaking her frayed polyester bra. She listened to the crickets while watching her son play, muttering his lines to himself as he went in a circle around the field. The moon was glowing above their heads. Winking at them, as Guy liked to say, on its way to brighter shores.

Opening his eyes, Guy asked her, "How do you think a man is judged after he's gone?"

How did he expect her to answer something like that?

"People don't eat riches," she said. "They eat what it can buy."

"What does that mean, Lili? Don't talk to me in parables. Talk to me honestly."

"A man is judged by his deeds," she said. "The boy never goes to bed hungry. For as long as he's been with us, he's always been fed."

Just as if he had heard himself mentioned, the boy came dashing from the other side of the field, crashing in a heap on top of his parents.

"My new lines," he said. "I have forgotten my new lines."

"Is this how you will be the day of this play, son?" Guy asked. "When people give you big responsibilities, you have to try to live up to them."

The boy had relearned his new lines by the time they went to bed.

That night, Guy watched his wife very closely as she undressed for bed.

"I would like to be the one to rub that piece of lemon on your knees tonight," he said.

She handed him the half lemon, then raised her skirt above her knees.

Her body began to tremble as he rubbed his fingers over her skin.

"You know that question I asked you before," he said, "how a man is remembered after he's gone? I know the answer now. I know because I remember my father, who was a very poor struggling man all his life. I remember him as a man that I would never want to be."

•

Lili got up with the break of dawn the next day. The light came up quickly above the trees. Lili greeted some of the market women as they walked together to the public water fountain.

On her way back, the sun had already melted a few gray clouds. She found the boy standing alone in the yard with a terrified expression on his face, the old withered mushrooms uprooted at his feet. He ran up to meet her, nearly knocking her off balance.

"What happened?" she asked. "Have you forgotten your lines?"

The boy was breathing so heavily that his lips could not form a single word.

"What is it?" Lili asked, almost shaking him with anxiety.

"It's Papa," he said finally, raising a stiff finger in the air.

The boy covered his face as his mother looked up at the sky. A rainbow-colored balloon was floating aimlessly above their heads.

"It's Papa," the boy said. "He is in it."

She wanted to look down at her son and tell him that it wasn't his father, but she immediately recognized the spindly arms, in a bright flowered shirt that she had made, gripping the cables.

•

From the field behind the sugar mill a group of workers were watching the balloon floating in the air. Many were clapping and cheering, calling out Guy's name. A few of the women were waving their head rags at the sky, shouting, "Go! Beautiful, go!"

Lili edged her way to the front of the crowd. Everyone was waiting, watching the balloon drift higher up into the clouds.

"He seems to be right over our heads," said the factory foreman, a short slender mulatto with large buckteeth.

Just then, Lili noticed young Assad, his thick black hair sticking to the beads of sweat on his forehead. His face had the crumpled expression of disrupted sleep.

"He's further away than he seems," said young Assad. "I still don't understand. How did he get up there? You need a whole crew to fly these things."

"I don't know," the foreman said. "One of my workers just came in saying there was a man flying above the factory."

"But how the hell did he start it?" Young Assad was perplexed.

"He just did it," the foreman said.

"Look, he's trying to get out!" someone hollered.

A chorus of screams broke out among the workers.

The boy was looking up, trying to see if his father was really trying to jump out of the balloon. Guy was climbing over the side of the basket. Lili pressed her son's face into her skirt.

Within seconds, Guy was in the air hurtling down towards the crowd. Lili held her breath as she watched him fall. He crashed not far from where Lili and the boy were standing, his blood immediately soaking the landing spot.

The balloon kept floating free, drifting on its way to brighter shores. Young Assad rushed towards the body. He dropped to his knees and checked the wrist for a pulse, then dropped the arm back to the ground.

"It's over!" The foreman ordered the workers back to work.

Lili tried to keep her son's head pressed against her skirt as she moved closer to the body. The boy yanked himself away and raced to the edge of the field where his father's body was lying on the grass. He reached the body as young Assad still knelt examining the corpse. Lili rushed after him.

"He is mine," she said to young Assad. "He is my family. He belongs to me."

Young Assad got up and raised his head to search the sky for his aimless balloon, trying to guess where it would land. He took one last glance at Guy's bloody corpse, then raced to his car and sped away.

The foreman and another worker carried a cot and blanket from the factory.

Little Guy was breathing quickly as he looked at his father's body on the ground. While the foreman draped a sheet over Guy's corpse, his son began to recite the lines from his play.

"A wall of fire is rising and in the ashes, I see the bones of my people. Not only those people whose dark hollow faces I see daily in the fields, but all those souls who have gone ahead to haunt my dreams. At night I relive once more the last caresses from the hand of a loving father, a valiant love, a beloved friend."

"Let me look at him one last time," Lili said, pulling back the sheet.

She leaned in very close to get a better look at Guy's face. There was little left of that countenance that she had loved so much. Those lips that curled when he was teasing her. That large flat nose that felt like a feather when rubbed against hers. And those eyes, those night-colored eyes. Though clouded with blood, Guy's eyes were still bulging open. Lili was searching for some kind of sign—a blink, a smile, a wink—something that would remind her of the man that she had married.

"His eyes aren't closed," the foreman said to Lili. "Do you want to close them, or should I?"

The boy continued reciting his lines, his voice rising to a man's grieving roar. He kept his eyes closed, his fists balled at his side as he continued with his newest lines.

"There is so much sadness in the faces of my people. I have called on their gods, now I call on our gods. I call on our young. I call on our old. I call on our mighty and the weak. I call on everyone and anyone so that we shall all let out one piercing cry that we may either live freely or we should die."

"Do you want to close the eyes?" the foreman repeated impatiently.

"No, leave them open," Lili said. "My husband, he likes to look at the sky."

Craft Questions

- What marks the story's beginning as an in medias res one?
- List the story's plot points, noting its multiple scenes. How is the presentation of the story related to its subjects and themes?
- What internal and external tensions are explored in the story?
- In what ways does the plot of the son's rehearsal for his performance parallel the plot of Guy's desire for freedom or escape? In what ways do the two plots diverge or interrupt each other?
- Danticat's story is rich with a sense of Haitian history, including the history of political and economic oppression. Discuss the ways that these social realities are woven into the story.

Exercises

Exercise 1: Plot Potential

Two people are standing on a city sidewalk waiting for a bus. Write a mini-story (1 page) about this event. Ask yourself these questions:

Who are these people?
When does this scene take place? What comes before/after?
What is their relationship to one another?
Where are they headed?

Objective: To practice placing characters in medias res and building the story from there.

Exercise 2: From Scenes to Plot

Read over a story in progress and mark up its scenes. Make a bulleted list of scenes, and try reordering them: first on your list, and then by cutting and pasting scenes to create a new draft. If the story is strictly chronological, see what would happen if you started with a later scene and circled back, or rearranged the story in another way. If the story is not chronological, try reordering it so that it is. Once you find a structure you like, read it over again to see if you need to add signal phrases or change verb tense for consistency and clarity.

Objective: To use scenes as building blocks for creating an effective plot.

Exercise 3: Writing the Flashback

Read over a story in progress and find a place where it would be useful to have a flashback. Try writing one with the aim of revealing more information about your central character's history, desires, and motivations. See if you can weave the flashback into your existing story.

Objective: To add temporal and psychological complexity to your story.

fourteen | setting

a sense of place

One of the most engaging aspects of crafting a short story is thinking about where the story is set. After all, if we consider the setting of our own lives, place is at the center of almost everything we do. Do we live in an urban or rural area? How does this area affect our literal view of things? How might it affect our interactions, the pace of our days? What specific sights, sounds, tactile sensations, and smells do we regularly experience? Even when we're lost, we're attuned to physical place: the landscape, landmarks, and sensory details around us.

Therefore, you'll need to keep in mind that your readers will generally want to know *where* they are fairly soon after a story begins. If your current story in-progress lacks a developed sense of place, you can consider this aspect of the story as you revise; you may end up adding more descriptive detail to help focus your story, or you may even decide to change the setting of a story in-progress entirely, as the story unfolds. In any case, you'll want to consider **setting**, not only *place*, but also *time of day*, *season*, and possibly *historical period*, early and often. Ultimately, setting not only creates an atmosphere for your story, but it can also be used to reveal aspects of your characters and their situations. And, as we'll see in this chapter, setting can also function symbolically, to heighten the themes of your story.

As you craft your story's setting, you'll be making important choices about how much detail to include, as well as its function within the story. Just as we started from the assumption that you are the expert on your characters, we'll start with a similar assumption here: that you know everything you can about your setting, whether or not you decide to include all of those specific details in your story itself. The extent to which you describe your setting will vary, but your story will benefit if your connection with a sense of setting is strong.

Actual and Imagined Places

What's the difference between setting a story in an unnamed city versus setting it in Harlem, New York? The difference between setting your story in a car at night versus setting it in a Corvette? The obvious answer is specificity. Since we've discussed the importance of including plenty of detail in your short stories, we might assume that specifying actual place is the way to go. But this isn't necessarily the case since both actual and imagined places carry with them potential drawbacks as well as benefits. And since no element works in isolation, the degree to which you develop the setting of your story depends on many other factors, including the scope of your story, as well as its style and tone.

Let's briefly review passages from several of the short stories we've read so far to think about their settings. As you read, consider the writer's choice to set the story either in an actual place or in an imagined one, keeping in mind that both actual and imagined places entail acts of creative imagination in fiction.

Jayne Anne Phillips's "Blind Girls"

> She knew it was only boys in the field, come to watch them drunk on first wine. A radio in the little shack poured out promises of black love and lips. Jesse watched Sally paint her with grenadine, dotting the sticky syrup on her arms. The party was in a shack down the hill from her house, beside a field of tall grass where black snakes lay like flat belts. The Ripple bottles were empty and Jesse told pornographic stories about various adults while everyone laughed; about Miss Hicks the Home-ec teacher whose hands were dimpled and moist and always touching them. It got darker and the stories got scarier.

Craft Questions

- What sensory details does Phillips use to describe the setting?
- What time of day is it?
- How does this setting contribute to the tone or mood of the story?
- How does Phillips's decision to create an imagined place, rather than a specific, actual one, affect our experience as readers?

Anne Beattie's "Snow"

I remember the cold night you brought in a pile of logs and a chipmunk jumped off as you lowered your arms. "What do you think you're doing in here?" you said, as it ran through the living room. It went through the library and stopped at the front door as though it knew the house well. This would be difficult for anyone to believe, except perhaps as the subject of a poem. Our first week in the house was spent scraping, finding some of the house's secrets, like wallpaper under wallpaper. In the kitchen, a pattern of white-gold trellises supported purple grapes as big and round as ping-pong balls. When we painted the walls yellow, I thought of the bits of grape that remained underneath and imagined the vine popping through, the way some plants can tenaciously push through anything. The day of the big snow, when you had to shovel the walk and couldn't find your cap and asked me how to wind a towel so that it would stay on your head—you, in the white towel turban, like a crazy king of snow. People liked the idea of our being together, leaving the city for the country.

Craft Questions

- Where and when is the story set?
- What details does Beattie use to bring the setting to life?
- How does the season contribute to this love story?
- Why do you think Beattie sets the story in "the country," as opposed to setting it in a particular rural area?

Sherman Alexie's "What You Pawn I Will Redeem"

I'm a Spokane Indian boy, an Interior Salish, and my people have lived within a hundred-mile radius of Spokane, Washington, for at least ten thousand years. I grew up in Spokane, moved to Seattle twenty-three years ago for college, flunked out after two semesters, worked various blue- and bluer-collar jobs, married two or three times, fathered two or three kids, and then went crazy. Of course, crazy is not the official definition of my mental problem, but I don't think asocial disorder fits it, either, because that makes me sound like I'm a serial killer or something. I've never hurt another human being, or, at least, not physically. I've broken a few hearts in my time, but we've all done that, so I'm nothing special in that regard. I'm a boring heartbreaker, too. I never dated or married more than one woman at a time. I didn't break hearts into pieces overnight. I broke them slowly and carefully. And I didn't set any land-speed records running out the door. Piece by piece, I disappeared. I've been disappearing ever since.

I've been homeless for six years now.

Craft Questions

- What's the relevance of the protagonist's background in Spokane, Washington?
- What does the use of the actual location, the streets of Seattle, add to the story?
- Looking back on Alexie's story, discuss the use of times of day and night for individual sections. What's the role of time in the story?

As you can see from these examples, there's no one right way to develop your setting. As usual, it's probably best to begin with your own intuition, then to think carefully about this aspect of your story as you develop it, with the help of your classmates, professor, workshop group, or writing friends. Here's one word of caution, however: base your setting on places you actually know. If your setting is an actual place, it will be easier to describe if you've spent time there, instead of relying on movies or others' recollections. Similarly, if you decide to leave place open-ended, such as a country house in the winter, your setting will be believable if you've spent time in such a place. If you've never experienced a heavy snowfall, it might be more difficult to describe its characteristics and the feeling associated with it as accurately and deeply as someone who grew up experiencing snowy winters.

Time and Season

In reviewing the above examples, we've not only taken note of actual versus imagined places, but time of day and season as well. In some cases, you may not choose to include these details, if you aim to keep a reader off guard, uncertain, or uneasy. However, in many cases, you'll want to make use of these markers of time in order to contribute to the story's atmosphere and themes. Whereas Alexie's story uses time of day most directly, many stories are set during some portion of the day or night or both. And including descriptive details that indicate season is often a wonderful way to enhance your story.

As you read the following short-short story by contemporary United States writer Mary Robison (b. 1949), you'll be able to detect the strong influence of both time of day and season on the story's plot and themes. The setting of "Yours" is so important, in fact, that it's difficult to imagine this evocative, haunting story without it.

Yours

Allison struggled away from her white Renault, limping with the weight of the last of the pumpkins. She found Clark in the twilight on the twig-and-leaf-littered porch behind the house.

He wore a wool shawl. He was moving up and back in a padded glider, pushed by the ball of his slippered foot.

Allison lowered a big pumpkin, let it rest on the wide floorboards.

Clark was much older—seventy-eight to Allison's thirty-five. They were married. They were both quite tall and looked something alike in their facial features. Allison wore a natural-hair wig. It was a thick blonde hood around her face. She was dressed in bright-dyed denims today. She wore durable clothes, usually, for she volunteered afternoons at a children's day-care center.

She put one of the smaller pumpkins on Clark's long lap. "Now, nothing surreal," she told him. "Carve just a *regular* face. These are for kids."

In the foyer, on the Hepplewhite desk, Allison found the maid's chore list with its cross-offs, which included Clark's supper. Allison went quickly through the day's mail: a garish coupon packet, a bill from Jamestown Liquors, November's pay-TV program guide, and the worst thing, the funniest, an already opened, extremely unkind letter from Clark's relations up North. "You're an old fool," Allison read, and, "You're being cruelly deceived." There was a gift check for Clark enclosed, but it was uncashable, signed as it was, "Jesus H. Christ."

Late, late into this night, Allison and Clark gutted and carved the pumpkins together, at an old table set on the back porch, over newspaper after soggy newspaper, with paring knives and with spoons and with a Swiss Army knife Clark used for exact shaping of tooth and eye and nostril. Clark had been a doctor, an internist, but also a Sunday watercolorist. His four pumpkins were expressive and artful. Their carved features were suited to the sizes and shapes of the pumpkins. Two looked ferocious and jagged. One registered surprise. The last was serene and beaming.

Allison's four faces were less deftly drawn, with slits and areas of distortion. She had cut triangles for noses and eyes. The mouths she had made were just wedges—two turned up and two turned down.

By one in the morning they were finished. Clark, who had bent his long torso forward to work, moved back over to the glider and looked out sleepily at nothing. All the lights were out across the ravine.

Clark stayed. For the season and time, the Virginia night was warm. Most leaves had been blown away already, and the trees stood unbothered. The moon was round above them.

Allison cleaned up the mess.

"Your jack-o'-lanterns are much, much better than mine," Clark said to her.

"Like hell," Allison said.

"Look at me," Clark said, and Allison did.

She was holding a squishy bundle of newspapers. The papers reeked sweetly with the smell of pumpkin guts.

"Yours are *far* better," he said.

"You're wrong. You'll see when they're lit," Allison said.

She went inside and came back with yellow vigil candles. It took her a while to get each candle settled, and then to line up the results in a row on the porch railing. She went along and lit each candle and fixed the pumpkin lids over the little flames.

"See?" she said.

They sat together a moment and looked at the orange faces.

"We're exhausted. It's good night time," Allison said. "Don't blow out the candles. I'll put in new ones tomorrow."

That night, in their bedroom, a few weeks earlier in her life than had been predicted, Allison began to die. "Don't look at me if my wig comes off," she told Clark. "Please."

Her pulse cords were fluttering under his fingers. She raised her knees and kicked away the comforter. She said something to Clark about the garage being locked.

At the telephone, Clark had a clear view out back and down to the porch. He wanted to get drunk with his wife once more. He wanted to tell her, from the greater perspective he had, that to own only a little talent, like his, was an awful, plaguing thing; that being only a little special meant you expected too much, most of the time, and liked yourself too little. He wanted to assure her that she had missed nothing.

He was speaking into the phone now. He watched the jack-o'-lanterns. The jack-o'-lanterns watched him.

Craft Questions

- What details does Robison use to make the setting of the story specific and memorable?
- How does the season contribute to the mood and tone of the story?
- What's the first hint you get of the story's climax?
- How does the passage of time—from day to night—contribute to your growing awareness of the story's plot and themes?

Historical Fiction

Although many of the stories we've read so far have been contemporary, taking place roughly in our time period, it's possible that you're working on a story or an idea for a story that takes place before you were born. Or you may find yourself curious about an even earlier time period, such as the roaring twenties or the Victorian era. If you already know a lot about the time period in which you intend to set your story, that will be helpful. If not, you'll want to do some research to help render the time period realistically.

For writing fiction, this sort of research involves learning enough so that you can imaginatively and accurately project yourself into the time period you've chosen. There are several ways that you can begin to do this:

- If you know someone who lived during the period, speak with them about their experiences. Get a sense of what it was like to watch television in black and white, how it felt to see the first computer, or what kinds of common phrases were used at a particular moment in time in everyday speech.

- Read newspapers, books, magazines, and letters from the time period to see how people wrote and thought. Watch movies to see how people dressed, comported themselves, and spoke, keeping in mind that movies are not always realistic.

- Search the internet and library for pictures and information on the period, focusing on material that may be relevant for building the world of your story and forgetting details that may not be as useful.

- If you're writing on an earlier time period you lived through, do some free writing on your memories and discuss some of these memories with friends who also lived through the period.

As always, use your intuition when deciding on and researching a particular period for your short story. If you find yourself slipping into clichés, you may want to lessen the emphasis on time period or dispense with the historical period altogether. However, if a particular time period seems relevant to the story you have to tell, immerse yourself in it and see if you can bring your readers along with you.

Setting and Symbolism

If we look back on the stories we've read so far and read ahead to the one included at the end of this chapter, we'll discover that setting can be handled in many different ways. Some stories develop the setting in detail, whereas in others, setting plays a less-obvious role. Some are actual; some are imagined. Some seem to function symbolically, and others simply provide a sense of place and atmosphere. Whatever the case, however, the setting *is* connected to all other aspects of the story.

So, as you develop your own stories, and as you begin to develop your own aesthetic and way of doing things, you'll necessarily be considering the function of setting in *your writing*. As you try out different methods, keep in mind that that's what you're doing: experimenting. Every serious writer goes through the process of trial and error, of imitation, missteps, and discoveries. This is part of what makes developing the art and craft of fiction so much fun!

This spirit of experimentation and play will serve you well as you consider whether your setting might function symbolically, since you'll want to keep it subtle if it does. The story that follows uses setting symbolically, albeit in different ways. As you read (and write!) see if you can discover the ways in which symbolism begins to suggest itself, remembering that for something to work symbolically, it first has to paint a vivid picture. And then, gradually, that picture—those images, objects, or details—begins to suggest meanings beyond the literal. Before we know it, ideas multiply and combine, and we find ourselves in the verdant space of the imagination as it works through questions that very well may affect our lives, as well as our characters' lives. In other words, symbolism is one way to explore the connectedness of things. But you'll have to see if it suits you and your story.

Reading

Margaret Atwood (b. 1939)
Death by Landscape

Now that the boys are grown up and Rob is dead, Lois has moved to a condominium apartment in one of the new waterfront developments. She is relieved not to have to worry about the lawn, or about the ivy pushing its muscular little suckers into the brickwork, or the squirrels gnawing their way into the attic and eating the insulation off the wiring, or about strange noises. This building has a security system, and the only plant life is in pots in the solarium.

Lois is glad she's been able to find an apartment big enough for her pictures. They are more crowded together than they were in the house, but this arrangement gives the walls a European look: blocks of pictures, above and beside one another, rather than one over the chesterfield, one over the fireplace, one in the front hall, in the old acceptable manner of sprinkling art around so it does not get too intrusive. This way has more of an impact. You know it's not supposed to be furniture.

None of the pictures is very large, which doesn't mean they aren't valuable. They are paintings, or sketches and drawings, by artists who were not nearly as well known when Lois began to buy them as they are now. Their work later turned up on stamps, or as silk-screen reproductions hung in the principals' offices of high schools, or as jigsaw puzzles, or on beautifully printed calendars sent out by corporations as Christmas gifts to their less important clients. These artists painted after the first war, mostly in the twenties and thirties and forties; they painted landscapes. Lois has two Tom Thompsons, three A.Y. Jacksons, a Lawren Harris. She has an Arthur Lismer, she has a J.E.H. MacDonald. She has a David Milne. They are pictures of convoluted tree trunks on an island of pink wave-smoothed stone, with more islands behind; of a lake with rough, bright, sparsely wooded cliffs; of a vivid river shore with a tangle of bush and two beached canoes, one red, one gray; of a yellow autumn woods with the ice-blue gleam of a pond half-seen through the interlaced branches.

It was Lois who'd chosen them. Rob had no interest in art, although he could see the necessity of having something on the walls. He left all the decorating decisions to her, while providing the money, of course. Because of this collection of hers, Lois's friends—especially the men—have given her the reputation of having a good nose for art investments.

But this is not why she bought the pictures, way back then. She bought them because she wanted them. She wanted something that was in them although she could not have said at the time what it was. It was not peace:

she does not find them peaceful in the least. Looking at them fills her with a wordless unease. Despite the fact that there are no people in them or even animals, it's as if there is something, or someone, looking back out.

When she was thirteen, Lois went on a canoe trip. She'd only been on overnights before. This was to be a long one, into the trackless wilderness, as Cappie put it. It was Lois's first canoe trip, and her last.

Cappie was the head of the summer camp to which Lois had been sent ever since she was nine. Camp Manitou, it was called; it was one of the better ones, for girls, though not the best. Girls of her age whose parents could afford it were routinely packed off to such camps, which bore a generic resemblance to one another. They favored Indian names and had hearty, energetic leaders, who were called Cappie or Skip or Scottie. At these camps you learned to swim well and sail, and paddle a canoe, and perhaps ride a horse or play tennis. When you weren't doing these things you could do Arts and Crafts, and turn out dingy, lumpish clay ashtrays for your mother—mothers smoked more then—or bracelets made of colored braided string.

Cheerfulness was required at all times, even at breakfast. Loud shouting and the banging of spoons on the tables were allowed, and even encouraged, at ritual intervals. Chocolate bars were rationed, to control tooth decay and pimples. At night, after supper, in the dining hall or outside around a mosquito-infested campfire ring for special treats, there were singsongs. Lois can still remember all the words to "My Darling Clementine," and "My Bonnie Lies Over the Ocean," with acting-out gestures: a rippling of the hands for "the ocean," two hands together under the cheek for "lies." She will never be able to forget them, which is a sad thought.

Lois thinks she can recognize women who went to these camps and were good at it. They have a hardness to their handshakes, even now; a way of standing, legs planted firmly and farther apart than usual; a way of sizing you up, to see if you'd be any good in a canoe—the front, not the back. They themselves would be in the back. They would call it the stern.

She knows that such camps still exist, although Camp Manitou does not. They are one of the few things that haven't changed much. They now offer copper enameling, and function-less pieces of stained glass baked in electric ovens, though judging from the productions of her friends' grandchildren the artistic standards have not improved.

To Lois, encountering it in the first year after the war, Camp Manitou seemed ancient. Its log-sided buildings with the white cement in between the half-logs, its flagpole ringed with whitewashed stones, its weathered gray dock jutting out into Lake Prospect, with its woven rope bumpers and its rusty rings for tying up, its prim round flowerbed of petunias near the office door, must surely have been there always. In truth, it dated only from the first decade of the century; it had been founded by Cappie's parents, who'd thought of camping as bracing to the character, like cold showers, and had been passed along to her as an inheritance and an obligation.

Lois realized later that it must have been a struggle for Cappie to keep Camp Manitou going during the Depression and then the war, when money did not flow freely. If it had been a camp for the very rich, instead of the merely well-off, there would have been fewer problems. But there must have been enough Old Girls, ones with daughters, to keep the thing in operation, though not entirely shipshape: furniture was battered, painted trim was peeling, roofs leaked. There were dim photographs of these Old Girls dotted around the dining hall, wearing ample woolen bathing suits and showing their fat, dimpled legs, or standing, arms twined, in odd tennis outfits with baggy skirts.

In the dining hall, over the stone fireplace that was never used, there was a huge molting stuffed moose head, which looked somehow carnivorous. It was a sort of mascot; its name was Monty Manitou. The older campers spread the story that it was haunted and came to life in the dark, when the feeble and undependable lights had been turned off or, due to yet another generator failure, had gone out. Lois was afraid of it at first, but not after she got used to it.

Cappie was the same: you had to get used to her. Possibly she was forty, or thirty-five, or fifty. She had fawn-colored hair that looked as if it was cut with a bowl. Her head jutted forward, jigging like a chicken's as she strode around the camp, clutching notebooks and checking things off in them. She was like their minister in church: both of them smiled a lot and were anxious because they wanted things to go well; they both had the same overwashed skins and stringy necks. But all this disappeared when Cappie was leading a sing-song or otherwise leading. Then she was happy, sure of herself, her plain face almost luminous. She wanted to cause joy. At these times she was loved, at others merely trusted.

There were many things Lois didn't like about Camp Manitou, at first. She hated the noisy chaos and spoon banging of the dining hall, the rowdy sing-songs at which you were expected to yell in order to show that you were enjoying yourself. Hers was not a household that encouraged yelling. She hated the necessity of having to write dutiful letters to her parents claiming she was having fun. She could not complain, because camp cost so much money.

She didn't much like having to undress in a roomful of other girls, even in the dim light, although nobody paid any attention, or sleeping in a cabin with seven other girls, some of whom snored because they had adenoids or colds, some of whom had nightmares, or wet their beds and cried about it. Bottom bunks made her feel closed in, and she was afraid of falling out of top ones; she was afraid of heights. She got homesick, and suspected her parents of having a better time when she wasn't there than when she was, although her mother wrote to her every week saying how much they missed her. All this was when she was nine. By the time she was thirteen she liked it. She was an old hand by then.

Lucy was her best friend at camp. Lois had other friends in winter, when there was school and itchy woolen clothing and darkness in the afternoons, but Lucy was her summer friend.

She turned up the second year, when Lois was ten and a Bluejay. (Chickadees, Bluejays, Ravens, and Kingfishers—these were the names Camp Manitou assigned to the different age groups, a sort of totemic clan system. In those days, thinks Lois, it was birds for girls, animals for boys—wolves and so forth—though some animals and birds were suitable and some were not: never vultures, for instance; never skunks, or rats.)

Lois helped Lucy to unpack her tin trunk and place the folded clothes on the wooden shelves, and to make up her bed. She put her in the top bunk right above her, where she could keep an eye on her. Already she knew that Lucy was an exception to a good many rules; already she felt proprietorial.

Lucy was from the United States, where the comic books came from, and the movies. She wasn't from New York or Hollywood or Buffalo, the only American cities Lois knew the names of, but from Chicago. Her house was on the lakeshore and had gates to it, and grounds. They had a maid, all of the time. Lois's family only had a cleaning lady twice a week.

The only reason Lucy was being sent to *this* camp (she cast a look of minor scorn around the cabin, diminishing it and also offending Lois, while at the same time daunting her) was that her mother had been a camper here. Her mother had been a Canadian once but had married her father, who had a patch over one eye, like a pirate. She showed Lois the picture of him in her wallet. He got the patch in the war. "Shrapnel," said Lucy. Lois, who was unsure about shrapnel, was so impressed she could only grunt. Her own two-eyed, unwounded father was tame by comparison.

"My father plays golf," she ventured at last.

"*Everyone* plays golf," said Lucy. "My *mother* plays golf."

Lois's mother did not. Lois took Lucy to see the outhouses and the swimming dock and the dining hall with Monty Manitou's baleful head, knowing in advance they would not measure up.

This was a bad beginning; but Lucy was good-natured, and accepted

Camp Manitou with the same casual shrug with which she seemed to accept everything. She would make the best of it, without letting Lois forget that this was what she was doing.

However, there were things Lois knew that Lucy did not. Lucy scratched the tops off all her mosquito bites and had to be taken to the infirmary to be daubed with Ozonol. She took her T-shirt off while sailing, and although the counselor spotted her after a while and made her put it back on, she burned spectacularly, bright red, with the X of her bathing-suit straps standing out in alarming white; she let Lois peel the sheets of whispery-thin burned skin off her shoulders. When they sang "Alouette" around the campfire, she did not know any of the French words. The difference was that Lucy did not care about the things she didn't know, whereas Lois did.

During the next winter, and subsequent winters, Lucy and Lois wrote to each other. They were both only children, at a time when this was thought to be a disadvantage, so in their letters they pretended to be sisters or even twins. Lois had to strain a little over this, because Lucy was so blond, with translucent skin and large blue eyes like a doll's, and Lois was nothing out of the ordinary—just a tallish, thinnish, brownish person with freckles. They signed their letters LL, with the L's entwined together like the monograms on a towel. (Lois and Lucy, thinks Lois. How our names date us. Lois Lane, Superman's girlfriend, enterprising female reporter; I Love Lucy. Now we are obsolete, and it's little Jennifers, little Emilys, little Alexandras and Carolines and Tiffanys.)

They were more effusive in their letters than they ever were in person. They bordered their pages with X's and O's, but when they met again in the summers it was always a shock. They had changed so much, or Lucy had. It was like watching someone grow up in jolts. At first it would be hard to think up things to say.

But Lucy always had a surprise or two, or something to show, some marvel to reveal. The first year she had a picture of herself in a tutu, her hair in a ballerina's knot on the top of her head; she pirouetted around the swimming dock, to show Lois how it was done, and almost fell off. The next year she had given that up and was taking horseback riding. (Camp Manitou did not have horses.) The next year her mother and father had been divorced, and she had a new stepfather, one with both eyes, and a new house, although the maid was the same. The next year, when they had graduated from Bluejays and entered Ravens, she got her period, right in the first week of camp. The two of them snitched some matches from their counselor, who smoked illegally, and made a small fire out behind the furthest outhouse, at dusk, using their flashlights. They could set all kinds of fires by now; they had learned how in Campcraft. On this fire they burned one of Lucy's used sanitary napkins. Lois is not sure why they did this or whose idea it was. But she can remember the feeling of deep satisfaction it gave her as the white fluff singed and the blood sizzled, as if some wordless ritual had been fulfilled.

They did not get caught, but then they rarely got caught at any of their camp transgressions. Lucy had such large eyes, and was such an accomplished liar.

This year Lucy is different again: slower, more languorous. She is no longer interested in sneaking around after dark, purloining cigarettes from the counselor, dealing in black market candy bars. She is pensive, and hard to wake in the mornings. She doesn't like her stepfather, but she doesn't want to live with her real father either, who has a new wife. She thinks her mother may be having a love affair with a doctor; she doesn't know for sure, but she's seen them smooching in his car, out on the driveway, when her stepfather wasn't there. It serves him right. She hates her private school. She has a boyfriend, who is sixteen and works as a gardener's assistant. This is how she met him: in the garden. She describes to Lois what it is like when he kisses her: rubbery at first, but then your knees go limp. She has been forbidden to see him and threatened with boarding school. She wants to run away from home.

Lois has little to offer in return. Her own life is placid and satisfactory, but there is nothing much that can be said about happiness. "You're so lucky," Lucy tells her, a little smugly. She might as well say *boring*, because this is how it makes Lois feel.

Lucy is apathetic about the canoe trip, so Lois has to disguise her own excitement. The evening before they are to leave, she slouches into the campfire ring as if coerced and sits down with a sigh of endurance, just as Lucy does.

Every canoe trip that went out of camp was given a special send-off by Cappie and the section leader and counselors, with the whole section in attendance. Cappie painted three streaks of red across each of her cheeks with a lipstick. They looked like three-fingered claw marks. She put a blue circle on her forehead with fountain-pen ink, and tied a twisted bandanna around her head and stuck a row of frazzle-ended feathers around it, and wrapped herself in a red and black Hudson's Bay blanket. The counselors, also in blankets but with only two streaks of red, beat on tom-toms made of round wooden cheeseboxes with leather stretched over the top and nailed in place. Cappie was Chief Cappeosota. They all had to say "How!" when she walked into the circle and stood there with one hand raised.

Looking back on this, Lois finds it disquieting. She knows too much about Indians: this is why. She knows, for instance, that they should not even be called Indians, and that they have enough worries without other people taking their names and dressing up as them. It has all been a form of stealing.

But she remembers too that she was once ignorant of this. Once she loved the campfire, the flickering of light on the ring of faces, the sound of the fake tom-toms, heavy and fast like a scared heartbeat; she loved Cappie in a red blanket and feathers, solemn, as a Chief should be, raising her hand and saying, "Greetings, my Ravens." It was not funny, it was not making fun. She wanted to be an Indian. She wanted to be adventurous and pure, and aboriginal.

"You go on big water," says Cappie. This is her idea—all their ideas—of how Indians talk. "You go where no man has ever trod. You go many moons." This is not true. They are only going for a week, not many moons. The canoe route is clearly marked, they have gone over it on a map, and there are prepared campsites with names that are used year after year. But when Cappie says this—and despite the way Lucy rolls up her eyes—Lois can feel the water stretching out, with the shores twisting away on either side, immense and a little frightening.

"You bring back much wampum," says Cappie. "Do good in war, my braves, and capture many scalps." This is another of her pretenses: that they are boys, and bloodthirsty. But such a game cannot be played by substituting the word squaw. It would not work at all.

Each of them has to stand up and step forward and have a red line drawn across her cheeks by Cappie. She tells them they must follow the paths of their ancestors (who most certainly, thinks Lois, looking out the window of her apartment and remembering the family stash of daguerreotypes and sepia-colored portraits on her mother's dressing table—the stiff-shirted, black-coated, grim-faced men and the beflounced women with their severe hair and their corsetted respectability—would never have considered heading off onto an open lake in a canoe, just for fun).

At the end of the ceremony they all stood and held hands around the circle and sang taps. They did not sound very Indian, thinks Lois. It sounded like a bugle call at a military post, in a movie. But Cappie was never one to be much concerned with consistency, or with archaeology.

After breakfast the next morning they set out from the main dock, in four canoes, three in each. The lipstick stripes have not come off completely and still show faintly pink, like healing burns. They wear their white denim sailing hats, because of the sun, and thin-striped T-shirts, and pale baggy shorts with the cuffs rolled up. The middle one kneels, propping her rear end against the rolled sleeping bags. The counselors going with them are Pat and Kip. Kip is no-nonsense; Pat is easier to wheedle or fool.

There are white puffy clouds and a small breeze. Glints come from the little waves. Lois is in the bow of Kip's canoe. She still can't do a j-stroke very well, and she will have to be in the bow or the middle for the whole trip. Lucy is behind her; her own j-stroke is even worse. She splashes Lois with her paddle, quite a big splash.

"I'll get you back," says Lois.

"There was a stable fly on your shoulder," Lucy says.

Lois turns to look at her, to see if she's grinning. They're in the habit of splashing each other. Back there, the camp has vanished behind the first long point of rock and rough trees. Lois feels as if an invisible rope has broken. They're floating free, on their own, cut loose. Beneath the canoe the lake goes down, deeper and colder than it was a minute before.

"No horsing around in the canoe," says Kip. She's rolled her T-shirt sleeves up to the shoulder; her arms are brown and sinewy, her jaw determined, her stroke perfect. She looks as if she knows exactly what she is doing.

The four canoes keep close together. They sing, raucously and with defiance; they sing "The Quarter Master's Store" and "Clementine" and "Alouette." It is more like bellowing than singing.

After that the wind grows stronger, blowing slantwise against the bows, and they have to put all their energy into shoving themselves through the water.

Was there anything important, anything that would provide some sort of reason or clue to what happened next? Lois can remember everything, every detail; but it does her no good.

They stopped at noon for a swim and lunch, and went on in the afternoon. At last they reached Little Birch, which was the first campsite for overnight. Lois and Lucy made the fire while the others pitched the heavy canvas tents. The fireplace was already there, flat stones piled into a U. A burned tin can and a beer bottle had been left in it. Their fire went out, and they had to restart it. "Hustle your bustle," said Kip. "We're starving."

The sun went down, and in the pink sunset light they brushed their teeth and spat the toothpaste froth into the lake. Kip and Pat put all the food that wasn't in cans into a packsack and slung it into a tree, in case of bears.

Lois and Lucy weren't sleeping in a tent. They'd begged to be allowed to sleep out; that way they could talk without others hearing. If it rained, they told Kip, they promised not to crawl dripping into the tent over everyone's legs: they would get under the canoes. So they were out on the point.

Lois tried to get comfortable inside her sleeping bag, which smelled of musty storage and of earlier campers—a stale, salty sweetness. She curled herself up, with her sweater rolled up under her head for a pillow and her flashlight inside her sleeping bag so it wouldn't roll away. The muscles of her sore arms were making small pings, like rubber bands breaking.

Beside her Lucy was rustling around. Lois could see the glimmering oval of her white face.

"I've got a rock poking into my back," said Lucy.

"So do I," said Lois. "You want to go into the tent?" She herself didn't, but it was right to ask.

"No," said Lucy. She subsided into her sleeping bag. After a moment she said, "It would be nice not to go back."

"To camp?" said Lois.

"To Chicago," said Lucy. "I hate it there."

"What about your boyfriend?" said Lois. Lucy didn't answer. She was either asleep or pretending to be.

There was a moon, and a movement of the trees. In the sky there were stars, layers of stars that went down and down. Kip said that when the stars were bright like that instead of hazy, it meant bad weather later on. Out on the lake there were two loons, calling to each other in their insane, mournful voices. At the time it did not sound like grief. It was just background.

The lake in the morning was flat calm. They skimmed along over the glassy surface, leaving V-shaped trails behind them; it felt like flying. As the sun rose higher it got hot, almost too hot. There were stable flies in the canoes, landing on a bare arm or leg for a quick sting. Lois hoped for wind.

They stopped for lunch at the next of the named campsites, Lookout Point. It was called this because, although the site itself was down near the water on a flat shelf of rock, there was a sheer cliff nearby and a trail that led up to the top. The top was the lookout, although what you were supposed to see from there was not clear. Kip said it was just a view.

Lois and Lucy decided to make the climb anyway. They didn't want to hang around waiting for lunch. It wasn't their turn to cook, though they hadn't avoided much by not doing it, because cooking lunch was no big deal. It was just unwrapping the cheese and getting out the bread and peanut butter, but Pat and Kip always had to do their woodsy act and boil up a billy can for their own tea.

They told Kip where they were going. You had to tell Kip where you were going, even if it was only a little way into the woods to get dry twigs for kindling. You could never go anywhere without a buddy.

"Sure," said Kip, who was crouching over the fire, feeding driftwood into it. "Fifteen minutes to lunch."

"Where are they off to?" said Pat. She was bringing their billy can of water from the lake.

"Lookout," said Kip.

"Be careful," said Pat. She said it as an afterthought, because it was what she always said.

"They're old hands," Kip said.

Lois looks at her watch: it's ten to twelve. She is the watch-minder; Lucy is careless of time. They walk up the path, which is dry earth and rocks, big rounded pinky-gray boulders or split-open ones with jagged edges. Spindly balsam and spruce trees grow to either side; the lake is blue fragments to the left. The sun is right overhead; there are no shadows anywhere. The heat comes up at them as well as down. The forest is dry and crackly.

It isn't far, but it's a steep climb and they're sweating when they reach the top. They wipe their faces with their bare arms, sit gingerly down on a scorching-hot rock, five feet from the edge but too close for Lois. It's a lookout all right, a sheer drop to the lake and a long view over the water, back the way they've come. It's amazing to Lois that they've traveled so far, over all that water, with nothing to propel them but their own arms. It makes her feel strong. There are all kinds of things she is capable of doing.

"It would be quite a dive off here," says Lucy.

"You'd have to be nuts," says Lois.

"Why?" says Lucy. "It's really deep. It goes straight down." She stands up and takes a step nearer the edge. Lois gets a stab in her midriff, the kind she gets when a car goes too fast over a bump.

"Don't," she says.

"Don't what?" says Lucy, glancing around at her mischievously. She knows how Lois feels about heights. But she turns back. "I really have to pee," she says.

"You have toilet paper?" says Lois, who is never without it. She digs in her shorts pocket.

"Thanks," says Lucy.

They are both adept at peeing in the woods: doing it fast so the mosquitoes don't get you, the underwear pulled up between the knees, the squat with the feet apart so you don't wet your legs, facing downhill; the exposed feeling of your bum, as if someone is looking at you from behind. The etiquette when you're with someone else is not to look. Lois stands up and starts to walk back down the path, to be out of sight.

"Wait for me?" says Lucy.

Lois climbed down, over and around the boulders, until she could not see Lucy; she waited. She could hear the voices of the others, talking and laughing, down near the shore. One voice was yelling, "Ants! Ants!"

Someone must have sat on an anthill. Off to the side, in the woods, a raven was croaking, a hoarse single note.

She looked at her watch: it was noon. This is when she heard the shout.

She has gone over and over it in her mind since, so many times that the first, real shout has been obliterated, like a footprint trampled by other footprints. But she is sure (she is almost positive, she is nearly certain) that it was not a shout of fear. Not a scream. More like a cry of surprise, cut off too soon. Short, like a dog's bark.

"Lucy?" Lois said. Then she called. "Lucy!" By now she was clambering back up, over the stones of the path. Lucy was not up there. Or she was not in sight.

"Stop fooling around," Lois said. "It's lunchtime." But Lucy did not rise from behind a rock or step out, smiling, from behind a tree. The sunlight was all around; the rocks looked white. "This isn't funny!" Lois said, and it wasn't. Panic was rising in her, the panic of a small child who does not know where the bigger ones are hidden. She could hear her own heart. She looked quickly around; she lay down on the ground and looked over the edge of the cliff. It made her feel cold. There was nothing.

She went back down the path, stumbling; she was breathing too quickly; she was too frightened to cry. She felt terrible, guilty and dismayed, as if she had done something very bad by mistake, something that could never be repaired.

"Lucy's gone," she told Kip.

Kip looked up from her fire, annoyed. The water in the billy can was boiling. "What do you mean, 'Gone'?" she said. "Where did she go?"

"I don't know," said Lois. "She's just gone."

No one had heard the shout; but then, no one had heard Lois calling either. They had been talking among themselves, by the water.

Kip and Pat went up to the lookout and searched and called and blew their whistles. Nothing answered.

Then they came back down, and Lois had to tell exactly what had happened. The other girls all sat in a circle and listened to her. Nobody said anything. They all looked frightened, especially Pat and Kip. They were the leaders. You did not just lose a camper like this, for no reason at all.

"Why did you leave her alone?" said Kip.

"I was just down the path," said Lois. "I told you. She had to go to the bathroom." She did not say pee in front of people older than herself.

Kip looked disgusted.

"Maybe she just walked off into the woods and got turned around," said one of the girls.

"Maybe she's doing it on purpose," said another.

Nobody believed either of these theories.

They took the canoes and searched around the base of the cliff and peered down into the water. But there had been no sound of falling rock; there had been no splash. There was no clue, nothing at all. Lucy had simply vanished.

That was the end of the canoe trip. It took them the same two days to go back that it had taken coming in, even though they were short a paddler. They did not sing.

After that the police went, in a motorboat, with dogs; they were the Mounties and the dogs were German shepherds, trained to follow trails in the woods. But it had rained since, and they could find nothing.

Lois is sitting in Cappie's office. Her face is bloated with crying, she's seen that in the mirror. By now she feels numbed; she feels as if she has drowned. She can't stay here. It has been too much of a shock. Tomorrow her parents are coming to take her away. Several of the other girls who were on the canoe trip are also being collected. The others will have to stay, because their parents are in Europe or cannot be reached.

Cappie is grim. They've tried to hush it up, but of course everyone in camp knows. Soon the papers will know too. You can't keep it quiet, but what can be said? What can be said that makes any sense? "Girl vanishes in broad daylight, without a trace." It can't be believed; other things, worse things, will be suspected. Negligence, at the very least. But they have always taken such care. Bad luck will gather around Camp Manitou like a fog; parents will avoid it in favor of other, luckier places. Lois can see Cappie thinking all this, even through her numbness. It's what anyone would think.

Lois sits on the hard wooden chair in Cappie's office, beside the old wooden desk over which hangs the thumb-tacked bulletin board of normal camp routine, and gazes at Cappie through her puffy eyelids. Cappie is now smiling what is supposed to be a reassuring smile. Her manner is too casual: she's after something. Lois has seen this look on Cappie's face when she's been sniffing out contraband chocolate bars, hunting down those rumored to have snuck out of their cabins at night.

"Tell me again," says Cappie, "from the beginning."

Lois has told her story so many times by now, to Pat and Kip, to Cappie, to the police, that she knows it word for word. She knows it, but she no longer believes it. It has become a story. "I told you," she said. "She wanted to go to the bathroom. I gave her my toilet paper. I went down the path, I waited for her. I heard this kind of shout ..."

"Yes," says Cappie, smiling confidingly, "but before that. What did you say to one another?"

Lois thinks. Nobody has asked her this before. "She said you could dive off there. She said it went straight down."

"And what did you say?"

"I said you'd have to be nuts."

"Were you mad at Lucy?" says Cappie, in an encouraging voice.

"No," says Lois. "Why would I be mad at Lucy? I wasn't ever mad at Lucy." She feels like crying again. The times when she has, in fact, been mad at Lucy have been erased already. Lucy was always perfect.

"Sometimes we're angry when we don't know we're angry," says Cappie, as if to herself. "Sometimes we get really mad and we don't even know it. Sometimes we might do a thing without meaning to, or without knowing what will happen. We lose our tempers."

Lois is only thirteen, but it doesn't take her long to figure out that Cappie is not including herself in any of this. By *we* she means Lois. She is accusing Lois of pushing Lucy off the cliff. The unfairness of this hits her like a slap. "I didn't!" she says.

"Didn't what?" says Cappie softly. "Didn't what, Lois?"

Lois does the worst thing, she begins to cry. Cappie gives her a look like a pounce. She's got what she wanted.

...

Later, when she was grown up, Lois was able to understand what this interview had been about. She could see Cappie's desperation, her need for a story, a real story with a reason in it; anything but the senseless vacancy Lucy had left for her to deal with. Cappie wanted Lois to supply the reason, to be the reason. It wasn't even for the newspapers or the parents, because she could never make such an accusation without proof. It was for herself: something to explain the loss of Camp Manitou and of all she had worked for, the years of entertaining spoiled children and buttering up parents and making a fool of herself with feathers stuck in her hair. Camp Manitou was, in fact, lost. It did not survive.

Lois worked all this out, twenty years later. But it was far too late. It was too late even ten minutes afterwards, when she'd left Cappie's office and was walking slowly back to her cabin to pack. Lucy's clothes were still there, folded on the shelves, as if waiting. She felt the other girls in the cabin watching her with speculation in their eyes. Could she have done it? *She must have done it.* For the rest of her life, she has caught people watching her in this way.

Maybe they weren't thinking this. Maybe they were merely sorry for her. But she felt she had been tried and sentenced; and this is what has stayed with her: the knowledge that she had been singled out, condemned for something that was not her fault.

Lois sits in the living room of her apartment, drinking a cup of tea. Through the knee-to-ceiling window she has a wide view of Lake

Ontario, with its skin of wrinkled blue-gray light, and of the willows of Centre Island shaken by a wind, which is silent at this distance and on this side of the glass. When there isn't too much pollution she can see the far shore, the foreign shore, though today it is obscured.

Possibly she could go out, go downstairs, do some shopping; there isn't much in the refrigerator. The boys say she doesn't get out enough. But she isn't hungry, and moving, stirring from this space, is increasingly an effort.

She can hardly remember, now, having her two boys in the hospital, nursing them as babies; she can hardly remember getting married, or what Rob looked like. Even at the time she never felt she was paying full attention. She was tired a lot, as if she was living not one life but two: her own, and another, shadowy life that hovered around her and would not let itself be realized—the life of what would have happened if Lucy had not stepped sideways and disappeared from time.

She would never go up north, to Rob's family cottage or to any place with wild lakes and wild trees and the calls of loons. She would never go anywhere near. Still, it was as if she was always listening for another voice, the voice of a person who should have been there but was not. An echo.

While Rob was alive, while the boys were growing up, she could pretend she didn't hear it, this empty space in sound. But now there is nothing much left to distract her.

She turns away from the window and looks at her pictures. There is the pinkish island, in the lake, with the inter-twisted trees. It's the same landscape they paddled through, that distant summer. She's seen travelogues of this country, aerial photographs; it looks different from above, bigger, more hopeless: lake after lake, random blue puddles in dark green bush, the trees like bristles.

How could you ever find anything there, once it was lost? Maybe if they cut it all down, drained it all away, they might find Lucy's bones, sometime, wherever they are hidden. A few bones, some buttons, the buckle from her shorts.

But a dead person is a body; a body occupies space, it exists somewhere. You can see it; you put it in a box and bury it in the ground, and then it's in a box in the ground. But Lucy is not in a box or in the ground. Because she is nowhere definite, she could be anywhere.

And these paintings are not landscape paintings. Because there aren't any landscapes up there, not in the old, tidy European sense, with a gentle hill, a curving river, a cottage, a mountain in the background, a golden evening sky. Instead there's a tangle, a receding maze, in which you can become lost almost as soon as you step off the path. There are no backgrounds in any of these paintings, no vistas; only a great deal of foreground that goes back and back, endlessly, involving you in its twists and turns of trees and branch and rock. No matter how far back in you go, there will be more. And the trees themselves are hardly trees; they are currents of energy, charged with violent color.

Who knows how many trees there were on the cliff just before Lucy disappeared? Who counted? Maybe there was one more, afterwards.

Lois sits in her chair and does not move. Her hand with the cup is raised halfway to her mouth. She hears something, almost hears it: a shout of recognition or of joy.

She looks at the paintings, she looks into them. Every one of them is a picture of Lucy. You can't see her exactly, but she's there, in behind the pink stone island or the one behind that. In the picture of the cliff she is hidden by the clutch of fallen rocks towards the bottom; in the one of the river shore she is crouching beneath the over-turned canoe. In the yellow autumn woods she's behind the tree that cannot be seen because of the other trees, over beside the blue sliver of pond; but if you walked into the picture and found the tree, it would be the wrong one, because the right one would be further on. Everyone has to be somewhere, and this is where Lucy is. She is in Lois's apartment, in the holes that open inwards on the wall, not like windows but like doors. She is here. She is entirely alive.

Craft Questions

- Contrast the description of Lois's landscape pictures with the description of Camp Manitou and the wilderness.
- Note the structure of the story. Why might Atwood have decided to frame this story of tragedy with scenes from the present?
- What mood is created by these two time frames and places?
- Consider the title, "Death by Landscape." What might landscape symbolize or metaphorically suggest in the story?
- Is Canadian identity important to this story? Why or why not?

Exercises

Exercise 1: This Must Be the Place

Spend some time thinking about places that you know well. Pick one. Maybe it's your childhood home, your grandmother's porch, or a particular park that you've visited multiple times. How does this place look, feel, and smell? What mood does it create, what symbolic associations does it suggest? Free-write about this place, and return later to see if you can use some of your description for a new story or a story in progress.

Objective: To draw from your sensory impressions of an actual place in order to develop an imaginative setting.

Exercise 2: Mood and Place

On the left is a list of places, times, and weather. On the right are words that describe a mood. Pick one item from the left and one from the right. Write a passage in which the setting suggests the mood. Try for less obvious pairings. Feel free to incorporate a character.

a garden in the rain	exuberant
midnight in a parking lot	lovesick
1920, on the veranda	suspenseful
a winter morning	melancholy
in the ice-skating rink	saddened
the road that seems to go on forever	surprised
daybreak	fearful

Objective: To experiment with possible connections between setting and mood.

Exercise 3: Day and Night

Read over a story in progress to see if you've mentioned time of day. If so, see what happens to the story's mood if you change it (from day to night or night to day, for example). If you haven't yet mentioned time of day, try adding it into the story to amplify existing moods, tensions, or themes. Instead of writing a single paragraph of description, try describing the time of day in several separate sentences or passages, interspersed in the story.

Objective: To use time of day to contribute to the mood and tone of an existing story.

fifteen | style and tone

icebergs and castles

WHEN YOU THINK OF *style*, what comes to mind? Fashion? Interior decoration? A distinguishing quality more difficult to define? All of these definitions are relevant to our discussion, but, in fiction, **style** is largely a matter of the way in which a story is written, including the choice of words (**diction**) and the order in which they're presented (**syntax**), whereas the term **tone** describes the mood or feeling of a story. Ultimately, style and tone are interrelated, and as you craft your stories, you'll probably be developing them together without even realizing it. You're also likely developing the **voice** and **viewpoint** (see chapter 11) simultaneously; all of these elements work together.

The way in which your story is told and the mood it sets are determined by who is speaking and whether they're speaking in a specific voice, such as that of an unreliable first-person narrator or someone telling a story as if it's being spoken aloud. For example, a story told in the voice of an adolescent first-person narrator who uses slang and idiomatic expressions will necessarily have a different style and tone from one told in the voice of a distant, omniscient third-person narrator who uses more formal language and longer sentences.

As you focus on your story's style and tone, you'll also want to consider **verb tense**, the **narrative balance** between dialogue, thoughts, and action, as well as the relative presence or absence of **figurative** or **poetic language** (see chapter 10). When you're first drafting your story, continue to work intuitively. But when you go back to revise, you can consciously use these elements to create the style and tone you have in mind.

Sparse and Elaborate Styles

As you've surely noticed from the stories we've read so far, each one has its own unique style and tone; the options are seemingly endless. However, two general categories include **sparse** styles, or those devoid of much descriptive detail, figurative language, or lengthy sentences, and their opposite: **elaborate** styles. Although most stories arguably fall somewhere in between, it may be useful to observe and try out sharply contrasting styles, in order to identify your inclinations and strengths. With this in mind, read the following excerpts with an eye on their styles.

The first is the opening of "The Beast in the Jungle" by one of the great United States literary stylists, Henry James (1843–1916). As both a realist, concerned with the details of everyday life, and an early modernist, exploring complex states of interior consciousness, James's work is considered important, in part, because it ultimately defies categorization.

> What determined the speech that startled him in the course of their encounter scarcely matters, being probably but some words spoken by himself quite without intention—spoken as they lingered and slowly moved together after their renewal of acquaintance. He had been conveyed by friends an hour or two before at the house at which he was staying; the party of visitors at the other house, of whom he was one, and thanks to whom it was his theory, as always, that he was lost in the crowd, had been invited over to luncheon. There had been after luncheon much dispersal, all in the interest of the original motive, a view of Weatherend itself and the fine things, intrinsic features, pictures, heirlooms, treasures of all the arts, that made the place almost famous; and the great rooms were so numerous that guests could wander at their will, hang back from the principal group and in cases where they took such matters with the last seriousness give themselves up to mysterious appreciations and measurements.

The second example is the opening of contemporary United States writer, Tommy Orange's (b. 1982) story "The Team":

You'd been staring at a wall in your office for what amount of time you weren't sure. Time slipped away lately, as if behind a curtain then back out again as something else, here as an internet hole, there as a walk on your street you insisted on calling a hike with your wife and son, here as a book your eyes look at, that you don't comprehend, there as crippling depression, here as observing circling turkey vultures, there as your ever-imminent anxiety, here as a failed Zoom call, there as a home-schooling shift with your son, here as April, May already gone, there as the obsession over the body count, the nameless numbers rising on endless graphics of animated maps. Time was not on your side or anyone's, it was dreaming its waste with you, as you, hidden and loud as the sun behind a cloud. You were thinking of when you were last in public. This wasn't counting the masked and panicked weekly grocery-store runs, or the post-office-box scramble, you with your precariously stacked boxes of the unessential, keeping as much distance as you could from anyone you saw, especially after hearing a podcast that introduced you to the disgusting idea of mouth rain. You don't even make eye contact with anyone anymore, so afraid of you are the spread.

Craft Questions

- Do you consider each passage sparse or elaborate?
- Discuss the ways in which each passage's various elements—including diction, syntax, voice, and tone—contribute to its style.

Not only do these two passages illustrate stylistic choices, they emphasize historical lines of connection, given the fact that the work of proto-modernists such as James, in a sense, helped pave the way for contemporary postmodernists such as Orange. The same is true at the other end of the spectrum; take a look back on the connection between the sparse or minimalist tendencies of writers such as Beattie and Robison. In other words, our style doesn't come out of nowhere. Like so many things—speech patterns, mannerisms, thoughts—our style reflects the time in which we live, which itself reflects previous periods.

Now that you've taken a look at some sparse and elaborate passages, you may wonder how to use such techniques in your own writing. The simple answer is trial and error. You have to try out various stylistic options to begin to arrive at combinations that feel authentic and inspired. For fun, you may want to try to imitate (or even parody) some of the writers we've discussed.

Diction and Syntax

What kinds of words do you generally use when you speak? When you write? How do these words change according to context and audience? One way of beginning to answer these questions is to take a closer look at your default word choice or diction in the writing you've been doing recently, maybe in your latest short story. Ask yourself if the words you're using convey the overall style, tone, and mood you have in mind. Then take a closer look at your word choice within dialogue and ask whether these words seem natural for your characters.

Do you use a lot of *Latinate* words or those with Greek or Latin roots? If you're not sure, you can always use a good dictionary to look up the words' etymologies or origins. In general, English words that come from Latin or Greek tend to sound formal in comparison to those with English roots. Consider, for example, a Latinate word such as the verb form of *interrogate*. The *Oxford English Dictionary*'s etymology for the word includes: "Latin *interrogātus*, participial stem of *interrogāre*, < *inter* between, at intervals + *rogare* to ask." As you can see if you're familiar with French, the Latin word morphs into the French infinitive with the same meaning: *rogare*.

Now compare the word to an Anglo-Saxon synonym, *ask*. In this case, the *Oxford English Dictionary*'s etymological entry includes:

> Old English **ascian**, Old English **askede** (past tense, *rare*), early Middle English **ascie**, early Middle English **asskenn** (*Ormulum*), early Middle English **easki** (*south-west midlands*), early Middle English **escie** (*south-west midlands*), early Middle English **eski** (*south-west midlands*), early Middle English **eskie** (*south-west midlands*), Middle English **ascke**, Middle English **aski**, Middle English **asky**, Middle English **askye**, Middle English **assk**, Middle English **esce** (*south-west midlands*), Middle English **hask**, Middle English **haske**, Middle English–1600s **aske**, Middle English–**ask**, 1500s–**askt** (past tense and past participle, now *nonstandard*), 1600s **asck**; *Scottish* pre-1700 **alscyt** (past tense), pre-1700 **alsk**, pre-1700 to 1700s–**ask**.

This etymology offers more information than we need to know about a simple word that we use in everyday life! But it illustrates the point that *ask*, originally from Old English, wends its way through multiple regional Middle English dialects and through Scottish in the seventeenth and eighteenth centuries. In fact, English is a hybrid language through and through, as it is made up of bits and pieces from so many other languages with which it has come in contact over time. And the English language continues to morph and grow. In itself, this history constitutes a rich area of study for writers and lovers of language. For our purposes, however, it's useful to simply become attuned to whether the words we tend to use create a formal or informal tone and whether we're getting the most mileage we can out of the words we choose.

Here are a few questions to help you tune in to diction in your own and others' stories:

- Does the story's diction reflect the characters' ages, level of education, and station in life?
- How many words would a typical reader have to look up?
- Does the diction change in different parts of the story? If so, is there a clear reason for the change(s)?
- Whether sparse or elaborate, how does the diction contribute to the story's overall style and meaning?

By attempting to answer these questions, you'll get a sense of how diction is currently functioning and how to revise it.

What about using *dialect*: words or phrases that communicate regional or cultural ways of speaking? Although this technique can be difficult to render effectively without overdoing it or without it becoming a distraction, if you are familiar with a specific speech pattern, you may want to try using it sparingly to see if it adds to the texture, realism, and power of your writing. Don't shy away from using words and phrases that you use and hear in everyday life if they suit your story's characters and setting.

Clearly, it's difficult to think about diction without thinking about syntax: the order of words in phrases and sentences. In fact, sentence-structure not only creates rhythm, pace, and overall style, it can also affect meaning. For example, look back at this sentence in the James passage at the beginning of this chapter:

> He had been conveyed by friends an hour or two before at the house at which he was staying; the party of visitors at the other house, of whom he was one, and thanks to whom it was his theory, as always, that he was lost in the crowd, had been invited over to luncheon.

Craft Questions

- How would you describe the syntax of this passage? Is it long or short? Direct or indirect?
- How would you describe its pace?
- What ideas come up first, in the middle, and at the end of the sentence?
- What state of being does the sentence emphasize or even enact?

As a general rule, longer, complex sentences tend to read more slowly whereas shorter ones create a more abrupt, quicker pace. However, sometimes the opposite is true. Ultimately, syntax depends upon context. For instance, take a second look at the breathtaking ending of Alexie's "What You Pawn I Will Redeem":

> I took my grandmother's regalia and walked outside. I knew that solitary yellow bead was part of me. I knew I was that yellow bead in part. Outside, I wrapped myself in my grandmother's regalia and breathed her in. I stepped off the sidewalk and into the intersection. Pedestrians stopped. Cars stopped. The city stopped. They all watched me dance with my grandmother. I was my grandmother, dancing.

Craft Questions

- Discuss Alexie's use of repetition in this passage. How does it affect the tone of the story's ending?
- Discuss the passage's three shortest sentences. Do they slow down or speed up the pace of the passage? How does syntax impact your experience of this scene?
- Try rewriting the last sentence without changing or substituting any words. How does syntax alter meaning?

Verb Tense

Deciding on which verb tense to use for your story will probably come naturally. However, there are instances where reconsideration may yield reward. For most writers, the past tense is their default, and readers may not even notice past tense since we're generally accustomed to telling stories about things that happened in the past.

In contrast, the present tense is often more noticeable, and writers are using present tense more frequently today than they did in the past. A story told in the present tense may take on a greater sense of immediacy. And present tense makes it comparatively easy to switch back and forth between base-time and flashbacks if you so choose, as we discussed in chapter 13. The future tense appears infrequently for entire stories, but is the go-to tense for flash-forwards.

Beginning writers frequently encounter difficulties in keeping tense consistent, and unless you have a clear reason to switch, it's best to try to stay in one tense. This is sometimes simply a matter of rusty grammar, which can be caught by reading your story aloud or having someone read it aloud to you. In other cases, the switch in verb tense indicates a not yet fully realized idea. For example, maybe you *do* intend to switch from present to past to indicate a flashback, but you still need to provide a paragraph break or context clue to signal this intention.

Tone

Again, whereas style refers to the way in which your story is written, tone indicates its mood, feeling or atmosphere. In some ways, this is the subtlest element we've discussed, while also being significant. As we considered in our discussion of dialogue in chapter 12, *how* things are said, including where the emphasis falls, is often just as significant as *what* is said. The same can be said of *tone* in everyday life. Without even realizing it, we pick up all kinds of information on people's moods, states of mind, and situations through their tone of voice. In fact, from a very early age, even before we can speak ourselves, we are tuning in to these kinds of frequencies.

The tone of a short story can be variously described as *witty, humorous, bold, upbeat, gritty, arresting, poignant*, or *somber*. The list goes on. Look back on the stories we've discussed so far and see if you can describe their various tones. Then, if possible, compare your list with classmates or friends to see if you're in agreement. Since complex stories evoke various tones throughout, and since we all bring our own experiences to the reading we do, it's unlikely that you'll arrive at a single answer. Instead, you'll likely be able to identify a range of related possibilities.

Irony and Satire

Although most of the stories we've discussed so far can be characterized as more serious than humorous, plenty of great fiction employs some type of humor. Two of the most widely used forms of humor are **irony**, which involves a reversal of our normal expectations, and **satire**, which pokes fun at characters or situations through the use of exaggeration. Closely related to **sarcasm**, which mocks or expresses contempt, satire often holds up a mirror to faulty institutions, behaviors, or beliefs.

To identify and define these possibilities, let's take a look at the opening of "I Can Say Many Nice Things" by contemporary United States writer Ben Marcus (b. 1967):

> Fleming awoke in the dark and his room felt loose, sloshing so badly he gripped the bed. From his window there was nothing but a hallway, and if he craned his neck, a blown lightbulb swung into view. The room pitched up and down and for a moment he thought he might be sick. The word "hallway" must have a nautical

name. Why didn't they supply a glossary for this cruise? Probably they had, in the welcome packet he'd failed to read. A glossary. A history of the boat, which would be referred to as a ship. Sunny biographies of the captain and crew, who had always *dreamed* of this life. Lobotomized histories of the islands they'd visit. Who else had sailed this way. Famous suckwads from the past, slicing through this very water on wooden longships.

A welcome packet, the literary genre most likely to succeed in the new millennium. Why not read about a community you don't belong to, that doesn't actually exist, a captain and crew who are, in reality, if that isn't too much of a downer on your vacation, as indifferent to one another as any set of co-employees at an office or bank? Read doctored personal statements from underpaid crew members—because ocean life pays better than money!—who hate their lives but have been forced to buy into the mythology of working on a boat, separated now from loved ones and friends, growing lonelier by the second, even while they wait on you and follow your every order.

And yet, when Fleming thought about it, this welcome packet, fucked-up though it was, even though he hadn't read it, most certainly had more readers than he did. More people, for sure, read this welcome packet than had ever read any of his books or stories. This welcome packet commanded a bigger audience than he ever would with his sober, sentimental inventions of domestic lives he'd never lived, if that wasn't too flattering a description of the literary product he willed onto the page with less and less conviction every time he sat down. Maybe he'd actually learn something about writing if he read the welcome packet.

The room spun and he clutched the bed. It would be two straight weeks of this seesawing, punctuated by mind-raping workshop sessions in a conference room and the occasional blitz of tropical sun if he could stand it. He had planned to get in shape for this trip, just to medicate a minor quadrant of his self-loathing apparatus, but when that hadn't happened, when instead he had fattened further, he went out and bought new T-shirts, one size larger than last year. He looked okay in them. Not really that bad. He would just make sure not to take one off in public. Even in private, actually, he had cut down on the nudity. These days the shame followed him indoors.

Craft Questions

- Discuss the narrator and his situation. In what ways can his situation be considered ironic?
- Would you define the tone of this passage as satiric, sarcastic, or both? Why?
- Which words and phrases does Marcus use to create this particular style and tone?

Whatever styles and tones you end up creating in your short stories, it can be an adventure to try out various possibilities. Experimentation is part of the process of discovering the stories that resonate most deeply within you. As you explore, be prepared to admire stories that would be difficult, if not impossible, for you to tell in a believable, authentic way. Whereas we all contain a range of possible voices, subjects, styles, and tones, this doesn't mean that anything we try on will fit. It takes a certain fearlessness and honesty to try things and fail. And fail we must—before we succeed.

Readings

Jamaica Kincaid (b. 1949)
Girl

Wash the white clothes on Monday and put them on the stone heap; wash the color clothes on Tuesday and put them on the clothesline to dry; don't walk barehead in the hot sun; cook pumpkin fritters in very hot sweet oil; soak your little cloths right after you take them off; when buying cotton to make yourself a nice blouse, be sure that it doesn't have gum on it, because that way it won't hold up well after a wash; soak salt fish overnight before you cook it; is it true that you sing benna[1] in Sunday school?; always eat your food in such a way that it won't turn someone else's stomach; on Sundays try to walk like a lady and not like the slut you are so bent on becoming; don't sing benna in Sunday school; you mustn't speak to wharf-rat boys, not even to give directions; don't eat fruits on the street—flies will follow you; *but I don't sing benna on Sundays at all and never in Sunday school*; this is how to sew on a button; this is how to make a button-hole for the button you have just sewed on; this is how to hem a dress when you see the hem coming down and so to prevent yourself from looking like the slut I know you are so bent on becoming; this is how you iron your father's khaki shirt so that it doesn't have a crease; this is how you iron your father's khaki pants so that they don't have a

1 A Caribbean style of music associated with *carnival*.

crease; this is how you grow okra—far from the house, because okra tree harbors red ants; when you are growing dasheen, make sure it gets plenty of water or else it makes your throat itch when you are eating it; this is how you sweep a corner; this is how you sweep a whole house; this is how you sweep a yard; this is how you smile to someone you don't like too much; this is how you smile to someone you don't like at all; this is how you smile to someone you like completely; this is how you set a table for tea; this is how you set a table for dinner; this is how you set a table for dinner with an important guest; this is how you set a table for lunch; this is how you set a table for breakfast; this is how to behave in the presence of men who don't know you very well, and this way they won't recognize immediately the slut I have warned you against becoming; be sure to wash every day, even if it is with your own spit; don't squat down to play marbles—you are not a boy, you know; don't pick people's flowers—you might catch something; don't throw stones at blackbirds, because it might not be a blackbird at all; this is how to make a bread pudding; this is how to make doukona;[1] this is how to make pepper pot; this is how to make a good medicine for a cold; this is how to make a good medicine to throw away a child before it even becomes a child; this is how to catch a fish; this is how to throw back a fish you don't like, and that way something bad won't fall on you; this is how to bully a man; this is how a man bullies you; this is how to love a man, and if this doesn't work there are other ways, and if they don't work don't feel too bad about giving up; this is how to spit up in the air if you feel like it, and this is how to move quick so that it doesn't fall on you; this is how to make ends meet; always squeeze bread to make sure it's fresh; *but what if the baker won't let me feel the bread*?; you mean to say that after all you are really going to be the kind of woman who the baker won't let near the bread?

Craft Questions

- Pick out the aspects of the story that are unmistakably different from all the other works we have read.
- How do these stylistic choices influence the tone?
- What do we know about the characters?
- How is tension generated in the story?
- Is there a climax or tipping point? What changes from beginning to middle to end?

1 A traditional Antiguan dish.

Steven Schutzman
The Bank Robbery

The bank robber told his story in little notes to the bank teller. He held the pistol in one hand and gave her the notes with the other. The first note said:

> *This is a bank holdup because money is just like time and I need more to keep on going, so keep your hands where I can see them and don't go pressing any alarm buttons or I'll blow your head off.*

The teller, a young woman of about twenty-five, felt the lights that lined her streets go on for the first time in years. She kept her hands where he could see them and didn't press any alarm buttons. Ah danger, she said to herself, you are just like love. After she read the note, she gave it back to the gunman and said:

"This note is far too abstract. I really can't respond to it."

The robber, a young man of about twenty-five, felt the electricity of his thoughts in his hand as he wrote the next note. Ah money, he said to himself, you are just like love. His next note said:

> *This is a bank holdup because there is only one clear rule around here and that is* WHEN YOU RUN OUT OF MONEY YOU SUFFER, *so keep your hands where I can see them and don't go pressing any alarm buttons or I'll blow your head off.*

The young woman took the note, touching lightly the gunless hand that had written it. The touch of the gunman's hand went immediately to her memory, growing its own life there. It became a constant light toward which she could move when she was lost. She felt that she could see everything clearly as if an unknown veil had just been lifted.

"I think I understand now," she said to the thief, looking first in his eyes and then at the gun. "But all this money will not get you what you want." She looked at him deeply, hoping that she was becoming rich before his eyes.

Ah danger, she said to herself, you are the gold that wants to spend my life.

The robber was becoming sleepy. In the gun was the weight of his dreams about this moment when it was yet to come. The gun was like the heavy eyelids of someone who wants to sleep but is not allowed.

Ah money, he said to himself, I find little bits of you leading to more of you in greater little bits. You are promising endless amounts of yourself but others are coming. They are threatening our treasure together. I cannot pick you up fast enough as you lead into the great, huge quiet that you are. Oh money, please save me, for you are desire, pure desire, that wants only itself.

The gunman could feel his intervals, the spaces in himself, piling up so that he could not be sure of what he would do next. He began to write. His next note said:

> *Now is the film of my life, the film of my insomnia: an eerie bus ride, a trance in the night, from which I want to step down, whose light keeps me from sleeping. In the streets I will chase the wind-blown letter of love that will change my life. Give me the money, my Sister, so that I can run my hands through its hair. This is the unfired gun of time, so keep your hands where I can see them and don't go pressing any alarm buttons or I'll blow your head off with it.*

Reading, the young woman felt her inner hands grabbing and holding onto this moment of her life.

Ah danger, she said to herself, you are yourself with perfect clarity. Under your lens I know what I want.

The young man and woman stared into each other's eyes forming two paths between them. On one path his life, like little people, walked into her, and on the other hers walked into him.

"This money is love," she said to him. "I'll do what you want." She began to put money into the huge satchel he had provided.

As she emptied it of money, the bank filled with sleep. Everyone else in the bank slept the untroubled sleep of trees that would never be money. Finally she placed all the money in the bag.

The bank robber and the bank teller left together like hostages of each other. Though it was no longer necessary, he kept the gun on her, for it was becoming like a child between them.

Craft Questions

- How would you describe the story's style and tone?
- Compare the diction and syntax of the gunman's notes with the diction and syntax of the rest of the story. What do these differences add to the story?
- Discuss the story's use of figurative language and symbolism.
- What is the story about thematically?

Exercises

Exercise 1: Imitation and Variation

Find a passage you admire stylistically in any of the stories we've discussed. Paying close attention to diction and syntax, write an imitation. Next, rework your passage, keeping words, phrases, and sentences you like and changing those that sound forced to a more natural rhythm and tone.

Objective: To try on and borrow style elements for your own stories.

Exercise 2: Paragraph Style Redux

Rework one of your paragraphs from a story in progress by first using a sparse style and next an elaborate one. Consider diction, syntax, and the use of repetition. Read over your two versions and see what you learn from pushing yourself in these two different directions. Do you have a favorite or are there elements from each you like? How would you find your way back to some sort of middle ground, if that is, in fact, what you intend?

Objective: To push yourself to stylistic extremes to see if you can use one of these techniques, or something in between, to revise a story.

Exercise 3: Who's Listening, Anyway?

Imagine that you have just been released from a bank where there was a robbery and you are telling the story of what just happened to one of the following people. As you write, consider how you feel about the experience and try to convey that feeling.

Your mother
Your best friend
A bystander
A reporter

Alternately, try rewriting a passage from a story in progress by imagining a specific audience/listener.

Objective: To work with tone by imagining an interlocutor.

sixteen | revision

are we there yet?

By now you've hopefully developed a story or two that you like. And you've likely received some feedback on your creative work. How do you know when a story is finished? How can you tell when you've arrived at your final version? The short answer is: you can't. The process of revision is endless, depending upon your inclinations and proclivities as a writer. If you really want to create a beautiful, complete story, you'll be doing more than editing for typos and changing a few words here and there. For some fiction writers, revising involves re-envisioning and redrafting the entire story multiple times. For others, it involves cutting sections, moving sections or scenes, and adding missing elements. Some writers even continue revising after a story has been initially published.

The folio at the end of this chapter showcases a student story from its beginning stage of composition, through a marked draft, process statement, and completion, providing a visual model for revision. As you begin to find ways to revise that work for *you*, there are certain questions you can ask to help you determine when a story is finished *enough*: when you can stop working on it, turn it in for an assignment, or share it with others. Here's a list of general questions you can use alone or with a classmate to see if your story may be nearing completion:

- Does the story arouse initial curiosity?
- Does the story effectively avoid melodrama and cliché?
- What is the point of view? Is it consistent throughout?
- Who or what is the focus of the story? What is the story about thematically?
- Are the characters consistent, unique, and complex? Are the characters revealed in a realistic way?
- Is there a good balance between believable dialogue, description, and action?
- Is the structure and pace of the story effective? Are there scenes that should be tightened up, removed, expanded, or added?
- Is there dramatic tension in the story? How is it created?
- Is the setting of the story engaging? Does it contribute to the overall atmosphere and meaning of the story?
- Are the style and tone effective for this particular story?

Finding Strong Writing Models

If you're in a class, you may be wondering where to go next for help with your writing once the semester is over. As useful as it can be to take courses, keep in mind that creative writing, as a discipline, didn't really begin to take hold in United States colleges and universities until the mid-twentieth century. What did countless writers do before there were courses? They read and wrote. This text has stressed the importance of reading, discussing, studying, and imitating strong writing models to see how others who have come before you, as well as your contemporaries, have done the things you're trying to do now.

Even when you strongly dislike a story, there's something you can learn from it. We develop our own ways of doing things not only from admiration but also from objection. And the stories we read become part of our experience in subtler, less detectable ways; they're part of our internal landscape, just like the water we drink, the air we breathe, the food we eat, the dreams we dream, the movies we see, the stories we hear, the struggles we encounter. So, if you want to write great stories, you absolutely need to read great stories (and not so great ones too). Read voraciously and variously. You never know from where you will draw inspiration. Most fiction writers regularly read outside of their field for ideas, and, as we've discussed, this becomes especially important if you are writing on a different time period or incorporating ideas from a particular discipline such as cognitive science, philosophy, or natural history.

Libraries are treasure troves that many of us have forgotten in this age of easily accessible, digital information. Visit your public or school library to roam around, get lost, and find things you didn't even know existed.

Similarly, if you've got a good bookstore nearby, make a habit of visiting to check out new and old titles. And, of course, blogs, online journals, and other internet repositories are easy to find and often free to access. Appendix B offers a list of online resources. You can find journals online, check out their free samples, and subscribe if you're interested. This is a great way to stay current. In addition, platforms such as YouTube, Instagram, and online groups regularly feature literary work, whether performed or written. There are more ways than even before to access the spoken and written word.

Establishing Your Own Critique Circle

If there has been a workshop component to your studies, you've hopefully benefited from the deadlines, critiques, feedback, and support that a good workshop can offer. One way to keep receiving these benefits is to enroll in another creative writing course. However, if this isn't possible, you may want to consider forming your own critique circle. All you need is a few other writers and a space to meet (virtually or in-person). For more on what makes a workshop effective, see appendix A. But keep in mind that it's often most helpful if the writers involved are at a similar stage in their writing (e.g., beginning, intermediate, advanced). It's also helpful if participants have similar goals in mind and agree on the frequency and rigor of meetings.

For many established writers, individual writing companions can serve a similar purpose. Most of us have a few people to whom we send rough drafts for feedback, and for whom we return the favor. In fact, if you've met other writers in your recent writing adventures, you may already have begun what can become lifelong relationships. Otherwise, writing can be an awfully solitary practice. And if you haven't already found such companions, reach out in your community for meet-ups, book clubs, and writing groups at bookstores, libraries, community centers, colleges, and universities. If the first group you try isn't a good fit, keep looking. Once you find a supportive community, however small, you'll be happy you did.

Readings

Folio: A Story in Progress

The following folio consists of an annotated early draft, a final draft, and a process statement by my former student, Emily Bazelak. As you read, compare Emily's approaches to revision with your own.

—Title—

A townhouse,

a dog cage and

a little girl inside it. She's curled in on herself, her eyes half open. She blinks sleepily, her top eyelashes never reaching her bottom ones. There is a towel wet with urine underneath her. She holds a dry corner of it to her bruised face.

Josie!

I run towards the cage, suddenly in a warehouse. I found her. *I found her.*

Josie we need to leave. It's okay, you're okay. We need to leave.

The little girl doesn't move. She holds the towel to her cheek like she either hasn't heard me or doesn't have strength enough to care.

My fear feels like electric currents coursing around my bones, licking every nerve on their path from my toes to my skull. My skin vibrates with the energy of it. My soul is trying to break out of my body, and with a single exhale, I know I'd be free from whatever hell I'm currently in. So I keep my mouth shut tight, and I don't breathe.

Josie's here. She's alive.

I desperately go for a lock or something, anything, to open the cage trapping Josie inside, but there isn't one. There's not even a door, just rusted bars locking her in like a dog. I start kicking and grunting and kicking harder, but it doesn't budge.

Josie is sitting now. The towel is gone. She's wearing the clothes she had on the day she went missing — a navy blue skirt with white polka dots and a grey hoodie. She's speaking to me, but no sound is coming from her mouth.

God, I just need some way to break these bars.

Someone's behind me. I know it like he tapped me on my shoulder, but I'm certain he's at least ten feet away. I spin around, ready to tear apart the monster who dared ~~to~~ take my little sister away from me. Just one good look at him, at his face, that's all I need.

But he's only a shadow, standing amongst dozens of crates, each filled with a growling, drooling dog. He doesn't move and the jolting terror returns. I don't care who he is anymore, I don't care, I just want to get Josie out of here and run.

Frantically, I turn back, but Josie is gone. Two little girls have taken her place in the cage. They stare at me expectantly~~, and~~ then begin to shriek, high pitched and blood curdling like the audio feedback of an amateur using a microphone.

This is a dream. I know it is.

I know it is, so I try to force my eyes open, but God, it hurts.

It hurts, it hurts, it hurts but

add space

I'm awake.

Only my eyes shoot open. I don't spring up in my bed or anything like those people who have nightmares in movies, who holler and choke loud enough that some loved one immediately rushes in to make sure they're okay. It always seems like they're waiting right outside the door for the other's nightmare to peak, which is much more creepy than comforting, if you ask me. Nothing in my life is that dramatic. insert scratching the wall or scratching herself (racoon cat claw marks later)

change — I'm simply [awkward] back in my one bedroom apartment, trying to keep my eyes open long enough for the nightmare to recede before going back to sleep. There're no cages, no dogs, but I can make out the two lumpy forms of Nyah and Cozzie lying beside me.

The sun is already rising, and I can hear the sounds of morning through the thin walls — a few lost birds chirping, trash bags hitting the concrete and our neighbors aggressively greeting one another. Cars are honking and screeching along, too, but that's not unique to the morning.

My brain is still trying to force me back to sleep. I'm about to resort to holding my eyeballs open with my fingers, but when I go to bring my hands to my face, I start at the flash of neon pink on my usually bare nails.

For a second, my sleep-drunken mind explains to me that I haven't woken up at all: this is just another nightmare, Lia, because only then would you have ever painted your nails. At least Nyah and Cozzie are sleeping and not substituting as faulty amplifiers, right?

I give in and close my eyes again, actually comforted.

change: no murderers in opening dream

[The lack of murderers after five seconds of waiting is what convinces me I'm truly and painfully awake.] My eyes burst back open and this time I do sit straight up, my right hand instinctively shooting in front of my face to get a closer look. It isn't nail polish at all, it's bright pink highlighter.

I have to give it to Nyah, who I immediately recognize as the culprit. She's the one person on this planet who would *dare* to find an ~~alternative~~ *alternate* way to do my nails after I explained to her, only hours before, how much I hate it.

Nyah is always coming up with new ways to make me "girlier." She insists if I change my style and grow my hair out, more people will like me. ~~Despite my best efforts to teach her about the patriarchy and how we, as women, shouldn't do things we don't want to just to please others, she never cares~~.

Plus, she loves to argue.

"Come on just let me paint them," She whined last night as I pulled the blanket up to her and her older sister, Cozzie's, chins. "You won't be doing it just so boys will like you."

"Oh yeah? Who am I doing it for then because it certainly isn't for myself," I counteracted.

"Do it for me!"

"I already do too much for you." I meant it as a joke, but I saw it strike a chord. She winced then and took her eyes off of mine, directing them towards her fiddling thumbs, the blanket tucked tightly under her armpits.

"Besides," I said, trying to remedy the situation the only way I know how, through faulty justification, "I don't own any nail polish, anyway."

Unfortunately, though, I did own highlighters.

add space

I get grudgingly out of bed, now fully awake, to wash the pink highlighter off.

She didn't falter because she felt bad about overlooking all I've done for her and her sister, ~~I think as I stand up,~~ she was simply pretending to so I would think I'd won. That whole time she was plotting how to get want she wanted.

Nyah always manages to find another way, a talent that not only drives me insane on a daily basis, but is also probably what I admire most about her. I would never tell her that, though.

I rub my eyes, making sure to keep my nails from touching my face and look down at the two girls. They're sleeping peacefully on the make-shift bed I set up for us the day I brought them home — an old mattress with no head bored, two pillows, and some white sheets I got at a Sears closing sale. My last one was just the couch.

My bright pink rage* fades a little, and I can't help but note how beautiful Nyah and Cazzie look — beautiful in a way only children can be. With mouths puckered and long eyelashes tickling their cheeks, they hold one another, still enjoying whatever mystical lands their minds have dreamt up. They look like angels, and I'm reminded of Josie again in that cage clutching her towel. Probably realizing by then that her older sister will never find her.

It's almost enough to make me forget about my neon fingernails altogether, but as soon as that thought tries to fade and the familiar grief tries to creep in, I glimpse the pink highlighter grasped loosely in Nyah's hand.

God, why can't kids just listen!

I look at the wall next to them where three sets of frantic claw marks have ruined the paint because four days ago they thought it was a good idea to bring a stray cat in here. *Four days ago*, and now this. I'm suddenly so angry and sad and annoyed all at once that it nearly overwhelms me. It's funny how your eyes never let you miss out on beautiful moments, but your mind is always right there rushing in to remind you of the ugly reality.

Still, I take a deep breath and decide not to give Nyah a hard time about it, even though a part of me really wants to. Instead, I turn away from the slumbering demons and walk to my closet of a bathroom to rinse the highlighter off, all the while priding myself on how mature I'm being. Shaken, but content enough, I close the bathroom door behind me and turn on the sink.

I'm still half asleep, mind you, so when someone starts wildly banging on the bathroom door, naturally I jump to the high heavens, an electric jolt of shock rattling through every bone in my body, It's similar to the fear in my dream but much more startling. The sheer amount of water I splash everywhere with my instinctive attempt to shield myself from the noise is frankly impressive.

* reference nightmare here

"Don't wash it off!" Nyah screeches, loud enough that she might as well be in the small space with me. I swear to go she was fast asleep a few seconds ago, "It looks pretty!"

"Son of a-" I yank open the door startling her back, a feat that momentarily gives me a surge of joy, but I don't let it show. "Stop screaming! Someone's gonna complain about the noise, and then we'll all be living on the street. Is that what you want, Nyah?"

"What I want for you is to stop being so stubborn, and let me make you look less like a toe!"

"Oh I'm the one who looks like a toe?" I huff before turning my fury on the demon [still] snuggled in bed, "Cozzie, tell your sister to show me some respect."

Cozzie doesn't answer, not that I really expect her to, having only heard her voice a handful of times since we've met~~, or, as my savior complex likes to put it, since I saved them from an angry cashier threatening to call the police~~.

[add space]

That fateful day, Nyah had been wearing a silky white dress with pink flowers decorating the material and a pale pink ribbon tied around her waist. I remember finding it odd that she was dressed for Easter Sunday when it was a Wednesday in July.

Cozzie, on the other hand, had on an oversized t-shirt that might as well have been a dress, too. Nyah told me later that her sister had outgrown all of her shorts and had deemed it too hot to wear pants, so she simply did without either. However, this wasn't what first struck me most about the second little girl; it was the black and blue ring surrounding her left eye, strikingly visible despite her dark complexion.

I watched from the chip isle~~, my hand halfway towards a bag of Cheatos,~~ as Cozzie shoved a gallon of milk under Nyah's dress, then proceeded to shove a box of cereal under her own big shirt. My first concern wasn't about the shoplifting per say, but rather that the little girl in the white dress wasn't going to fool anyone by pretending to be pregnant with her milk baby. They were clearly amateurs at this.

Even now, I'm not sure why I did it ~~(again, probably just my savior complex at work)~~, but I came to their rescue. I put on my best if-you-don't-listen-to-me-Im'ma-whoop-yo-ass voice that I'd learned from years of using it on my own little sister. I lectured them on how stealing was wrong, and how they're lucky I didn't let the good man call 911, and how they should be ashamed of themselves, and blah, blah, blah. I turned back to the cashier to explain to him that they were my delinquent little sisters. I could tell by his wide eyes and fidgeting hands that I made him nervous. I relished in that for a moment, in the power I held over everyone in that room. Then, I smiled politely, payed for the girls' stuff (I'm a saint, I know), and we left the seizure-inducing fluorescent lighting of the 7/11 behind us forever. And by forever, I mean until next Tuesday when we needed more milk.

"Why don't you have any hair?" Nyah asked me the moment we stepped outside into the mucky heat of the city. She was still hobbling under the weight of the milk gallon because I never offered to help her carry it, and when I heard the question, I was glad I didn't.

"Really? You don't thank someone by questioning their hairstyle, kid."

"Was it cancer?"

"Was it wha-," I whipped around and stared directly down at the big brown eyes looking back up at me. Little did I know, this would become a common occurrence between Nyah and me. "No, it wasn't cancer," I retorted a little too aggressively, "I chose to shave my head because I hated having hair. It was too heavy and it cost too much money. That's it."

She puckered her lips in concentration as she took the rest of me in. From my slides to my basketball shorts up over my plain blue t-shirt and back to my bald head. She decided, "I don't like it."

I just stared at her for a few seconds. The sun was burning the back of my neck as I encompassed Nyah in my shadow. Cozzie came back into view, her arms crossed over the box of Lucky Charms she took. Her black eye looked worse in the sun, a tint of red amidst the dark bruise meant it was recent. She never offered to help Nyah carry the milk either.

This overwhelming feeling of desperation hit me then, like it always hits me when I see unsupervised kids walking around the city. We didn't live in the suburbs, where crimes were committed quietly, and I could understand why parents naively believed their children would be fine walking home alone. We lived where men sat on their front steps, where trash piled up at the street corners, and where just two days ago a sixteen year-old kid was shot and killed by someone not much older than himself. It was some drug thing, I was told.

These two little girls were stealing milk and cereal. Where we lived, there was most certainly a reason why.

“What’re your names, anyway?” I asked them in a much quieter tone than I had used with them thus far. It seemed to mellow the younger one out a bit.

“I’m Nyah and that’s Cozzie. She’s my big sister,” and as an afterthought, “She doesn’t talk much.”

“That’s alright. Your mouth is big enough for the both of you,” I replied, not unkindly.

Nyah shot her tongue out at me and I instinctively shot!! ~~shit~~ mine back at her. Then I remembered that she was probably seven and I was twenty-two, so I collected myself. I started up the street towards my apartment, hoping Nyah and Cozzie would follow but not really knowing why.

They did.

“I’m Julia by the way,” I said over my shoulder, “but you guys can call me Lia.”

“I like the name Lia,” answered Nyah in a strained voice from behind me. I smiled and took the milk from her. She sighed in relief and smoothed out her lacey dress like a lady might smooth out a napkin on her lap at a fancy dinner. “Oh thank god,” She exhaled, “I thought you guys were gonna make me carry that the whole way. I mean I would’ve because I’m not a pussy, but it was so italicize heavy.”

I was startled by the language, I’m not going to lie, but I chose not to acknowledge it. Instead, we kept walking until we got to my depressingly small apartment with its stained brick on the outside and a hallway that smelled like cat piss leading to my front door. It didn't actually dawn on me how tiny it was until the three of us got inside.

add space

That was two months ago, and unfortunately, my place hasn't gotten any bigger, but there are sporadic claw marks decorating the walls now. ~~Whatever.~~

As much as I huff and complain, I do have love having Nyah and Cozzie around. I love the life that's been brought back into this ugly, little apartment I took over after my mom passed. Josie and I used to sleep in the same room I share with Nyah and Cozzie now. Our favorite game was to throw stuffed animals into the ceiling fan at top speed and see who could catch them first. We got so many bumps and bruises from colliding with walls or smashing heads with each other in our desperate attempt to stop a blue bunny's death fall from the sky.

Happy, sad, angry — all at once.

Suddenly, all I want is to go back to sleep before work in a few hours. The thought of work brings me back from my daydreaming, and I look down to see my hand resting in Nyah's. She's reapplying the faux pas (italicize?) nail polish.

"You're such a little brat," I say to her. My eyes ~~suddenly~~ so heavy I consider letting myself go right this instant, to stop fighting real life and just sleep. To give in to the nightmare if I have to. I'd probably crush Nyah, though, so I stay standing, making no attempt ^to remove my hand from hers.

"At least she doesn't look like a toe." This was Cozzie's voice, small and crunchy like she stopped working on maturing it when she was five or so. Nyah starts laughing hysterically, and I can't help it, I laugh, too.

"Lia's an entire foot, that's what I think!" Nyah screeches in delight, releasing my half-finished hand. I take a pillow and knock her onto the bed. The two sisters squeal and take up their own pillows to fight back.

That's how we continue on for a few minutes, all arms and giggles and pure joy. Meanwhile, the neighborhood has really started to wake up.

(most likely)

Between our screams, I hear people talking and smoking on their front steps, a woman cursing as the sound of her keys hit the pavement, and the exhaust of a school bus coming to a stop deep in the distance.

lie

I ~~lay~~ myself on top of them both, keeping their wiggling contained. "Alright, alright, enough. Let's go back to sleep for a while before I gotta get to work," I say. They go still.

indent

"Can't you stay home, just this once? It's so boring when you're not here," Nyah says. ~~I roll off of them onto my side of the bed, closest to the door. I've tried to get them as much as possible to keep them occupied while I'm gone. My living room is filled with coloring books and dress up clothes, most of which I don't even remember I got until I see them using it.~~

"I only work weekdays. We'll spend the entire weekend together this week, okay?"

"I'll bring a racoon in here this time; I swear to God."

"Nyah, please... "

"Fine. I'll just color then, I guess."

I'm not wholly convinced she's telling the truth, but enough to roll over them and take them both my arms and drift back to sleep.

—

(to be continued...)

Class Notes / Ideas

— get a grip on who these characters are/were

— what if Nyah and Cozzie aren't real?

— she finds two other girls once they are gone?

— why/how did Josie go missing?

Final Draft
Nyah and Cozzie's Soliloquy

A townhouse,
a dog cage and
a little girl inside it. She's curled in on herself, her eyes half open. She blinks sleepily, her top eyelashes never reaching her bottom ones. There is a towel wet with urine underneath her. She holds a dry corner of it to her bruised face.

Josie!

I run towards the cage. In a warehouse. I found her. *I found her.*

Josie we need to leave. It's okay, you're okay, but we need to leave.

The little girl doesn't move. She holds the towel to her cheek like she either hasn't heard me or doesn't have strength enough to care.

My fear feels like electric currents coursing around my bones, licking every nerve on their path from my toes to my skull. My skin vibrates with the energy of it. My soul is trying to break out of my body, and with a single exhale, I know I'd be free from whatever hell I'm currently in. So I keep my mouth shut tight, and I don't breathe.

Josie's here. She's alive.

I desperately go for a lock or something, anything, to open the cage trapping Josie inside, but there isn't one. There's not even a door, just rusted bars locking her in like a dog. I start kicking and grunting and kicking harder, but it doesn't budge.

Josie is sitting now. The towel is gone. She's wearing the clothes she had on the day she went missing—a navy blue skirt with white polka dots and a grey hoodie. She's speaking to me, but no sound is coming from her mouth.

God, I just need some way to break these bars.

Someone's behind me. I know it like he tapped me on my shoulder, but I'm certain he's at least ten feet away. I spin around, ready to tear apart the monster who dared to take my little sister away from me. Just one good look at him, at his face, that's all I need.

But he's only a shadow, standing amongst dozens of crates, each filled with a growling, drooling dog. He doesn't move and the jolting terror returns. I don't care who he is anymore, I don't care, I just want to get Josie out of here and run.

Frantically, I turn back, but Josie is gone. Two little girls have taken her place in her cage. They stare at me expectantly, and then begin to shriek, high pitched and blood curdling like the audio feedback of an amateur using a microphone.

This is a dream. I know it is.

I know it is, so I try to force my eyes open, but God it hurts.

It hurts, it hurts, it hurts but

I'm awake.

Only my eyes shoot open. I don't spring up in my bed or anything like those people who have nightmares in movies, who holler and choke loud enough that some loved one immediately rushes in to make sure they're okay. It always seems like they're waiting right outside the door for the other's nightmare to peak, which is much creepier than comforting, if you ask me. Nothing in my life is that dramatic. Once I woke up clawing at my chest, convinced Josie was literally in my heart, after a well-meaning, old neighbor told me she would always be there, but that's it. Usually I'm back in my one-bedroom apartment, trying to keep my eyes open long enough for the nightmare to recede before going back to sleep, like I am now. There're no cages, no dogs, but I can make out the two lumpy forms of Nyah and Cozzie lying beside me.

The sun is already rising, and I can hear the sounds of morning through the thin walls—a few lost birds chirping, trash bags hitting the concrete and our neighbors aggressively greeting one another. Cars are honking and screeching along, too, but that's not unique to the morning.

My brain is still trying to force me back to sleep. I'm about to resort to holding my eyeballs open with my fingers, but when I go to bring my hands to my face, I start at the flash of neon pink on my usually bare nails.

For a second, my sleep-drunken mind explains to me that I haven't woken up at all: this is just another nightmare, Lia, because only then would you have ever painted your nails. At least Nyah and Cozzie are sleeping and not substituting as faulty amplifiers, right?

I give in and close my eyes again, actually comforted.

I wait, but nothing happens. I'm truly and painfully awake.

Shit.

My eyes pop open, and this time I do sit straight up, my right hand instinctively shooting in front of my face to get a closer look. It isn't nail polish at all, it's bright pink highlighter.

I have to give it to Nyah, who I immediately recognize as the culprit. She's the one person on this planet who would *dare* to find an alternate way to do my nails after I explained to her, only hours before, how much I hate it.

Nyah is always coming up with new ways to make me "girlier." She insists if I change my style and grow my hair out, more people will like me. I've come up with dozens of excuses at this point as to why I don't want to be girly, but she never believes any of them. She's a smart kid.

Plus, she loves to argue.

"Come on just let me paint them," She whined last night as I pulled the blanket up to her and her older sister, Cozzie's, chins. "You won't be doing it just so boys will like you."

"Oh yea? Who am I doing it for then because it certainly isn't for myself," I counteracted.

"Do it for me!"

"I already do too much for you." I meant it as a joke, but I saw it strike a chord. She winced then and took her eyes off of mine, directing them towards her fiddling thumbs, the blanket tucked tightly under her armpits.

"Besides," I said, trying to remedy the situation the only way I knew how, through faulty justification, "I don't own any nail polish, anyway."

Unfortunately, though, I did own highlighters.

I get grudgingly out of bed, now fully awake, to wash the pink highlighter off.

She didn't falter because she felt bad about overlooking all I've done for her and her sister, she was simply pretending to, so I would think I'd won. That whole time she was plotting how to get want *she* wanted. Nyah always manages to find another way, a talent that not only drives me insane on a daily basis, but is also probably what I admire most about her. I would never tell her that, though.

I rub my eyes, making sure to keep my nails from touching my face and look down at the two girls. They're sleeping peacefully on the makeshift bed I set up for us the day I brought them home—an old mattress with no headboard, two pillows, and some white sheets I got at a Sears closing sale. My last one was just the couch.

My bright pink rage fades a little, and I can't help but note how beautiful Nyah and Cozzie look—beautiful in a way only children can be. With mouths puckered and long eyelashes tickling their cheeks, they hold one another, still enjoying whatever mystical lands their minds have dreamt up. They look like angels, and I'm reminded of Josie again in that cage clutching her towel. Probably realizing by then that her older sister will never find her.

It's almost enough to make me forget about my neon fingernails altogether, but as soon as that thought tries to fade and the familiar grief starts to creep in, I glimpse the pink highlighter grasped loosely in Nyah's hand.

God, why can't kids just listen!

I look at the wall next to them where three sets of frantic claw marks have ruined the paint because four days ago they thought it was a good idea to bring a stray cat in here. *Four days ago*, and now this. I'm suddenly so angry and sad and annoyed all at once that it nearly overwhelms me. It's funny how your eyes never let you miss out on beautiful moments, but your mind is always right there rushing in to remind you of the ugly reality.

Still, I take a deep breath and decide not to give Nyah a hard time about it, even though a part of me really wants to. Instead, I turn away from the slumbering demons and walk to my closet of a bathroom to rinse the highlighter off, all the while priding myself on how mature I'm being. Shaken, but content enough, I close the bathroom door behind me and turn on the sink.

I'm still half asleep, mind you, so when someone starts wildly banging on the bathroom door, naturally I jump to the high heavens, an electric jolt of shock rattling through every bone in my body. It's similar to the fear in my dream but much more startling. The sheer amount of water I splash everywhere with my instinctive attempt to shield myself from the noise is frankly impressive.

You're awake, you're awake, you're awake.

"Don't wash it off!" Nyah screeches, loud enough she might as well be in the small space with me. I swear to god she was fast asleep a few seconds ago. "It looks pretty!"

"Son of a—" I yank open the door startling her back, a feat that momentarily gives me a surge of joy, but I don't let it show. "Stop screaming! Someone's gonna complain about the noise, and then we'll *all* be living on the street. Is that what you want, Nyah?"

"What I want is for you to stop being so stubborn, and let me make you look like less of a toe!"

"Oh I'm the one who looks like a toe?" I huff before turning my fury on the demon still snuggled in bed, "Cozzie, tell your sister to show me some respect."

Cozzie doesn't answer, not that I really expect her to, having only heard her voice a handful of times since we've met.

That fateful day, Nyah had been wearing a silky white dress with pink flowers decorating the material and a pale pink ribbon tied around her waist. I remember finding it odd that she was dressed for Easter Sunday when it was a Wednesday in July. Cozzie, on the other hand, had on an oversized t-shirt that might as well have been a dress, too. Nyah told me later that her sister had outgrown all of her shorts and had deemed it too hot to wear pants, so she simply did without either. However, this wasn't what first struck me most about the second little girl; it was the black and blue ring surrounding her left eye, strikingly visible despite her dark complexion.

I watched from the chip aisle as Cozzie shoved a gallon of milk under Nyah's dress, then proceeded to shove a box of cereal under her own big shirt. My first concern wasn't about the shoplifting per se, but rather that the little girl in the white dress wasn't going to fool anyone by pretending to be pregnant with her milk baby. They were clearly amateurs at this.

Even now, I'm not sure why I did it, but I came to their rescue. I put on my best if-you-don't-listen-to-me-Im'ma-whoop-yo-ass voice that I'd learned from years of using it on my own little sister. I lectured them on how stealing was wrong, and how they're lucky I didn't let the good man call 911, and how they should be ashamed of themselves, and blah, blah, blah. I turned back to the cashier to explain to him that they were my delinquent little sisters. I could tell by his wide eyes and fidgeting hands that I made him nervous. I relished in that for a moment, in the power I held over everyone in that room. Then, I smiled politely, payed for the girls' stuff (I'm a saint, I know), and we left the seizure-inducing fluorescent lighting of the 7/11 behind us forever. And by forever, I mean until next Tuesday when we needed more milk.

"Why don't you have any hair?" Nyah asked me the moment we stepped outside into the mucky heat of the city. She was still hobbling under the weight of the milk gallon because I never offered to help her carry it, and when I heard the question, I was glad I didn't.

"Really? You don't thank someone by questioning their hairstyle, kid."

"Was it cancer?"

"Was it wha—," I whipped around and stared directly down at the big brown eyes looking back up at me. Little did I know, this would become a common occurrence between Nyah and me. "No, it wasn't cancer," I retorted a little too aggressively, "I chose to shave my head because I hated having hair. It was too heavy and it cost too much money. That's it."

She puckered her lips in concentration as she took in the rest of me. From my slides to my basketball shorts up over my plain blue t-shirt and back to my bald head. She decided, "I don't like it."

I just stared at her for a few seconds. The sun was burning the back of my neck as I encompassed Nyah in my shadow. Cozzie came into view then, her arms crossed over the box of Lucky Charms she took. Her black eye looked worse in the sun, a tint of red amidst the dark bruise meant it was recent. She never offered to help Nyah carry the milk either.

This overwhelming feeling of desperation hit me then, like it always hits me when I see unsupervised kids walking around the city. We didn't live in the suburbs, where crimes were committed quietly, and I could understand why parents naively believed their children would be fine walking home alone. We lived where men sat on their front steps, where trash piled up at street corners, and where just two days ago a sixteen-year-old kid was shot and killed by someone not much older than himself. It was some drug thing, I was told.

These two little girls were stealing milk and cereal. Where we lived, there was most certainly a reason why.

"What're your names, anyway?" I asked them in a much quieter tone than I had used with them thus far. It seemed to mellow the younger one out a bit.

"I'm Nyah and that's Cozzie. She's my big sister," and as an afterthought, "She doesn't talk much."

"That's alright. Your mouth is big enough for the both of you."

Nyah shot her tongue out at me and I instinctively shot mine back at her. Then I remembered that she was probably seven and I was twenty-two, so I collected myself. I started up the street towards my apartment, hoping Nyah and Cozzie would follow but not really knowing why.

They did.

"I'm Julia by the way," I said over my shoulder, "but you guys can call me Lia."

"I like the name Lia," answered Nyah in a strained voice from behind me. I smiled and took the milk from her. She sighed in relief and smoothed out her lacey dress like a lady might smooth out a napkin on her lap at a fancy dinner. "Oh thank god," she exhaled, "I thought you guys were gonna make me carry that the whole way. I mean I would've because I'm not a pussy, but it was *so* heavy."

I was startled by the language, I'm not going to lie, but I chose not to acknowledge it. Instead, we kept walking until we got to my depressingly small apartment with its stained brick on the outside and a hallway that smelled like human piss leading to my front door. It didn't actually dawn on me how tiny it was until the three of us got inside.

That was two months ago, and unfortunately, my place hasn't gotten any bigger, but there are sporadic claw marks decorating the walls now.

As much as I huff and complain, I do love having Nyah and Cozzie around. I love the life that's been brought back into this ugly, little apartment I took over after my mom passed. Josie and I used to sleep in the same room I share with Nyah and Cozzie now. Our favorite game was to throw stuffed animals into the ceiling fan at top speed and see who could catch them first. We got so many bumps and bruises from colliding with walls or smashing heads with each other in our desperate attempt to stop a blue bunny's death fall from the sky.

Happy, sad, angry—all at once.

Suddenly, all I want is to go back to sleep before work in a few hours. The thought of which brings me back from my daydreaming, and I look down to see my hand resting in Nyah's. She's reapplying the *faux* nail polish.

"You're such a little brat," I say to her. My eyes so heavy I consider letting myself go right this instant, to stop fighting real life and just sleep. To give in to the nightmare if I have to. I'd probably crush Nyah, though, so I stay standing, making no attempt to remove my hand from hers.

"At least she doesn't look like a toe." This was Cozzie's voice, small and crunchy like she stopped working on maturing it when she was five or so.

Nyah starts laughing hysterically, and I can't help it, I laugh, too.

"Lia's an entire foot, that's what I think!" Nyah screeches in delight, releasing my half-finished hand. I take a pillow and knock her onto the bed. The two sisters squeal and take up their own pillows to fight back.

That's how we continue on for a few minutes, all arms and giggles and pure joy. Meanwhile, the neighborhood has really started to wake up. Between our screams, I hear people talking and (most likely) smoking on their front steps, a woman cursing as the sound of her keys hit the pavement, and the exhaust of a school bus coming to a stop deep in the distance.

I lie myself on top of them both, keeping their wiggling contained. "Alright, alright, enough. Let's go back to sleep for a while before I gotta get to work," I say.

They go still.

"Can't you stay home, just this once? It's so boring when you're not here," Nyah says.

"I only work weekdays. We'll spend the entire weekend together this week, okay?"

"I'll bring a racoon in here this time; I swear to God."

"Nyah, please ..."

"Fine. I'll just color then, I guess."

I'm not wholly convinced she's telling the truth, but enough to roll over and take them both in my arms and drift back to sleep.

–

Work was hard and long and stupid, so while I walk home, I try to relax by thinking how nice it would be to be a tree in the Amazon. For one thing, do plants realize how lucky they are to be able to photosynthesize? It would be such a blessing to not have to worry about food right now and what I should get Nyah, Cozzie and me for dinner tonight. If I didn't need to eat, I wouldn't need to work because I wouldn't need money for food, and therefore, wouldn't be stressed all the time about work being so hard and long and stupid.

If I was a tree, specifically an Amazonian one, I could just stand and exist, which is all I really want. I wouldn't have to deal with people, like the men at the bar, who feel the need to tell me which sports teams they're rooting for and which presidential candidate they'd most likely bang. They completely ignore all of my social cues that practically scream how badly I want them to drop dead. To be able stay still and breathe in fresh air rather than the hot sewage steam that encompasses me now as I pass over a manhole—that's all I ask.

Amazon trees are huge and indestructible but beautiful, too. My hand instinctively goes to my bald head. I suddenly miss my long hair, and my sister and her long hair, so much I feel my throat constrict. An old neighbor said to me after Josie went missing that she always knew such a pretty thing with that kind of hair would get lost in the city one day and we'd never see her again.

"That long black hair made her a target," she'd said, "Lem'me tell you, men go after pretty little things with long hair they can grab onto and a skirt they can easily get under. I think baby girl would be right here with us still if she'd not been wearing what she was. Always with those pretty little skirts and that pretty long hair. Your mamma's lived here her whole life, she should'a known better. Well, no use thinking too hard about it now, I guess. She'll always be in our hearts. God, that pretty little thing, what a shame."

I shaved my head that night with shaky hands in a gas station bathroom. I cursed my mother for letting us grow up in a place where such bad things happened and for making us feel safe in such a deadly environment. Josie and I were loved; we were cuddled when we had nightmares and we sat down to dinner every night and said our prayers. My mom would take my hand, I'd take Josie's, and Josie would take my mom's, and we'd thank God for another good day. From the second we learned Josie was gone, my mom and I never ate dinner or said our prayers together again. Instead, I took to cursing her before bed, much like a prayer, until the day she finally died. I might've missed her, if it wasn't her fault I had to miss Josie so much.

There are no trees in our neighborhood, and for some reason this is what reminds me about the forest fires in the Amazon last year. Josie would've been one of the trees those farmers burnt down, and I'd somehow be left standing alone there, too.

God, I wish my thoughts didn't turn on me so violently all the time.

Luckily, I'm distracted as I pass under the streetlight I make sure to visit every night. (I would've pretended it was a tree, but I don't want to anymore.) Taped to the lamppost are photos of missing children. I always wondered if rich people really do put up signs like this when their dogs go missing like I've seen in movies. What's worse is that it works; there's a tearful reuniting of human and dog set to music that's sure to make the audience cry if they weren't already. Some of these kids have been missing for years, and there's no one left to cry for them.

The light overhead illuminates Josie's smiling face, so I can see the twinkle in her almond eyes even though it's dark. We used her sixth-grade school picture for the posters. She proudly curled her own hair that morning with the curling iron my mom bought her for her 11th birthday. I remember her begging for it for weeks, even though her hair was naturally curly to begin with. Her ringlets in the picture are all different lengths and widths, and the top of her head is haloed in frizzy fly-aways. She would flip her head upside down and swing it back, her hair cascading like a crashing wave, to make it more "voluptuous."

I hate that she even knew that word. Nothing about her was voluptuous yet. Josie was a child; an 11-year-old girl. All of these missing girls with their picture-day hair were *children*.

I trace my finger along her name, "Josephine Johnson," and I let my eyes wander along the pole.

JOSEPHINE JOHNSON, MISSING SINCE: July 17, 2013
AYANA GILMORE, MISSING SINCE: April 3, 2015
SARA WASHINGTON, MISSING SINCE: November 21, 2018
COZZIE HALL

My heart crashes into my stomach, and I feel lightheaded. Cozzie Hall? My Cozzie Hall? Has someone reported her and Nyah missing? They told me no one would notice if they were gone. I distinctly remember Nyah asking me if I thought they would be stealing milk and cereal at a 7/11 if anyone cared about them. Cozzie's black eye reaffirming the same. My legs go numb as I look to the left of Cozzie's stoic face and see her little sister's giant gap-toothed grin staring back at me.

NYAH HALL, MISSING SINCE: February 2, 2010
February 2, 2010.

I force my feet to walk. The orange glow of the streetlights seems threatening all of a sudden. They feel like helicopter spotlights, and each one I escape gets me caught in another.

Nyah, Cozzie, Ayana, Josie.

I walk past a couple arguing in broken English, past empty beer cans and smoking cigarette butts, past trash bags thrown to the curb.

Townhouses and dog cages.

My ears are ringing, and I claw at my chest, thinking that maybe if I can get my heart some air, the pressure will release.

She'll always be in our hearts.

I collide with my front door, typing the wrong numbers into the keypad at first, but managing to get it right with my second attempt. As I'm going to push the door open, a flash of neon pink on my usually bare nails makes me stop short, but it's not nail polish, at all, I realize quickly. It's bright pink highlighter.

It hurts, it hurts, it hurts but

Amazon trees on fire.

I know who the culprit is.

Process Statement

Revision is a process and one that's entirely unique to each writer. For me, I typically start my stories knowing exactly what the beginning, middle and end are going to be. Then, by the next week or so, every idea I was so certain about completely changes. The most helpful thing for me when revising is to ask for my peers' opinions and to talk it out with them. Sometimes I'll give them options between this and that and let them decide which plotline they would rather read, but other times they'll have brilliant ideas that I never even considered before. It's still scary for me to let people read my writing, but I remind myself to take their ideas as advice rather than judgment. Still, it can definitely be hard for me to cut things out, so whenever I do, I never delete them. I copy and paste the line or paragraph to a new document. You never know; what doesn't work in one story might work perfectly in another! I keep all my drafts, both marked up and not, for that very reason. Physically marking up drafts is so important for me. I tend to change the font and size of the text before I print out physical copies to revise, too, because it helps me to catch mistakes I may not have noticed after looking at my work the same way for so long. All in all, my revision process is rooted in looking at my work from various perspectives, whether they are my own or somebody else's.

For this short story, I found my initial inspiration while subconsciously observing how other women comport themselves in public, especially when their behavior and appearance so drastically differ from my own. Lia became a reflection of one particular girl that I noticed in a 7/11 convenience store—hence why I decided Lia should first meet Nyah and Cozzie in a 7/11, as well. She had brown skin that was a little darker than mine, she was wearing basketball shorts and a plain t-shirt, and she had a completely shaved head (a look I *wish* I could pull off the way she did). Simply from her walk from the chip aisle to the register and out the door, I could feel confidence and strength radiating from her, two things I had very little of at that point in my life. I vividly remember thinking to myself: Is that all it takes? Would shaving my head and wearing men's clothes make me feel safe for once? Is her reimagining of the feminine style a shield that actively protects her or merely gives the illusion of safety? And so, this story largely became an exploration of that, but I don't think anyone would've been able to tell that from my first draft. What began as an admittedly shallow conflict of a girl not wanting to have anything to do with her nails being painted pink became a depiction of what often felt to me were inescapable nightmares inherent in being a young woman in today's society.

There was a similar reason behind my choice of setting. I've spent my entire life in a town bordering Philadelphia very closely, yet I haven't spent as much time in the city as one may expect. In fact, whenever I've shown interest in going, words of caution have always been proffered to me. While those words may come from good intention, along the way, they have instilled in me a nervousness and anxiety about the city, especially being a girl. I wanted to find a way to emulate what it feels to be caught between trying to be safe and overreacting; that is why Lia's reality is so often blurred with delusion. The hardest part of revision was subjecting Lia's character to the eyes and ears of others as she evolved because the more she did, the more of my own fears were revealed. However, in doing so, both she and I were able to grow far more than had we been left in a draft.

Craft Questions

- The questions at the end of the earlier draft came up in workshop. In what ways does Emily's final draft address or answer those questions? What information does she add to the story, and how does that information affect your reading?
- Reflect on Emily's scene construction and use of white space. Would you consider using visible sections in your stories? Why or why not?
- Emily notes that she is missing a title in the earlier draft. How does her final title affect your understanding of the story? Look back over some of the titles of stories we've read, and discuss your methods for titling your own stories.
- Note Emily's use of lyrical repetition of phrases. What does this technique add to the story, in terms of style, tone, and meaning?

Exercises

Exercise 1: "Parting Is Such Sweet Sorrow"

Look at one of your stories and ask yourself this question: wherein lies the resonance in the ending and what accomplishes that resonance? Could a physical object be incorporated in your ending to amplify the resonance?

Objective: To strengthen your story's ending by trying out various possibilities.

Exercise 2: But What's It About?

Take one of your finished stories, and complete the following sentence: This story is about.... Have friends or classmates read your story and complete the same sentence. It is not important that all the answers are the same, of course, but they should be related.

Objective: To ensure that the thematic content you have in mind is clearly communicated.

Exercise 3: Hearing Your Way

Read your most recent story aloud. As you read, circle words, phrases, and clauses that don't sound as pleasing as they might. When you are finished, go back and rewrite those areas that sounded "off" and repeat the process.

Objective: To catch awkward or ungrammatical diction and syntax by hearing the story read aloud.

PART III | APPENDICES

appendix a | workshopping

If you're in a creative writing class or writing group, you've likely participated in some sort of workshopping activities—or else you're about to do so. A writing **workshop**, in which you exchange and discuss works in progress, generally gives you a chance to receive feedback from others engaged in the craft. In addition, in the context of a college-level course, workshops may be geared toward helping you to sharpen your analytical skills; by learning to articulate your ideas about others' work, you're learning how to critically assess your own. And, at best, a workshop can provide a nourishing, sustaining form of support: no small thing for those of us engaged in the generally solitary work of writing. In fact, most of us continue some form of creative exchange for our entire writing lives.

What do we need to know as we approach a workshop, especially if we're participating for the first time? What's useful to keep in mind? And what ideas can we let go of? What can go wrong? Whether you're in a course or planning to set up an informal writing workshop of your own, by keeping the following in mind, you'll increase your chances of having a productive, enriching experience.

What to Share

Since you'll be sharing drafts of works in progress, it's helpful to share pieces that you genuinely want to revise. This can be tricky if you find that you're someone who isn't used to doing much revision. To benefit from a workshop, however, you'll need to suspend this reticence, at least temporarily; trust that others may have some insight that could be useful or interesting, whether or not you take all of their suggestions to heart.

Imagine that you're in a laboratory; this is just an experiment. Try this. Try that. See what results you achieve, and hold off on making any conclusions as you get started. There will be time for judging outcomes later. It's also useful to have a few questions about your own piece. Be honest with yourself. Are there places where you seem to fumble? Ideas you'd like to develop but aren't sure how? Workshop is an excellent forum to get other minds and perspectives thinking over your concerns.

On the other hand, if you bring a draft that's *too* loose, the group may not know what kind of feedback to offer. So, choose something that's at least far enough along to have some sort of shape, driving idea, or plan. This will also help you feel more confident in presenting it. And whether you're exchanging work digitally or in hard copy, choose a standard font and font size, consider double-spacing, use page numbers, and proofread before submitting. Workshops are usually most effective if pieces are distributed ahead of time to give participants time to read, digest, and make notes for discussion. However, reading and responding on the spot can also be fun if the group is comfortable running with more loosely formulated ideas.

The Group

Speaking of comfort within the workshop group, it's essential. Most of us are sensitive about sharing our writing, especially at first. It can feel like we're naked in front of a group and it takes some skill to make sure that everyone feels as relaxed and comfortable as possible, so that the workshop functions as a positive, generative experience that inspires growth. This is why so many creative writing professors will try to draw out all participants early and often, making space for quieter voices as well as more confident ones. This is also a reason to break a workshop into smaller groups (if it seems too large for close exchange). Although such steps are helpful, it's also up to the participants to engage each other with interest, respect, and support, even if there are members of the group that seem difficult or who stand out as different from the majority.

Workshops shouldn't be competitive, cliquey, or intimidating. I speak from experience, not only as someone who has led many of them, but as a longtime participant as well. In fact, the first workshop I attended as an undergraduate student was such a negative experience that I stopped writing for almost a year afterwards. I felt misunderstood and singled out as the only participant writing abstract, experimental poems; everyone else in the group seemed to favor straightforward narrative verse. Although the professor was individually supportive and encouraging, the group dynamics left me feeling discouraged and even bullied. If you find yourself in such a situation, I suggest speaking to the workshop leader privately early on (something I wish I'd done). If they take their responsibility seriously, they'll participate in group discussions to make sure that you don't feel alienated.

This may seem like simple advice that can be boiled down to *be nice*. But it's more complicated than that. How can you offer incisive commentary, constructive criticism, and helpful suggestions while remaining considerate of others' differences? One answer is to avoid generalizing, ad hominem comments (e.g., *you always write confusing lines*) and opt instead for descriptive, personally framed feedback (e.g., *line 9, while intriguing, is difficult for me to paraphrase*). In other words, we can learn a great deal just by describing what is or is not happening for us as we read.

Similarly, it's our job as a participant to be honest about where we're coming from before leaping into assessing another's work. Although we may have a completely different background and/or aesthetic from another, it's our job not to impose our own sensibilities. Instead, we need to learn to really listen to others' voices and aspirations. This is also what makes a good workshop so engaging and even life changing. The bonding that can occur, across various divides, is like no other, because ultimately, when we're talking about our writing we're also talking about ourselves (whether or not the work is autobiographical). We can learn so much from each other's perspectives.

Methods

Once you've prepared your piece or read the other pieces that are up for discussion ahead of time, it's important to make some notes on your thoughts to take with you into workshop. If your workshop is face-to-face, it's a good idea to have hard copies of the drafts on hand; if you're meeting virtually, you should be able to readily access those drafts as well as any notes you may have made. This way, everyone will be ready to dive into discussion in a focused, productive way.

Before discussion begins, it's useful to hear the piece (or part of it) read aloud, preferably by someone other than the writer. This allows the group to settle in by *listening* to the writer's voice before jumping in with their voices and opinions. It also allows the writer to hear their own work, maybe for the first time. Both participants and the writer may also be able to catch awkward phrases, typos, and other faulty moves by hearing the piece read aloud. Rather than discussing these issues at this point, it may be more useful to simply take note of them.

In the past, it was common to ask the writer whose work was up for discussion to remain silent and simply take notes. Sometimes the writer would be invited to respond or raise questions at the end. The idea behind this method was that the work should *stand for itself*, without explanation, defense, or elaboration. Although this method has some benefits, over the years, I've found that it's problematic in a couple of important ways. First, it denies the writer agency at a time when they're already feeling vulnerable and even powerless. I'm not sure that this kind of boot camp atmosphere produces the desire to keep creating. After all, we *do* need to feel some sense of confidence, which is different from foolish pride or arrogance, when we sit down to write or revise.

The next issue that I've found with adhering to a workshop gag order is that since the piece is *in progress*, it is often unrealistic to ask it to stand for itself. In fact, a little background information on what the writer was thinking, trying to achieve, or struggling with, can be helpful to hear before starting group discussion. Although your professor or workshop leader may also provide a focused list of questions or may lead the discussion in a certain direction, it's often useful to begin with the writer's own concerns and to circle back on them at some point in the discussion.

So, my suggestion is to begin by asking the writer to briefly raise any questions, concerns, or ideas they'd like the group to be aware of beforehand. If the writer is reluctant to speak up, so be it. But most of the time, they're relieved to have some say in how the discussion will go. Once the writer has spoken, they are then asked to remain *relatively* quiet in order to just listen and take notes on the discussion. However, if they feel the need to speak up to clarify something, without defending it per se or indulging in excessive explanation, they're free to do so.

A first step when approaching another's work is to ask yourself:

- What aesthetic, politics, and ideas does this piece seem to explore?
- Is this piece living up to the expectations that it, itself, has created?

Asking these questions will help you to guard against imposing your own style or trying to rewrite the piece according to how you would do it. It also foregrounds subject matter, which is always significant.

At the outset, I've found that it's useful to start with the strengths of the piece, not only to build comfort and trust on the part of the writer, but also because learning to clearly identify what's most promising or unique in our own work seems to lead us more to quickly to a path of growth. By focusing on the positive, by identifying with *it*, we're also gently letting go of what doesn't work as well for us, what territory is not ours to explore, whatever dead ends we've run into.

On the flip side, workshops can devolve into cheering sessions without much food for thought, if we're not careful. As you discuss the work, try to avoid frequently saying *I like* or *I love* (easier said than done), and instead be as specific as you can about what the piece is already achieving. Questions to consider include

- What emotions, ideas, questions, does the piece communicate?
- Where exactly is the piece doing something unique?
- What specifically are you most excited about and why?

Try your best to describe your experience of reading the piece without interjecting lengthy stories from your own life. Again, this is a matter of listening and focusing on another's world.

Next, the group may want to move into critique and suggestions. General questions to consider include

- Where does the draft seem to lack focus or energy?
- What might the writer want to think about when returning to the draft to revise?
- Are there parts of the piece that could be tightened up?
- Are there interesting thematic and/or aesthetic directions that are merely hinted at, without being fully developed?

In some cases, especially if the group has worked with each other before, it may be useful to include comments and ideas for future work. For example, you may suggest that the writer try writing more pieces like the one under discussion or that they experiment with a new technique or direction next time. This sort of holistic commentary can be particularly helpful for a group at the portfolio stage at the end of a semester.

Afterwards

After your draft has been workshopped, make sure that your notes are in order. Then, put the draft aside for a little while (a few days, a week), if you can afford to take the time, allowing it to simmer. This remains one of the most mysterious aspects of creative production, but it's one that countless writers and artists use successfully. To make a creative leap, to resolve the inevitable contradictions and ambivalences with which we wrestle, we often benefit from returning later with a fresh perspective. It's often at this point that we know intuitively what changes to make and what to leave as is.

Speaking of contradictions, you're sure to receive conflicting suggestions. In fact, it's not uncommon to receive radically different responses to the same piece or body of work. Once you've listened and taken note of those various ideas, it's ultimately *your* job to determine which to take and which to put aside. This can be difficult to sift through at first. However, the more experienced you become with gathering different viewpoints, the more you'll actually welcome the process of deciding among the various possibilities (including the possibility of returning to aspects of your original draft). In the end, this process will help you to hone your craft. Ultimately, even the suggestions that you end up rejecting can help you more clearly articulate the goals and aspirations you hold dear for the piece.

After you've workshopped others' work, you may be asked to give some sort of written feedback in the form of notes or commentary. This will likely help you to review some of the main ideas discussed. But even if you don't give written feedback, it's valuable to spend some time during and after the workshop reflecting on ideas that may be useful for your own work. In this way, workshopping benefits the readers as much as the writer whose work is under discussion. If the conversation has gone deep enough, it has touched on aesthetic concerns or technical issues that may be useful to you, as well, as you move forward.

Finally, although the workshop is not meant to be evaluative or competitive, it is inevitable to come out of it sometimes feeling that you've either gained approval or been told that you still have lots of work to do. Try not to get either too confident or too discouraged by others' responses. Of course, this is easier said than done! We're social creatures after all, and, for the most part, our writing is meant to be read by others. So, naturally we care what others think. However, if we can try to temper this by some sense of equanimity, balance, and inner confidence, we'll fare much better in the long run. In fact, in this regard, the workshop can serve as a safe haven in which to practice cultivating a tougher skin when it comes to acceptance and rejection: something almost all creatives have to work to achieve.

Did I remind you to have fun? Having your work up for discussion can often cause apprehension ahead of time, but can just as often cause a desire for more after it's over. After all, it's not often in life that we have others' undivided attention on our work, our concerns, our hopes and dreams. If you give generously of yourself as both a writer and responder in workshop, you'll be glad you did. Everyone will benefit!

appendix b | writing resources

IF YOU'VE SEARCHED THE web for writing resources, you've no doubt found a plethora of information, including informational and educational websites, sites of literary agents and book coaches, writers' blogs and online workshop groups, literary journals and magazines, book publishers, writing competitions, and more. In fact, we're inundated with so much information these days there's a need for a quick guide or selection of some of the most legitimate, useful tools from among this ever-proliferating list. So, here's a curated list of those websites, followed by tips on the process of seeing your way into print. Again, this list is in no way exhaustive; it's simply a starting point for you to create your own tailored list: suited to *your* interests, needs, and goals.

Websites for Writers

The Academy of American Poets (*poets.org*)
Founded in 1934 to support poets and to foster the appreciation of contemporary poetry, the Academy of American Poets is the producer of many national poetry initiatives, including activities for National Poetry

Month in April. Their website includes a searchable database by poem and poet, sound recordings from the Academy's archive, a glossary of poetic terms, event listings by region, and more.

Association of Writers and Writing Programs (awpwriter.org)
AWP provides resources and information for writers, college and university creative writing programs, and conferences and cultural centers. Although you'll need to join the organization to attend their annual conference and receive their magazine, their website lists opportunities for grants, awards, and publication.

Canadian Authors Association (canadianauthors.org)
Canadian Authors Association provides writers in every genre programs, services, and resources in both the craft and the business of writing. A non-profit, membership-based organization, their website includes resources for members and visitors alike.

Community of Literary Magazines and Presses (clmp.org)
The Community of Literary Magazines and Presses (formerly the Council of Literary Magazines and Presses) represents small publishers creating print and digital books, magazines, online publications, chapbooks and zines. Among their activities are an annual conference, literary awards, and small press and literary magazine fairs. Their website includes news about the world of literary magazine and small press publishing, event listings, and a directory of independent literary publishers.

The Favorite Poem Project (favoritepoem.org)
This site was founded under the auspices of the U.S. Poet Laureate. It contains sound and video recordings of thousands of poets reading their favorite poems.

League of Canadian Poets (poets.ca)
Founded in 1966, the League of Canadian Poets is the professional organization for established and emerging Canadian poets. The League organizes events, networking opportunities, projects, publications, mentoring, and awards. Visiting the League's website is a great way to learn about their programming.

National Writing Awards (magazine-awards.com)
In addition to listing information about its awards, the site of this Canadian organization maintains a list of literary magazines. This is a useful site to use when you're ready to start submitting work for publication.

New Pages (*newpages.com*)
New Pages features news, information, and guides to literary magazines, independent publishers, creative writing programs, alternative periodicals, indie bookstores, writing contests, and more. This is a useful site to use when you're ready to start submitting work for publication.

Poetry Daily (*poems.com*)
Poetry Daily is an anthology of contemporary poetry. Each day, it publishes and emails subscribers a new poem from new books, magazines, and journals.

Poetry Foundation (*poetryfoundation.org*)
The Poetry Foundation, publisher of *Poetry* magazine, is an independent literary organization. The site contains an extensive database of poets, poetry, and other related resources.

Poetry Society of America (*poetrysociety.org*)
This site contains information about the Poetry Society of America, the United States' oldest poetry organization, founded in 1910. It includes tributes to poets who have passed away and other features, as well as information about contests, residencies, conferences, bookstores, and organizations promoting poetry.

Poets & Writers Magazine (*pw.org*)
Poets & Writers publishes a print magazine and its website offers a list of resources, including databases and articles on publishing and promotion; information on readings, workshops, and conferences; and a submission calendar. This is a useful source to use when you're ready to start submitting work for publication.

Writer's Digest (*writersdigest.com*)
Writer's Digest magazine hosts this comprehensive site, which features resources for poets, fiction writers, and nonfiction writers, including articles, prompts, and information on publication.

Getting Published

Once you've been writing for a while and have written some pieces that you consider strong and finished (or as finished as any piece of writing can be), you may begin to think about submitting your work for publication. Before we get into the nitty-gritty of publication, however, consider a few questions: *Why do I want to publish now? What do I stand to gain? And what do I risk by starting this process now?*

The process of seeing your way into print can be arduous and even demoralizing, especially if you're not quite ready. Most writers are rejected many times before they experience their first acceptance. And, even when you are accepted for publication, it's possible to later regret publishing early work, if, again, you're not quite ready. Although *being ready* may be difficult to define, I do find that writers who are fairly secure in their identity as writers, who know they're going to continue despite acceptance or rejection, tend to fare better in the process than do those for whom creative writing is brand new. Ultimately, to sustain a life as a published writer, you need to have belief in your abilities and a self-motivated drive to keep going.

Literary Journals and Magazines

Once you are, in fact, ready to begin, the traditional first step is to explore literary journals and magazines with an eye toward finding some that seem to be a good fit for your work: aesthetically, formally, and thematically. Although there are hundreds of literary magazines, you'll need to search around a bit to find them. Since most bookstores have stopped carrying them, you may need to visit your library to find some hard copies to peruse. Of course, you can also look them up online by using one of the guides listed above, such as Poets & Writers or New Pages. Most often, you'll be able to read a handful of pieces from a recent issue online. However, if you want to read an entire issue, you may need to purchase it or subscribe, unless it's a free online journal.

So, let's say you've found a few journals that look like possible fits for your work. Take a look at their websites for submission information. Some journals only read submissions at a particular time of year. Many journals specify how many poems and what length of story to submit. And although most require that you submit online, some still require a snail-mailed submission. Whatever the instructions, follow them carefully. Otherwise, your work may be left unread.

Many journals these days use the service Submittable. Although it's free for you to establish an account and start submitting work through this service, some journals do, in fact, charge a small reading fee to submit your work. And unfortunately, only larger journals and magazines will offer any payment if your work is accepted. So, the bottom line is that you're submitting to these journals simply in hopes that others will read your work.

Each manuscript you send out should be accompanied by a cover letter, unless the publication clearly requests that you *not* attach one. In the case of Submittable and other online portals, you'll need to post this letter in the comments box. Your cover letter should be brief and polite. Here's an example:

Dear Editors,

Attached is my story "Name of Story" for your consideration in *Name of Journal.* My work has been published in *list other journals or venues here.*

Many thanks for your consideration.

Best Wishes,

Your Name

Your address, email, and phone number

What if you don't have any previous publication credits to list here? You could mention what school you attend, what you're studying, and/or where you live. Whatever you decide to include, be sure to keep it brief (one to two sentences). Editors generally don't have the time to wade through lengthy letters.

Can you submit the same story or poem to two different publications? That depends on whether the journal accepts *simultaneous submissions.* Review this policy before sending out and keep a list of your submissions to keep track of where you've already sent what. If the piece is accepted by a journal, you'll need to remember to withdraw it immediately from consideration by the other journal to which it was submitted. You can withdraw easily on Submittable. Otherwise, you may have to write a quick email letting an editor know that the piece was accepted elsewhere.

The most difficult time comes next: the time of waiting. Most often it takes months for a journal to get back to you, and most of the time, especially when you're first starting out, you *will* receive rejections. However, sometimes you'll receive an acceptance. Or you may receive a request to edit the work you submitted before it's published or to submit new work at a later date. These encouragements are meaningful. Enjoy them! Ideally, you'd forget about your submissions until you hear back, and rather than get discouraged by rejection, you'd send your work out to a new venue right away. However, this is easier said than done.

If your piece has been rejected by many different venues, you may want to ask yourself or someone you trust if you should revise or reconsider. However, most often, rejection doesn't mean that your work is unpublishable. It may be that you simply haven't found the right fit or that you've stumbled upon insurmountable competition. In any case, it's a good idea to expect rejection when you're first starting out and to be prepared to keep trying despite the odds.

Other Forms of Publication

Another way to get started publishing your work is to self-publish it on a blog, website, social media account, other open resource, or in a handmade publication such as a zine. Platforms such as YouTube and TikTok are also increasingly popular modes for artistic expression. Just as it's helpful to check out journals before you submit work to them, be sure to think through the ramifications of your post or use of a self-publishing platform before you put your work out there. Questions to consider include:

- What are the platform's strengths and weaknesses?
- Will the platform do my piece justice?
- Will I be able to publish the piece elsewhere if I've already posted it? (Oftentimes, journals require that the piece not have previously appeared.)

With these caveats in mind, you may find just the right platform for your work, without having to wait months for an editor's opinion.

Whatever path you take, remember to enjoy the creative work you do for its own sake. I'll leave you with a poem I wrote about this very subject:

Song

An awfully pleasing song in the branches.
A song that reaches as far as an eye can see.
Despite the annoyances, despite the contrivances,
despite the ridiculous need to sing to be.
The branches fright when what they sing
is pleasing. As far as an edge,
the need to sing to be.

permissions acknowledgments

Alexie, Sherman. "What You Pawn I Will Redeem," from *Ten Little Indians*. Copyright © 2003 by Sherman Alexie. Reprinted in electronic format by permission of Nancy Stauffer Associates, on behalf of the author. Reprinted in softcover by permission of Grove/Atlantic, Inc. Any third-party use of this material, outside of this publication, is prohibited.

Ashbery, John. "Street Musicians," from *Houseboat Days*. Copyright © 1975, 1976, 1977, 1999 by John Ashbery. Reprinted by permission of Georges Borchardt, Inc., on behalf of the author.

Atwood, Margaret. "Death by Landscape," from *Wilderness Tips*. Copyright © 1991 O.W. Toad Ltd. Reprinted in Canada by permission of Emblem/McClelland & Stewart, a division of Penguin Random House Canada Limited. All rights reserved. Any third-party use of this material, outside of this publication, is prohibited. Interested parties must apply directly to Penguin Random House Canada Limited for permission. Reprinted in the US and EU by permission of Doubleday, an imprint of the Knopf Doubleday Publishing Group, a division of Penguin Random House LLC. All rights reserved. Reprinted in the UK and Commonwealth by permission of Bloomsbury Publishing Plc.

Bachinsky, Elizabeth. "Wolf Lake," from *Home of Sudden Service*, Nightwood Editions, 2006. Copyright © 2006 Elizabeth Bachinsky. Reprinted by permission of Nightwood Editions www.nightwoodeditions.com.

Beasley, Sandra. "Let Me Count the Waves," from *Count the Waves: Poems*. Copyright © 2015 by Sandra Beasley. Used by permission of W.W. Norton & Company, Inc.

Beattie, Ann. "Snow," from *Where You'll Find Me: And Other Stories*. Copyright © 1986 by Irony and Pity, Inc., and Ann Beattie. Reprinted in the UK and Commonwealth [paperback] and Worldwide [electronic format] by permission of ICM Partners. Reprinted in other territories [paperback] with the permission of Scribner, a division of Simon & Schuster, Inc. All rights reserved.

Beatty, Jan. "Blue Dress," *Mad River*. Copyright © 1996 Jan Beatty. Reprinted by permission of the University of Pittsburgh Press.

Bishop, Elizabeth. "One Art" and "Sestina," from *Poems*. Copyright © 2011 by The Alice H. Methfessel Trust. Publisher's Note and compilation copyright © 2011 by Farrar, Straus and Giroux. Reprinted by permission of Farrar, Straus and Giroux. All Rights Reserved.

Brooks, Gwendolyn. "We Real Cool" and "The Bean Eaters," from *The Bean Eaters*, 1960. Reprinted by consent of Brooks Permissions.

Brown, Stephanie. "Feminine Intuition," *Allegory of the Supermarket*, University of Georgia Press, 1999. Copyright © 1998 by Stephanie Brown. Reproduced by permission of the University of Georgia Press.

Bursk, Christopher. "Letter to a Great-great-grandson," from *A Car Stops and a Door Opens*. Copyright © 2017 by Christopher Bursk. Reprinted with the permission of The Permissions Company, LLC on behalf of CavanKerry Press, cavankerrypress.org.

Cisneros, Sandra. "Barbie-Q," from *Woman Hollering Creek*. Copyright © 1991 by Sandra Cisneros. Published by Vintage Books, a division of Penguin Random House, Inc., and originally in hardcover by Random House. Reprinted in the UK and Commonwealth by permission of Bloomsbury Publishing Plc. Used in other territories by permission of Susan Bergholz Literary Services, New York, NY and Lamy, NM. All rights reserved.

Crozier, Lorna. "Onions," from *The Blue Hour of the Day: Selected Poems*. Copyright © 2007 Lorna Crozier. Reprinted by permission of McClelland & Stewart, a division of Penguin Random House Canada Limited. All rights reserved. Any third-party use of this material, outside of this publication, is prohibited. Interested parties must apply directly to Penguin Random House Canada Limited for permission.

cummings, e.e. "when faces called flowers float out of the ground," from *Complete Poems: 1904–1962*, edited by George J. Firmage. Copyright © 1950, 1978, 1991 by the Trustees for the e.e. cummings Trust. Copyright © 1979 by George James Firmage. Used by permission of Liveright Publishing Corporation.

Danticat, Edwidge. "A Wall of Fire Rising," from *Krik? Krak!* Copyright © 1991, 1995 by Edwidge Danticat. Reprinted by permission of Soho Press, Inc. All rights reserved.

Dickinson, Emily. "My Life had stood—a Loaded Gun," *The Poems of Emily Dickinson: Reading Edition*, edited by Ralph W. Franklin, Cambridge, MA: The Belknap Press of Harvard University Press, Copyright © 1998, 1999 by the President and Fellows of Harvard College. Copyright © 1951, 1955 by the President and Fellows of Harvard College. Copyright © renewed 1979, 1983 by the President and Fellows of Harvard College. Copyright © 1914, 1918, 1919, 1924, 1929, 1930, 1932, 1935, 1937, 1942 by Martha Dickinson Bianchi. Copyright © 1952, 1957, 1958, 1963, 1965 by Mary L. Hampson. Used by permission. All rights reserved.

Dubus, Andre. "The Intruder," from *Dancing After Hours: Stories.* Copyright © 1995 by Andre Dubus. Reprinted in the UK and Commonwealth by permission of Philip G. Spitzer Literary Agency, on behalf of the author's estate. Used in other territories by permission of Alfred A. Knopf, an imprint of the Knopf Doubleday Publishing Group, a division of Penguin Random House LLC. All rights reserved.

Gerstler, Amy. "Advice From a Caterpillar," from *Dearest Creature.* Copyright © 2009 by Amy Gerstler. Used by permission of Penguin Books, an imprint of Penguin Publishing Group, a division of Penguin Random House LLC. All rights reserved.

Ginsberg, Allen. "A Supermarket in California," from *Collected Poems 1947–1980.* Copyright © 1956, 1961, 1984 by Allen Ginsberg. Reprinted in the UK and Commonwealth by permission of The Wylie Agency LLC. Used in other territories by permission of HarperCollins Publishers.

Glück, Louise. "Yellow Dahlia," from *Ararat.* Copyright © 1990 by Louise Glück. Reprinted in the UK and Commonwealth by kind permission of Carcanet Press, Manchester, UK. Used in other territories by permission of HarperCollins Publishers.

Harjo, Joy. "The Woman Hanging from The Thirteenth Floor Window," from *She Had Some Horses.* Copyright © 1983 by Joy Harjo. Used by permission of W.W. Norton & Company, Inc.

Hayden, Robert. "Those Winter Sundays," from *Collected Poems of Robert Hayden*, edited by Frederick Glaysher. Copyright © 1966 by Robert Hayden. Used by permission of Liveright Publishing Corporation.

Hayes, Terrance. "Over-aged, over grave, overlooked brother ..." taken from *American Sonnets for My Past and Future Assassin*, published by Penguin. Copyright © 2018 by Terrance Hayes. Reprinted in the UK and Commonwealth by permission of Penguin Books Limited. Used in other territories by permission of Penguin Books, an imprint of Penguin Publishing Group, a division of Penguin Random House LLC, in other territories. All rights reserved.

Hillman, Brenda. "Describing Tattoos to a Cop," from *Extra Hidden Life Among the Days*. Copyright © 2018 by Brenda Hillman. Published by Wesleyan University Press. Used by permission.

Jackson, Laura (Riding). "Postponement of Self," *Poems of Mythical Occasion*. Cassell: London, 1938. Reproduced courtesy of Cornell University Library.

Jess, Tyehimba. "Sissieretta Jones," from *Olio*. Copyright © 2016 by Tyehimba Jess. Used with permission of the author and Wave Books.

Kincaid, Jamaica. "Girl," from *At The Bottom of the River*. Copyright © 1983 by Jamaica Kincaid. Reprinted by permission of Farrar, Straus and Giroux. All Rights Reserved.

Knight, Etheridge. "Haiku 1–9," *The Essential Etheridge Knight*. Copyright © 1986 Etheridge Knight. Reprinted by permission of the University of Pittsburgh Press..

Komunyakaa, Yusef. "Facing it," from *Pleasure Dome: New and Collected Poems*. Copyright © 2001 by Yusef Komunyakaa. Published by Wesleyan University Press. Used by permission.

Le Guin, Ursula K. "Six Quatrains," first appeared in *So Far So Good*, published by Copper Canyon Press, 2018. Copyright © 2018 by Ursula K. Le Guin. Reprinted by permission of Ginger Clark Literary, LLC.

Lee, Li-Young. "Persimmons," from *Rose*. Copyright © 1986 by Li-Young Lee. Reprinted with the permission of The Permissions Company, LLC on behalf of BOA Editions, Ltd., boaeditions.org.

Lynch, Alessandra. "Admission," from *Daylily Called It a Dangerous Moment*. Copyright © 2017 by Alessandra Lynch. Reprinted with the permission of The Permissions Company, LLC on behalf of Alice James Books, www.alicejames.org.

Macari, Anne Marie. "From the Plane," from *She Heads into the Wilderness*. Copyright © 2008 by Anne Marie Macari. Reprinted with the permission of The Permissions Company, LLC on behalf of Autumn House Press.

Melnick, Lynn. "Twelve," .*Poetry*, July/August 2018. Used with permission of the author.

Merwin, W.S. "Late Spring," from *The Rain in the Trees*. Copyright © 1988 by W.S. Merwin. Reprinted in paperback by permission of Alfred A. Knopf, an imprint of the Knopf Doubleday Publishing Group, a division of Penguin Random House LLC. All rights reserved. Used in electronic format by permission of The Wylie Agency LLC.

Mullen, Harryette. "Sleeping with the Dictionary," from *Sleeping with the Dictionary*. Copyright © 2002 by the Regents of the University of California. Reprinted by permission of the University of California, conveyed by Copyright Clearance Center.

Nelson, Marilyn. "Fingers Remember," *Poetry*, December 2019. Reproduced by permission of the author, conveyed by Blue Flower Arts LLC.

Neruda, Pablo. "Ode to Tomatoes," from *Selected Odes of Pablo Neruda*, translation and introduction by Margaret Sayers Peden, published by the University of

California Press. Copyright © 1990 by The Regents of the University of California. From the Spanish original "Oda al tomate," *Odas Elementales*. Copyright © Pablo Neruda, 1954, and Fundación Pablo Neruda. Reproduced by permission of Agencia Literaria Carmen Balcells. English translation reproduced by permission of the University of California Press.

Nine haiku of Issa's from *The Essential Haiku: Versions of Basho, Buson & Issa*, edited and with an Introduction by Robert Hass (Ecco, 2013; Bloodaxe Books, 2013). Introduction and selection copyright © 1994 by Robert Hass. Reproduced in the UK and Commonwealth with permission of Bloodaxe Books, www.bloodaxebooks.com. Used in other territories by permission of HarperCollins Publishers.

Notley, Alice. "I the People," from *Grave of Light*. Copyright © 2006 by Alice Notley. Published by Wesleyan University Press. Used with permission.

O'Hara, Frank. "The Day Lady Died," from *Lunch Poems*. Copyright © 1964 by Frank O'Hara. Reprinted with the permission of The Permissions Company, LLC on behalf of City Lights Books, citylights.com.

Oppen, George. "Solution," from *Collected Poems*. Copyright ©1975 by George Oppen. Reprinted by permission of New Directions Publishing Corp.

Pancake, Ann. "Me and My Daddy Listen to Bob Marley," from *Me and My Daddy Listen to Bob Marley: Novellas & Stories*. Copyright © 2015 by Ann Pancake. Reprinted with the permission of The Permissions Company, LLC on behalf of Counterpoint Press, counterpointpress.com.

Phillips, Jayne Anne. "Blind Girls," from *Black Tickets*, Vintage Contemporaries, Random House, Inc., 2001. Copyright © 1975, 1976, 1977, 1978, 1979 Jayne Anne Phillips. Reprinted by permission of Janklow & Nesbit Associates, New York, on behalf of the author.

Plath, Sylvia. "Mad Girl's Love Song," from *The Bell Jar*. Copyright © 1971 by Harper & Row, Publishers, Inc. Reprinted in the US by permission of HarperCollins Publishers. Used in other territories by permission of Faber and Faber Ltd.

Queyras, Sina. "The Couriers," *My Ariel*. Copyright © 2017 Sina Queyras. Reproduced with the permission of Coach House Books, https://chbooks.com/.

Rader, Dean. "Cartography; or American Allegory I," from *Self Portrait as Wikipedia Entry*. Copyright © 2017 by Dean Rader. Reprinted with the permission of The Permissions Company, Inc., on behalf of Copper Canyon Press, coppercanyonpress.org.

Rankine, Claudia. "Some years there exists a wanting to escape—" taken from *Citizen: An American Lyric*, published by Penguin 2015 (pp. 139–46) [excerpted]. First published in the United States by Graywolf Press 2014. Copyright © 2014 by Claudia Rankine. Used in the UK and Commonwealth by permission of Penguin Books Limited. Reprinted in other territories with the permission of The Permissions Company, LLC on behalf of Graywolf Press, graywolfpress.org.

Revell, Donald. "Car Radio," *The Gaza of Winter*, University of Georgia Press, 1988. Copyright © 1988 by Donald Revell. Previously published in *Poetry*, January 1986. Reproduced by permission of the University of Georgia Press.

Rich, Adrienne. "Diving Into the Wreck," from *Collected Poems: 1950–2012*. Copyright © 2016 by the Adrienne Rich Literary Trust. Copyright © 1973 by W.W. Norton & Company, Inc. Used by permission of W.W. Norton & Company, Inc.

Rilke, Rainer Maria. "Rose, Oh Pure Contradiction," from *Selected Poetry of Rainer Maria Rilke*, edited and translated by Stephen Mitchell. Translation copyright © 1982 by Stephen Mitchell. Used by permission of Random House, an imprint and division of Penguin Random House LLC. All rights reserved.

Rimbaud, Arthur. "Ruts," from *Illuminations*, translated by Louise Varese. Copyright ©1957 by New Directions Publishing Corp. Reprinted by permission of New Directions Publishing Corp.

Robison, Mary. "Yours," from *An Amateur's Guide to the Night*. Copyright © 1981, 1982, 1983 Mary Robison. Used by permission of The Wylie Agency LLC.

Ruefle, Mary. "Recollections of My Christmas Tree," from *My Private Property*. Copyright © 2016 by Mary Ruefle. Used with permission of the author and Wave Books.

Schutzman, Steven. "The Bank Robbery," *TriQuarterly* Magazine 35, Winter 1976. Reproduced courtesy of the author.

Sexton, Anne. "In Celebration of My Uterus," from *Love Poems*, A Mariner Book, Houghton Mifflin Company, 1999. Copyright by Linda Gray Sexton and Loring Conant, Jr. 1981. Reprinted by permission of SLL/Sterling Lord Literistic, Inc.

Sharif, Solmaz. "Ground Visibility," from *Look: Poems*. Copyright © 2016 by Solmaz Sharif. Reprinted with the permission of The Permissions Company, LLC on behalf of Graywolf Press, graywolfpress.org.

Shockley, Evie. "mirror and canvas," from *semiautomatic*. Copyright © 2018 by Evie Shockley. Published by Wesleyan University Press. Used by permission.

Simic, Charles. "The World," from *The Book of Gods and Devils*. Copyright © 1990 by Charles Simic. Reprinted by permission of Mariner Books, an imprint of HarperCollins Publishers.

Simonds, Sandra. "Red Wand," from *The Sonnets*, Bloof Books, 2014. Copyright © 2014 Sandra Simonds. Reproduced by permission of Bloof Books on behalf of the author. https://bloofbooks.com/

Smith, Danez. "The 17-Year-Old & the Gay Bar," *Poetry*, February 2017. Used with permission of the author.

Stallings, A.E. "Another Lullaby for Insomniacs," *Hapax*, TriQuarterly Books/ Northwestern University Press, 2006. Copyright © 2006 by A.E. Stallings. All rights reserved. Reproduced by permission of Northwestern University Press.

Stern, Gerald. "Galaxy Love," from *Galaxy Love: Poems*. Copyright © 2017 by Gerald Stern. Used by permission of W.W. Norton & Company, Inc.

Stewart, Susan. "Lessons From Television," *Columbarium.* Copyright © 2003 The University of Chicago. Republished with permission of The University of Chicago Press conveyed through Copyright Clearance Center, Inc.

Tate, James. "Distance From Loved Ones," from *Distance From Loved Ones.* Copyright © 1990 by James Tate. Published by Wesleyan University Press. Used with permission.

Trinidad, David. "Slicker," from *The Late Show*, published by Turtle Point Press. Copyright © 2007 by David Trinidad. Used by permission of Turtle Point Press.

Vuong, Ocean. "Aubade with Burning City," from *Night Sky with Exit Wounds.* Copyright © 2016 by Ocean Vuong. Reprinted in the UK and Commonwealth by permission of Penguin Books Limited. Reprinted in other territories with the permission of The Permissions Company, LLC on behalf of Copper Canyon Press, coppercanyonpress.org.

Williams, William Carlos. "This Is Just to Say," from *The Collected Poems: Volume I, 1909–1939.* Copyright ©1938 by New Directions Publishing Corp. Reprinted by permission of New Directions Publishing Corp.

Wright, C.D. "Flame" and "Clockmaker with Bad Eyes," from *Steal Away: Selected and New Poems.* Copyright © 1996, 2002 by C.D. Wright. Reprinted with the permission of The Permissions Company, LLC on behalf of Copper Canyon Press, coppercanyonpress.org.

Wright, James. "A Blessing" and "Lying in a Hammock," from *The Branch Will Not Break.* Copyright © 1963 by James Wright. Published by Wesleyan University Press. Used with permission.

Yau, John. "Overnight," from *Bijoux in the Dark*, Letter Machine Editions, 2018. Copyright © 2018 John Yau. Reproduced with permission.

Young, Kevin. "Ode to the Hotel Near the Children's Hospital," from *Dear Darkness: Poems.* Copyright © 2008 by Kevin Young. Reprinted in the UK and Commonwealth by permission of Massie & McQuilkin Literary Agents, on behalf of the author. Used in other territories by permission of Alfred A. Knopf, an imprint of the Knopf Doubleday Publishing Group, a division of Penguin Random House LLC. All rights reserved.

★

The publisher has made every attempt to locate all copyright holders of the articles published in this text and would be grateful for information that would allow correction of any errors or omissions in subsequent editions of the work.

index